THE COMPLETE
FILM
Production
HANDBOOK

Eve Light Honthaner

Lone Eagle Publishing Company
Los Angeles, California

THE COMPLETE FILM PRODUCTION HANDBOOK

Copyright © 1993 Eve Light Honthaner

Lone Eagle Publishing Company
2337 Roscomare Road - Suite Nine
Los Angeles, CA 90077-1851
310/471-8066 • FAX 310/471-4969
1/800-FILMBKS

Printed in the United States of America

Cover photograph by Toris von Wolfe

ISBN 0-943728-41-X

A Guide to Music Clearance reprinted with permission by The Clearing House, Ltd.

Library of Congress Cataloguing in Publication Data

Honthaner, Eve Light, 1950—
      The complete film production handbook/by Eve Light Honthaner
          p.   cm.
      ISBN 0-943728-41-X
      1.   Motion Pictures—production and direction—Handbooks, manuals, etc.
      I. Title.
      PN1995.9.P7H66   1993
      791.43'0232—dc20   93-90433
                                          CIP

TABLE OF CONTENTS

INTRODUCTION   vii

HOW TO USE THIS BOOK   ix

Chapter 1
PRE-PRODUCTION
Introduction   1
Pre-Production Schedule   2
Pre-Production Checklist   3

Chapter 2
ESTABLISHING COMPANY POLICIES
Inventories   7
Production Assistants/Runners   7
   Employees Driving Their Own Vehicles
   For Business Purposes   7
Mileage Reimbursement   8
Additional Taxable Income   8
Invoicing   8
Purchase Orders   8
Check Requests   8
Petty Cash   8
Distribution   9
Recycling   9
Product Placement   9
General Safety Guidelines   9
Better Safe Than Sorry   9

Chapter 3
INSURANCE REQUIREMENTS
Errors and Omissions   11
Comprehensive General Liability   11
Hired, Loaned Or Donated Auto Liability   12
Hired, Loaned Or Donated Auto Physical
Damage   12
Workers' Compensation and
Employer's Liability   12
Guild/Union Accident Coverage   13
Production Package   13
Cast Insurance   13
Negative Film & Videotape/Direct
Physical Loss   13
Faulty Stock, Camera and Processing   13
Props, Sets and Scenery, Costumes
and Wardrobe   13
Miscellaneous Rented Equipment   13
Office Contents   13
Extra Expense   14

Third Party Property Damage   14
Supplemental (or Optional) Coverages   14
   Umbrella (Excess Liability)   14
   Aircraft   14
   Watercraft   14
   Railroads Or Railroad Facilities   14
   Valuables   14
   Livestock Or Animals   14
Claims Reporting Procedures   15
Submitting Claims   15
Insurance Claim Worksheets
   Theft   16
   Damage   17
   Cast-Extra Expense-Faulty Stock   18
   Automobile Accident   19-20

Chapter 4
SETTING-UP PRODUCTION FILES
Movie For TV or Features   21
Series Files   21
General Production Files   21
Episode Files   22

Chapter 5
TALENT
Follow-Through After An Actor
Has Been Set   23
Street Performe Categories   24
Work Calls   25
The Work Week   25
Consecutive Employment   26
Performer Categories   26
Employment of Minors   26
Taft/Hartley   27
SAG Extras   27
Nudity   28
Working With Animals   28
SAG Offices   29

Chapter 6
SAG, DGA, WGA—FORMS AND REPORTS
Notice of Tentative Writing Credits   31
Screen Actors Guild Forms
   Daily Contract For Television
     Motion Pictures
     or Videotapes   33-34
   Minimum Three-Day Contract
     for Television, Motion Pictures
     or Videotapes   35-36

Minimum Free Lance	
Weekly Contract	37-38
Daily Stunt Performer Contract	39-40
Stunt Performer Minimum Free Lance	
Weekly Contract	41-42
Daily Contract For Theatrical	
Motion Pictures	43-44
Minimum Free Lance Contract For	
Theatrical Motion Pictures	45
Daily Stunt Performer Contract—	
for Theatrical Motion Pictures	46
Stunt Performer Minimum Freelance	
Weekly Contract for	
Theatrical Motion Pictures	47-48
Taft/Hartley Report	49
Taft/Hartley Report—SAG Extras	50
SAG Extra Voucher	51
Theatrical and Television Sign-In	52
Actors Production Time Report	52
Casting Data Report	55-56
Casting Data Report For	
Stunt Performers	57-58
Casting Data Report—Low Budget/	
Affirmative Action	59-60
Final Cast List Information Sheet	61-62
Member Report—	
ADR Theatrical/Television	63
Directors Guild of America Forms	
Weekly Work List	64
Employment Data Report	65-66
Writers Guild of America Forms	
Notice Of Tentative Screen Credits	
Theatrical	67
Notice Of Tentative Screen Credits	
Television	68

Chapter 7
STANDARD PRODUCTION FORMS
AND FORMATS

Script Revisions	69
Forms	71-80
Breakdown Sheet	71
Day-Out-Of-Days	72
Call Sheet	73-74
Production Report	75-76
Check Request	77
Purchase Order	78
Petty Cash Accounting	79
Received Of Petty Cash Slip	80
Shooting Schedule	81
One-Line Schedule	82
Crew List	83
Cast List	84
Executive Staff List	85
Contact List	86

Chapter 8
DEAL MEMOS

Cast Deal Memo	88
Crew Deal Memo	89
Writer's Deal Memo	90
Writing Team Deal Memo	91
DGA—Director Deal Memorandum	92
DGA—UPM and Assistant Director	
Deal Memorandum	93
Extra Talent Voucher	94

Chapter 9
CLEARANCES & RELEASE FORMS

Likeness	95
Location	95
Names	95
Names of Actual Businesses	
or Organizations	95
Photograph or Likeness of Actual Person	96
Telephone Numbers	96
License Plates	96
Street Address	96
Depiction of Identification of	
Actual Products	96
Film and Video Clips	96
Music	96
Location Agreement	97-98
Personal Release	99
Personal Release—Payment	100
Group Release	101
Use Of Name	102
Use Of Trademark Or Logo	
Use Of Literary Material	103
Use Of Still Photograph(s)	
Person In Photo/Payment	104
Person In Photo/Free	105
Copyrighted Owner/Payment	106
Copyrighted Owner/Free	107
Wording For Multiple Signs	
In A Studio Taping Or Filming	
Before A Live Audience	108
In An Area During The Taping	
or Filming Of A Show	109
Supplying A Film/Tape Clip Of Your Show	
For Promotional Purposes	110
Product Placement Release	111-112
Film/Tape Footage Release	113-114
Request For Videocassette	115

Chapter 10
MUSIC CLEARANCE

A Guide to Music Clearance	117

Chapter 11
MISCELLANEOUS PRODUCTION FORMS

Abbreviated Production Report	127
Daily Cost Overview	128
Cast Information Sheet	129
Box/Equipment Rental Inventory	130
Inventory Log	131
Purchase Order Log	132
Crew Start-up and Data Sheet	133
Time Cards/Invoices —	
Weekly Checklist	134

Individual Petty Cash Account 135
Invoice 136
Cash or Sales Receipt 137
The Check's in the Mail 138
Mileage Log 139
Raw Stock Inventory 140
Daily Raw Stock Log 141
Request For Pick Up 142
Request For Delivery 143
Drive-To 144
Walkie-Talkie Sign-Out Sheet 145
Beeper Sign-Out Sheet 146
Vehicle Rental Sheet 147

Chapter 12
LOCATIONS
Introduction 149
Location Information Sheet 150
Location List 151
Request To Film During
    Extended Hours 152

Chaper 13
DISTANT LOCATION
Additional Checklist For
    Distant Location 153
Working With the Hotel 153
Shipping Dailies 154
Forms
    Travel Movement 156
    Hotel Room Log 157
    Hotel Room List 158
    Meal Allowance 159
    Sample Travel Memo to
        Cast and Crew 160-161

Chapter 14
IMMIGRATION, CUSTOMS
    AND VISA INFORMATION
Filming In A Foreign Country 163
Temporarily Employing Talent
    and Technical Personnel
    from Other Countries 164

Chapter 15
A LITTLE POST PRODUCTION
Sample Post Production Schedule 167
Basic Post Production Terminology 169
Screen Credits
    Introduction 170
    Sample Main Titles
        Movie For Television 173
        Theatrical Motion Picture 173
        Movie For Television 174
        Theatrical Motion Picture) 175-176
    Standard Delivery Requirements 177

INDEX 181

INDEX OF FORMS (Blank & Filled In) 195

TEAR-OUT BLANK FORMS 196
        From Chapter 3
Insurance Claim Worksheets
Theft 197
Damage 198
Cast/Extra Expense/Faulty Stock 199
Automobile Accident 201-202

        From Chapter 6
Screen Actors Guild Forms
Daily Contract for Television
    Motion Pictures or Videotapes 203-204
Minimum Three-Day Contract for
    Television, Motion Pictures or
    Videotape 205-206
Minimum Freelance Weekly Contract
    for Television, Motion Pictures
    or Videotape 207-208
Daily Stunt Performer
    Contract for Television,
    Motion Pictures or Videotape 209-210
Stunt Performer Minimum Freelance
    Weekly Contract for Television,
    Motion Pictures or Videotape 211-212
Daily Contract for
    Theatrical Motion Pictures 213
Minimum Freelance Contract
    for Theatrical Motion Pictures 215-216
Daily Stunt Performer
    Contract for Theatrical Motion
    Pictures 217-218
Stunt Performer Minimum Freelance
    Weekly Contract—Motion Pictures 219
Taft-Hartley Report 220
Taft-Hartley Report—SAG Extras 221
SAG Extra Voucher 222
Theatrical and Television Sign-In 223
Actors Production Time Report 224
Casting Data Report 225-226
Casting Data Report for
    Stunt Performers 227-228
Casting Data Report—
    Low Budget/Affirmative Action 229-230
Final Cast List Information Sheet 231-232
Member Report—
    ADR Theatrical/Television 233
Directors Guild of America Forms
Weekly Work List 234
Employment Data Report 235-236

Writers Guild of America Forms
Notice of Tentative
    Screen Credits—Theatrical 237
Notice of Tentative
    Screen Credits—Television 238

From Chapter 7

Breakdown Sheet	239
Day-out-of-Days	240
Call Sheet	241-242
Production Report	243-244
Check Request	245
Purchase Order	246
Petty Cash Accounting	247
Received of Petty Cash Slip	248

From Chapter 8

Cast Deal Memo	249
Crew Deal Memo	250
Writer's Deal Memo	251
Writing Team Deal Memo	252
DGA Director Deal Memo	253
DGA UPM and Assistant Director Film Deal Memo	254
Extra Talent Voucher	255

From Chapter 9

Location Agreement	257-258
Personal Release	259
Personal Release—Payment	260
Group Release	261
Use of Name	262
Use of Trademark or Logo	263
Use of Literary Material	264
Use of Still Photographs (Copyrighted Owner, Not Person in Photo)	265
Use of Still Photographs (Person in Photo/Free)	266
Use of Still Photographs (Person in Photo/Payment)	267
Use of Still Photographs (Copyrighted Owner, Not Person in Photo/Free)	268
Wording for Multiple Signs	269
Film/Tape Clip for Promotional Uses	270
Product Placement Release	271-272
Film/Tape Footage Release	273-274
Request for Videocassette	275

From Chapter 11

Abbreviated Production Report	276
Daily Cost Overview	277
Cast Information Sheet	278
Box/Equipment Rental Inventory	279
Inventory Log	280
Purchase Order Log	281
Crew Start-up and Data Sheet	282
Time Car/Invoices Weekly Checklist	283
Individual Petty Cash Account	284
Invoice	285
Cash or Sales Receipt	286
The Check's in the Mail	287
Mileage Log	288
Raw Stock Inventory	289
Daily Raw Stock	290

Request for Pick-up	291
Request for Delivery	292
Drive-to	293
Walkie-Talkie Sign-out Sheet	294
Beeper Sign-out Sheet	295
Vehicle Rental Sheet	296

From Chapter 12

Location Information Sheet	297
Location List	298
Request to Film During Extended Hours	299

From Chapter 13

Travel Movement	300
Hotel Room Log	301
Hotel Room List	302
Meal Allowance	303
Travel Memo to Cast and Crew	305-306

INTRODUCTION

I assembled my first production manual while working as a production executive for an independent production company several years ago. I felt it was important to standardize forms, releases and procedures on all the company's shows; to provide important information needed to set-up and run a production; and for everyone to know, up front, what the company's policies were. It contained material I had either saved or put together at one time or another to help me on a particular show, or something created to simplify my job or to avoid specific problems I had previously encountered. I designed some of the forms and some are a compilation of the best of other forms I had used over the years.

I took the manual with me to the next company I worked for and the next show and the show after that, continually using it, adding to it, and sharing the information with the people I worked with. My co-workers were the first to encourage me to have the manual published so I could pass this collection of information on to other companies and individuals who would be able to use it on a day-to-day basis.

This industry-related reference book is different from most others as it will not teach you how to budget or breakdown a script. It does not include information on videotape production or live television and *very* little on post production. It does not contain much in the way of union and/or guild rules and rates or information on how to find various services, equipment, locations, crews, etc.,—all of which can be found in other books and manuals. What it does contain, however, is a detailed guide to *film* production for production personnel based solely on the scope of my experience and on what I feel is important to know...information you will not necessarily find in other publications.

Use this book as a **guideline**. The information provided under *Company Policies* and *Miscellaneous Forms* are suggestions; and although all of the enclosed forms, releases and deal memos have been approved by an attorney, I suggest you have your own attorney look everything over before you use them. Your attorney may also want to make changes or add riders which relate to the specifics of your production.

Since I began assembling the enclosed material, several new production-related computer software programs have come on the market. Although some of the forms contained in this book such as the *Breakdown Sheet* and *Day-Out-Of-Days* and samples of things such as the *Production Schedule* and *One-Line Schedule* are functions automatically prepared by these software programs, I have kept them in the book for those who are still learning or wish to breakdown and schedule their show manually and for those who do not yet own the software. Most of what this manual does contain cannot be found on a software program.

The major studios put out their own production manuals, but most independent production companies do not. Having your own manual will not only save you time and keep you more organized, but it adds a touch of professionalism to the smallest of production units.

One last thing: for all you new and prospective line producers, production managers and production coordinators who may not have had the experience of working in Production, it is *extremely* hard work. You are the first to arrive in the morning and the last to leave at night. You have the most responsibility and are the first one to get blamed if anything goes wrong. Your work can never be called "artistic", the fruits of your labor can rarely be seen on the screen, and you will work just as hard on a bad movie (sometimes harder) as you do on a good one. I can honestly say, however, that Production can be a lot of fun. There is something extremely satisfying (and even exciting at times, when you're not too tired or too crazed to get excited) about putting all the pieces together and watching a movie happen. It is great to work with and meet new people all the time, wonderful to travel to different locations and constantly experience new challenges.

Work as hard as you can, learn as much as you can, never be afraid to ask questions, treat your crew well, be flexible, do not yell, and be of good humor. The work is too difficult not to be able to have fun while you're doing it.

With very special thanks to my husband Ron, Nick Abdo, Patricia O'Brien, Marc Federman, Phil Wylly, Cindy Quan, Liam O'Brien and Linda English. And to them, along with other friends and associates who urged me to have the manual published and supplied me with their encouragement and help—thank you with all my heart. Without your nudging, I'd still be working on it.

Eve Light Honthaner

How To Use This Book

The Complete Film Production Handbook contains many forms: standard production forms, deal memos, release forms and an assortment of miscellaneous forms to help you be more organized. To illustrate how each form is to be completed, they have all been fully, or partially, filled out.

We have used an assortment of names and situations—all fictitious. The name of our production company is **XYZ Productions** and the name of the show is The Watcher. However, note that from situation to situation, **The Watcher** is either a feature film, or a television serieswith the current episode being, **Boy's Night Out**.

Also included is a complete set of blank forms which can be torn out (perforated pages) and filled in.

ABBREVIATIONS

Throughout the book, the following abbreviations are used:

UPM	Unit Production Manager
POC	Production Office Coordinator
DP	Director of Photography
AD	Assistant Director
SAG	Screen Actors Guild
DGA	Directors Guild of America
WGA	Writers Guild of America

To avoid the awkwardness of "he/she", "him/her" and "his/hers", when referring to people in specific positions who can either be men or women, we have elected to alternate the use of the masculine and the feminine throughout the book. Note that all references should be applied equally to men and women.

CHAPTER I

PRE-PRODUCTION

Pre-production is the period of time used to plan and prepare for the filming and completion of your film. It is the time to:

GET STARTED

Establish your production company

Set-up production offices

Hire a crew

Finalize your script and budget

Arrange for insurance and completion bond

Schedule your shoot

Become signatory to the unions or guilds you wish to sign with, and post any necessary bonds

Cast your show

Find your locations

Build and decorate your sets

Wardrobe actors

Order film, equipment, vehicles and catering

Book travel and hotel accommodations

Prepare all agreements, releases, contracts and paperwork

Plan stunt work and special effects

Line up special requirements such as picture vehicles, animals, mock-ups, miniatures, etc.

Set-up accounts with labs; set-up editing rooms; schedule routing of dailies; plan your post production schedule, hire post production crew and pre-book scoring, looping and dubbing facilities

Clear copyrighted music to be used in your picture

PLAN AHEAD TO AVOID PROBLEMS

Arrange for *cover sets* should the weather turn bad while filming exteriors

Know where you can exchange or get additional equipment if needed *at any time*

Keep names, phone numbers and resumes of additional crew members should you suddenly need an extra person or two

Line up alternate locations should your first choice not be available

The lower the budget, the more prep time you should have. Lower-budgeted films don't have extra time or money, so it is imperative to be completely prepared. Ironically, the films needing the most prep time are the ones that can least afford it. Many independent producers prepare as much as they can while waiting for their funding, although they are somewhat limited until they can officially hire key department heads.

Many variables, such as budget and script requirements, determine your pre-production schedule. The following is an example of what a reasonable schedule (barring any extraordinary circumstances) might look like based on a six-week shoot with a *modest* budget of $4—$6 million.

An ideal pre-production schedule allows one and-a-half weeks of prep for each week of shooting. Accordingly, a six-week shoot should have a nine-week prep period. The following eight-week schedule, however, should be more than sufficient as well as cost effective.

PreProduction Schedule

WEEK NUMBER ONE *(8 weeks of prep)*
Starting Crew:
- Producers
- Director
- Production Manager and/or Line Producer
- Production Accountant
- Location Manager
- Casting Director
- Secretary/Receptionist
- Production Assistant Number One

To Do:
- Establish your company, if not done earlier
- Set-up production offices
- Finalize script and budget
- Start filling out union/guild signatory papers
- Firm up insurance coverage
- Begin casting
- Start lining-up your crew
- Start scouting locations
- Open accounts with vendors

WEEK NUMBER TWO *(7 weeks of prep)*
Starting Crew:
- Production Designer

To Do:
- Start music clearance procedures using either your attorney or a music clearance service to determine if the rights are available and how much the sync license fees are.

WEEK NUMBER THREE *(6 weeks of prep)*
Starting Crew:
- Art Director
- Set Designer
- Production Coordinator
- Assistant Location Manager

WEEK NUMBER FOUR *(5 weeks of prep)*
Starting Crew:
- First Assistant Director
- Wardrobe Supervisor
- Transportation Coordinator
- Property Master
- Set Decorator
- Production Assistant Number Two

WEEK NUMBER FIVE *(4 weeks of prep)*
Starting Crew:
- Production Secretary
- Assistant Accountant
- Costumer Number One
- Assistant Property Master
- Lead Person

To Do:
- At the end of this week, you should be ready for your first production meeting.

NOTE: *Depending on script requirements, the Production Designer will determine the start dates of the Construction Coordinator and Construction crew. The Production Manager will determine the start dates of the Stunt Coordinator and Special Effects crew.*

WEEK NUMBER SIX *(3 weeks of prep)*
Starting Crew:
- Second Assistant Director
- Transportation Captain
- Swing Crew

WEEK NUMBER SEVEN *(2 weeks of prep)*
Starting Crew:
- Director of Photography
- Key Grip
- Gaffer
- Costumer Number Two
- Extra Casting, if needed

WEEK NUMBER EIGHT *(final week of prep)*
Monday
Starting Crew:
- Script Supervisor
- Production Assistant Number Three, Set Production Assistant
- Additional Drivers (as needed)

To Do:
- Post any neeeded bond with the Screen Actors Guild (SAG), otherwise you cannot clear your actors through Station 12 or give them work calls
- Complete your casting and send out contracts
- Finalize selection of locations
- Order all equipment, vehicles, raw stock, expendables and catering

Thursday
Starting Crew:
- Best Boy, Electric
- Best Boy, Grip
- Hair Stylist
- Makeup Artist
- 1st Assistant Cameraman

To Do:
- Final Location Scout For Camera, Grip, Electric

Friday
Starting Crew:
- Sound Mixer
- Production Van Driver

To Do:
- Final Production Meeting

PRE-PRODUCTION CHECKLIST

STARTING FROM SCRATCH
- [ ] Find a good attorney who specializes in entertainment law
- [ ] Establish company structure (i.e., Corporation or partnership)
- [ ] Obtain business licenses from city, county and, or state
- [ ] Apply to the IRS for a Federal ID number
- [ ] If you've established a corporation, you'll need a corporate seal and a minutes book
- [ ] Obtain Workers Compensation and General Liability insurance
- [ ] Open a bank account
- [ ] Secure a Completion Bond (if applicable)
- [ ] Start lining-up your staff and crew

LEGAL
Your company's Legal or Business Affairs Department or an outside entertainment attorney should do this work.
- [ ] Secure the rights to the screenplay
- [ ] Negotiate (or review) and prepare the contract for the writer of the screenplay
- [ ] Review all Financing and Distribution Agreements
- [ ] Order Copyright and Title Reports
- [ ] Prepare contracts for principal cast
- [ ] Prepare SAG contract riders
- [ ] Prepare contracts for the Producer, Director, Director of Photography, Production Designer and Costume Designer
- [ ] Prepare minors' contracts
- [ ] Review E & O (errors and omissions) Insurance
- [ ] Review contracts regarding literary material to make sure all required payments are made
- [ ] Review permits and other documents having potential legal significance
- [ ] Prepare (or approve) all necessary release forms
- [ ] Start music clearance procedures

SET-UP PRODUCTION OFFICE
- [ ] Order furniture
- [ ] Have phone system installed
- [ ] Copier machine
- [ ] Typewriters
- [ ] Computer(s)
- [ ] Fax machine(s)
- [ ] Office supplies
- [ ] Bottled water
- [ ] Coffee maker
- [ ] Refrigerator
- [ ] Extra keys to office (keep list of who has keys)
- [ ] Order beepers for key personnel
- [ ] Prepare department head envelopes for messages and approving bills

PAPERWORK
- [ ] Sign union and, or guild contracts (if applicable)
- [ ] Open accounts with vendors
- [ ] Set-up production files
- [ ] Assemble supply of production forms
- [ ] Prepare contact list
- [ ] Prepare chart-of-accounts for coding bills
- [ ] Start purchase order log
- [ ] Prepare and distribute inventory logs
- [ ] Start raw stock inventory
- [ ] If a television series, prepare a list of episodes, production dates, Director, Writer and Editor for each show
- [ ] Prepare DGA deal memos
- [ ] Prepare crew deal memos
- [ ] Give start slips and tax information to payroll
- [ ] Prepare crew list
- [ ] Prepare Crew Start-Up and Data Sheet

CAST-RELATED
- [ ] SAG bond (if applicable)
- [ ] Finalize casting
- [ ] Prepare cast lists
- [ ] Station 12 cast members
- [ ] Cast deal memos
- [ ] Prepare SAG contracts
- [ ] Schedule designated cast for medical exams (cast insurance)
- [ ] Actors' checklist—doctor exam, Wardrobe notified, contract received, contract signed, script received, etc.
- [ ] Wardrobe fitted
- [ ] Line-up stunt doubles and photo doubles
- [ ] Dialogue Coach
- [ ] Schedule rehearsal(s)
- [ ] Schedule hair, makeup tests
- [ ] Work permits for minors
- [ ] Welfare Worker(s), Teacher(s)
- [ ] Line up an extras casting agency
- [ ] Interview stand-ins and extras
- [ ] Obtain a good supply of Extra vouchers

SCRIPT, SCHEDULES
- [ ] Finalize script
- [ ] Script typed
- [ ] Script duplicated
- [ ] Script distributed to cast and crew
- [ ] Script to research company
- [ ] Breakdown script, prepare a production board
- [ ] Prepare a One-line schedule

- ❑ Prepare a Day-out-of-days
- ❑ Prepare a Shooting schedule
- ❑ Have the script timed

PREPARE BREAKDOWNS OF
- ❑ Atmosphere
- ❑ Production Vehicles
- ❑ Picture Vehicles
- ❑ Stunts
- ❑ Special Effects
- ❑ Locations

BUDGETARY
- ❑ Finalize budget
- ❑ Cash flow chart
- ❑ Send script, budget and schedule to the completion bond company

INSURANCE
- ❑ Send script and budget to insurance companies for bids
- ❑ Secure insurance coverage
- ❑ Secure special insurance coverage for aircraft, boats, railroad, etc.
- ❑ Prepare Certificates of Insurance for vehicles, equipment and locations
- ❑ Send travel, stunt and effects breakdown to Insurance Company
- ❑ Have a supply of Workers' Compensation accident forms and insurance information for office, 2nd Assistant Director and Company Nurse
- ❑ Select doctor approved by insurance company for director and cast physicals

PREPARE PRE-PRODUCTION SCHEDULE INCLUDING:
- ❑ Casting sessions
- ❑ Production meetings (Schedule at least two — more if time allows)
- ❑ Location scouts
- ❑ Rehearsals
- ❑ Pre-rigging

POST PRODUCTION-RELATED
- ❑ Set-up accounts for: lab, sound transfers, video transfers
- ❑ Set-up cutting room(s)
- ❑ Book scoring, looping and dubbing facilities and dates
- ❑ Route dailies
- ❑ Schedule screening of dailies
- ❑ Prepare a tentative post production schedule

LOCATIONS
- ❑ Location agreements
- ❑ Certificates of insurance
- ❑ Permits
- ❑ Fire and Police officers

- ❑ Security
- ❑ Intermittent Traffic Control
- ❑ Post for Parking
- ❑ Signed releases from neighbors
- ❑ Prepare maps to locations
- ❑ Heaters, fans, air conditioners
- ❑ Lay-out board, drop cloths
- ❑ Locate closest medical emergency facilities
- ❑ Power/Utilities
- ❑ Locate parking lot(s) if shuttling is necessary
- ❑ Extra tables, chairs, tent
- ❑ Allocate areas for extras, dressing rooms, eating, hair, makeup hair
- ❑ Allocate parking areas for equipment and vehicles
- ❑ Line-up strike and cleaning service

ORDER
- ❑ Raw stock
- ❑ Still film, Polaroid film
- ❑ Camera equipment*
- ❑ Empty cans, camera reports, black bags, cores (from lab)
- ❑ Steadicam
- ❑ Video Assist*
- ❑ Grip, electric equipment*
- ❑ Grip, electric, camera expendables
- ❑ Dolly(s), Crane(s), Condor(s)
- ❑ Generator(s)*
- ❑ Sound equipment*
- ❑ 1/4" Mag stock
- ❑ Walkie-talkies, bullhorns, headsets*
- ❑ Cellular phone(s)
- ❑ Portable VCR & monitor (if dailies are shown on set)*
- ❑ Catering

  * Most equipment rents on a weekly basis. If you are using the same equipment for the run of your show, you should be able to negotiate two- or three-day weekly rental rates with each of the equipment houses with whom you are dealing.

TRANSPORTATION
- ❑ Motor home(s), star wagon(s)
- ❑ Honeywagon(s)
- ❑ Camera car(s), process trailer(s)
- ❑ Water truck
- ❑ Production trailer
- ❑ Hair, makeup trailer
- ❑ Wardrobe trailer
- ❑ Crew cabs, vans
- ❑ Grip, electric truck
- ❑ Camera truck
- ❑ Prop truck
- ❑ Set dressing truck
- ❑ Fuel truck
- ❑ Picture cars

ANIMALS
- Locate the necessary animals/livestock
- Contact the American Humane Association for guidelines in the proper care, use, handling and safety of animals

Locate and hire competent:
- Animal handlers
- Trainers
- Wranglers

SPECIALTY ITEMS
- Technical advisor(s)
- Rear screen/process photography
- Stock footage
- Cycs
- Mock-ups
- Models
- Special makeup and, or hair pieces

Prepare a **Portable File Box** (or a legal-size accordion file) with the following paperwork to stay on the set at all times. This box should contain:

COPIES OF
- All signed location agreements
- All permits

BLANKS OF THE FOLLOWING
- Location agreements
- Call sheets
- Production reports
- Workers Compensation accident report forms
- Automobile accident report forms
- SAG contracts (a few of each kind)
- SAG Taft/Hartley report forms
- Crew deal memo forms
- Certificates of Insurance
- Check request forms
- Purchase orders
- Petty cash envelopes
- Release forms (an assortment)

EXTRA COPIES OF
- Staff and crew lists
- Scripts, script changes
- Cast lists
- Contact lists
- Shooting schedules
- Day-out-of-days
- Maps to the locations
- Start slips, W-4s, I-9s
- Extra vouchers

KEEP ON THE SET AT ALL TIMES
- A complete First Aid kit
- Aspirin, Tylenol
- Several flashlights
- An assortment of office supplies
- A typewriter and a small copy machine (if you have the room and the additional cost is within your budget)

Once the film (including post-production) has been completed and before the files are packed up and stored, prepare a **Final Production Book** containing all the pertinent information you may need to refer to at a later date. This book should contain: .

- Corporate (signatory papers) information
- Bank information (bank, contact, account number, copies of signature cards, etc.)
- Bank reconciliation
- Trial balance
- Final budget
- Final cost report
- Cast list, final SAG cast list
- Chart-of-accounts, vendor list
- Contact List (local and location)
- Final staff and crew list
- Crew deal memos
- Location list (including dates and deals)
- Call sheets
- Production reports
- Final shooting schedule
- Final day-out-of-days
- Key correspondence
- Copies of major deals
- Copies of signed union, guild contract agreements
- Information on insurance claims
- Final script
- Dates of delivery, delivery requirements
- Inventory logs, location of inventory

CHAPTER 2
ESTABLISHING COMPANY POLICIES

Whether you are producing one show or ten a year, your company should establish a set of policy guidelines. By doing this, you not only stay better organized and maintain tighter controls over your costs; but it is important for staff and crew members to know, coming in, what the company's policies are and what they are specifically responsible for.

Some production companies distribute memos to all new crew members listing their policies. Others attach a list of policies to each **Crew Deal Memo**—integrating the acceptance of these *rules* as a condition of employment.

The following are fairly standard industry policies.

INVENTORIES

Each department should keep an on-going inventory of all materials purchased, rented or built for your production, including prices, rental dates and serial numbers (wherever applicable). The production office will supply the **Inventory Log Forms**. At the completion of principal photography, each department should turn in all remaining inventory along with completed inventory logs to the production office.

Keep inventories on the following:

Equipment and tools
Set dressing, props
Wardrobe
Raw stock, videocassettes
Office supplies and equipment (including the serial numbers of typewriters, computers, editing equipment, VCRs, etc.)
Keys
Walkie-talkies, chargers, bullhorns (including the serial number of each)
Beepers
Supplies, expendables

PRODUCTION ASSISTANTS AND RUNNERS

Production Assistants and Runners should be responsible to the Production Coordinator or *one* other designated person only. They should not take directions from everyone in the office. The Production Coordinator (or other designated person) will organize each PA's duties and schedule runs based on production priorities. If an emergency arises and a PA is not available, the Production Coordinator will make alternate arrangements (another PA, messenger service, Transportation Driver, etc.)

Anyone requesting a pick-up or delivery must fill out a **Request for Pick-up** or **Request for Delivery** form, provided by the production coordinator. Place the completed form, along with any item to be delivered, in the PA's designated box. Each form will contain: 1) The name of the person requesting the pick-up (delivery) 2) When the item(s) need to be picked-up (delivered), 3) Street directions, 4) Whom to contact (pick-up from or deliver to), 5) Date and time of each pick-up (delivery), 6) Signature of recipient. Keep all completed pick-up (delivery) forms on file through the end of production.

PA's should call the Production Office after each run—unless they are on a pager—to see if they need to go elsewhere on their way back.

EMPLOYEES DRIVING THEIR OWN VEHICLES FOR BUSINESS PURPOSES

If an employee is driving a personal vehicle during the business day for business purposes and has an accident, insurance regulations specify that an employee's own insurance is primary. The Company's *non-owned auto liability policy* covers the production company—not the individual.

All employees using personal cars for business purposes—especially PA's and runners—need to show proof of auto insurance. Inform them of this policy.

MILEAGE REIMBURSEMENT

Tell your employees the mileage reimbursement rate. To qualify for mileage reimbursement, they must fill out **mileage logs** showing: beginning mileage, destination, purpose and ending mileage for each run. Estimated mileage is not acceptable. Mileage to and from home is not reimbursable.

Employees who receive mileage reimbursement are not reimbursed for gas receipts.

In order to be reimbursed for mileage expenses, submit the Mileage Log together with a properly filled out check request to the UPM or POC for approval. Once approved, the production office will pass it on to Accounting for payment.

ADDITIONAL TAXABLE INCOME

The Federal government has set an *allowable limit* for mileage reimbursement, drive-to and per diems. Any amount over such limit (see your accountant for limit guidelines) is considered taxable income and will be taxed along with weekly payroll checks.

Box rental monies are also considered taxable income, but are generally not taxed on a weekly basis. Those receiving box rentals will receive a 1099 at the end of the year

Box rental monies are also considered taxable income, but are generally not taxed on a weekly basis. Those receiving box rentals will instead receive a 1099 at the end of the year and each will be responsible for the taxes on this additional income.

INVOICING

The crew should turn in their invoices for salary, services, equipment, box rental, vehicle rental, car allowance or mileage reimbursement at the end of each week for payment the following week. Each invoice must include the employee's name, the corporation name, address and social security number (or Federal ID number). Include a complete description of what the invoice is for (e.g., services rendered or equipment rental) and a week-ending date on the invoice. The UPM must approve all invoices before payment can be made.

PURCHASE ORDERS

Use purchase orders whenever possible for purchases and, or rentals with vendors who have (or will have) an account with the company.

Obtain purchase orders from the POC or production accountant. Fill them out completely and have them approved *before* buying or renting. If the purchase order is for five hundred dollars ($500) or less, the Production Manager should approve it. If it is for more than $500, the Producer should approve it. If you don't know the exact amount of the purchase (rental) indicate an estimated amount that will not be exceeded. Distribute copies of each purchase order as follows:

1. To the Vendor (the original)
2. Production Manager
3. Accounting Dept.
4. Department Head

The POC should keep a running purchase order log indicating date, vendor, item(s) being purchased, rented, amount of purchase, rental, date of rental return and the department to which each PO is assigned. Also note in the log any purchases that will become part of the company's inventory at the end of the show.

CHECK REQUESTS

For payments that require a check, obtain a check request from the POC or the accounting department. Fill it out completely. The production manager must approve it before payment can be made. Be as complete as possible on the form including answers to such questions as: Is this a purchase? rental? location fee? petty cash advance? deposit? etc? If it's a deposit, is it *refundable* or should it be applied to the final bill? If this is a partial payment or the first of many, what are the terms of the purchase, rental or service and what is the total amount to be?

Indicate whether to mail the check or hold for pick up by the person making the request. Also indicate how quickly you need the check. Next week? Tomorrow? Immediately?

If *immediately*, and the UPM is not present, the UPM can give verbal approval (phone or walkie/talkie). If the UPM is not available, the producer can approve the request.

If the check request is for the purchase of tools, props, wardrobe, etc., (anything that can be considered inventory) note it on the check request so that it can be added to the Inventory Log.

PETTY CASH

Petty cash is used for small purchases that are not covered by a purchase order or check request—generally for items under $100, such as gas/oil for company vehicles, parking fees, expendable supplies, small props and miscellaneous office supplies.

Use a check request to request Petty Cash and follow the same procedures. Those receiving petty cash will receive a check in their name and a petty cash envelope to keep track of all petty cash expenditures.

Anyone receiving a petty cash advance from the production manager or accountant in CASH will need to sign a **Received of Petty Cash** slip acknowledging receipt of the cash. The person advancing the funds will also sign the slip. When turning in petty cash receipts, the person receiving the money should be responsible for finding and voiding the original Received of Petty Cash slip.

Number all receipts and tape them to 8-1/2" x 11" sheets of paper in sequence. Label and identify each clearly. List the corresponding numbers on the front of the envelope along with a description of each item. Petty cash should not to be used for salaries or box rentals and for meals only with the prior approval of the production manager.

Petty cash receipts should all be originals. Approximate costs are not generally accepted except for such things as phone calls and parking meters. Note any petty cash purchases for inventory items and add them to the inventory log.

Submit petty cash once a week, or before you run out of money. Date, list and total all expenditures. Do not seal the envelope. Once approved, accounting will issue you a check in the amount of your expenditures, keeping your initial draw at the same balance.

At the completion of principal photography and, or wrap, the balance of receipts, and remaining cash must be accounted for as quickly as possible.

DISTRIBUTION

When distributing copies of scripts, schedules, various lists, call sheets, production reports, etc., prepare a DISTRIBUTION LIST to ensure that everyone receives all necessary information. Your distribution list might look like this:
Name Title   Location   Phone No.   Ext.

RECYCLING

Use an box or trash can for empty drink cans and bottles. Place another empty box or can near the copier machine for paper that can be recycled (old scripts, outdated schedules, etc.) Make sure there are no paper clips or staples attached to the paper.

Have one of your production assistants or drivers locate the closest recycling center and drop off the recyclable items as often as it is convenient.

PRODUCT PLACEMENT

Before making a deal with a Product Placement firm or with an individual company for obtaining wardrobe, props, set dressing, vehicles, locations or services in exchange for on-air exposure and/or screen credits, discuss this with your production executive and/or attorney. If approved, a representative of the company supplying the item(s), service(s), location(s) will need to sign the appropriate release form(s).

GENERAL SAFETY GUIDELINES

In accordance with California Senate Bill 198, all California-based companies are required to post a list of General Safety Guildelines in the workplace. It has also become the practice to provide employees with a written list of guidelines and require them to sign a form acknowledging they have received a copy.

General Safety Guidelines cover such things as: the safe operation of equipment; accessibility to a phone and electrical panels; the proper disposals of waste; the proper storage of flammable liquids and chemicals; the wearing of safe clothing; keeping work areas clean; care in lifting heavy objects and performing difficult tasks (such as stunts and special effects); and being aware of the location and phone number of the nearest medical facility.

Although these procedures are regulated in California by CAL-OSHA (other states have similar safety programs); the Federal government is currently considering adopting a program like that of CAL-OSHA which would be consistent throughout the country.

When out of state production companies are filming in California, they are required to follow California safety regulations. In addition, union-signatory companies who are members of the Alliance of Motion Picture and Television Producers (AMPTP) are asked to voluntarily follow the same safety guidelines when filming in other states.

For more information on General Safety Guidelines, contact the AMPTP (818/995-3600) or CAL-OSHA (213/736-3041).

BETTER SAFE THAN SORRY

Being aware of safety guidelines and being as cautious as possible in the workplace is essential. Unfortunately, however, accidents do happen. Also, no production company—regardless of its size or stature—is immune to union greivances, law suits, insurance claims, etc. BE CAREFUL! It is too easy to get so busy on a shoot that a few little things fall between the cracks. But it is those little things than can turn into monsters and come back to haunt you later on.

Here are some guidelines that should be helpful:

To best protect one's own backside—and that of the company, keep careful inventories and note when something is lost or damaged.

When shooting at a practical location, remind your crew to be careful! Protect floors and carpeting to the best of your ability, cover furniture that is not being used and ask that valuables (not needed as set dressing) be put away for safe keeping by the owner(s).

Put as much information on the back of the production report as possible—including the slightest scratch anyone might receive. When a day passes and there are no injuries, note NO INJURIES REPORTED TODAY on the back of the production report.

When someone is injured, complete a Workers Compensation (Employer's Report of Injury) report ASAP and get it to the insurance agency. Also attach a copy to the daily production report.

Have an ambulance on the set on stand-by when you are doing stunts that are in the least bit complicated or dangerous. Always know where the closest emergency facility near your shooting location is located; and if you do not have an ambulance on the set, have a *designated* car and driver ready to take someone to the hospital if necessary.

Confirm all major decisions and commitments by writing a memo to the files. If you are having trouble with a crew member, keep a log of dates and incidents.

Do not sign a rental agreement for the use of equipment, motor homes, facilities, etc., until you or someone you trust can check out the quality...and know exactly what you're getting.

Favors are nice, but they can also backfire on you. Put as much in writing as you possibly can. For example: if you want to use a crew member's car in a chase sequence in exchange for having repairs made to the car, get a signed letter stating the terms of the exchange, releasing the company from any further responsibilities (once the repairs have been made.)

CHAPTER 3

INSURANCE REQUIREMENTS

Setting up insurance is one of the first things to do when starting any new production. The following pages will touch on the basics of motion picture insurance.

Standard motion picture and television coverages include the following:

ERRORS AND OMISSIONS

This coverage protects the insured (production company) against any liability resulting from any covered claim which may be made against the insured by reason of: 1) invasion of the right of privacy; 2) infringement of copyright or trademark; 3) libel, slander or other forms of defamation; or 4) unauthorized use of titles.

Delivery requirements might dictate whether this is to be a one-year or a three-year policy. A three-year policy is cost effective and renewals should continue at least throughout the distribution period.

COMPREHENSIVE GENERAL LIABILITY

This coverage includes bodily injury and property damage, contractual liability, personal injury and other forms of liability coverages.

A primary policy usually has a limit of $1,000,000 per occurrence, and evidence of this coverage is given in the form of a **Certificate of Insurance**.

Certificates of Insurance are issued by the production office (or in some cases, the Insurance Agency) to a third party (the certificate holder) as evidence of coverage.

Frequently, you will be requested to name a certificate holder as **Additional Insured** and/or **Loss Payee**. If a certificate holder is named as an Additional Insured, the insurance coverage will protect the certificate holder for claims arising out of the activities of the production company. A certificate holder who is named Loss Payee is the owner of a vehicle or equipment being used on your film. If there is a claim resulting from the loss or damage to their vehicle/equipment, reimbursement for the loss or damage would be paid to them.

Your insurance agency may require that you call their office to request Additional Insured or Loss Payee certificates when a certificate holder requests this additional coverage. There are times, however, when these certificates may be issued directly from the production office.

You can order certificates of insurance that specify:

Additional Insured—Managers or Lessors of Premises, which are issued to the owner(s) of each filming location; and **Additional Insured/Loss Payee—Equipment**, which are issued to the owners of rented equipment and vehicles.

Special coverages which involve the company's use of watercraft, aircraft or a railroad are always handled through your insurance representative. Certificates involving these activities are never issued by the production office.

When filling out a Certificate of Insurance on a rental vehicle or a picture vehicle, it is a good idea to include the make, model and ID number of the vehicle. If the value of the vehicle exceeds the limits of the policy, you will need additional coverage.

If you are doing a series, indicate the episode and production number on the certificate.

Give the top copy of the certificate (the original) to the owner of the vehicle, property or equipment. Send two copies to your insurance representative. Give one copy to your production executive, and keep one in the production files. If the certificate is for a vehicle, keep a copy in the vehicle's glove compartment.

HIRED, LOANED OR DONATED AUTO LIABILITY

This covers all company-owned, hired or leased vehicles used in connection with the production. Only vehicles that are being rented under the company's name and are issued certificates of insurance are covered under this policy. A certificate must be issued in order for the company's coverage to be primary.

If an employee has an accident while driving his personal car for company business, his own insurance is primary. The company's policy only insures the production company if the employee's coverage is insufficient.

Have your Transportation Coordinator keep a supply of Auto Accident Forms (Automobile Loss Notice) on the set at all times. If an accident occurs, make sure to fill one out and submit it to the insurance company immediately.

HIRED, LOANED OR DONATED AUTO PHYSICAL DAMAGE

This coverage insures company-owned, hired or leased vehicles against the risks of loss, theft or damage, (including collision) for all vehicles used in company-related activities. It covers vehicles rented from crew and/or staff members stating that the production company is assuming responsibility for the vehicles. This is true if the rental fee is paid by invoice or if there is a deal in writing.

If a vehicle is damaged as a result of more than one incident, make a note as to the specific damage caused by each incident, the date and time of each, what the vehicle was being used for (was it a picture vehicle or a production vehicle?) and how the accident occurred. The Insurance Company *will not* accept miscellaneous vehicle damage accumulated during the length of a production. It treats each occurrence as a separate accident, each with a separate deductible.

If you plan to use a picture vehicle for stunt work, include this information in your breakdown. Physical damage to vehicles used in stunts generally is not covered.

WORKERS' COMPENSATION AND EMPLOYER'S LIABILITY

All employees are entitled to Workers' Compensation benefits if they are injured or becomes ill directly resulting from or during the course of their employment. The benefits are established by state laws.

Workers' Compensation coverage is supplied by the payroll company or the "employer of record". If your employees are being paid through the production company, then the production company is responsible for obtaining their Workers' Compensation. If staff, crew, and cast members are being paid through a payroll company, then the payroll company will supply the coverage. Even if all employees are being paid through the payroll service, the production company should still carry a minimum Workers' Compensation policy to provide coverage for the "independent contractors" or volunteer labor that might be eligible for this coverage.

If your Workers' Compensation coverage is coming from more than one source, generate a memo indicating which staff, crew and cast members are covered under which policy. The memo should also include the following: information on each of the insurance companies (name, address and phone number); the name of an insurance agency or payroll company representative to report claims to; the policy numbers of each and a copy of the accident report form (Employer's Report of Injury) each insurance company uses. Make sure your Company Nurse (or First Aid Person) and/or Second Assistant Director has a copy of this memo and a supply of both accident forms on the set at all times.

When a staff, cast or crew member is injured on the set, fill out an Employer's Report of Injury form and note the incident on the back of the daily production report for that particular day. Send the report directly to the insurance agency or payroll company, keep a copy for the production files and send a copy to your production executive. Also attach an additional copy to the back of the production report. Forward all medical bills, doctor's reports, etc., to the respective insurance agency or payroll company.,

When applying for Workers' Compensation during pre-production, declare the need for coverage for employees hired in your state of your operations as well as coverage for any other state where you plan to shoot on location and hire local employees. Include an **All States' Endorsement** to your Workers' Compensation policy to protect the company if employees are hired from a state or states you had not initially declared.

If an employee is injured, she will receive benefits in accordance with the compensation laws of the state in which he was hired.

Six states—Nevada, Ohio, West Virginia, Wyoming, North Dakota and Washington State—are "monopolistic", meaning that you must purchase Workers' Compensation coverage directly from their state insurance program if you choose to hire employees from their state.

Your insurance agency representative and/or the State's Workers' Compensation fund will supply you with appropriate injury report forms. Reporting procedures are the same in every state.

The insurance agency will require a breakdown of all **stunts and special effects** prior to principal photography. They will also require detail as to safety procedures and the experience of the personnel involved. It is mandatory to confirm who the employer of record is for these employees. If the employer is other than the production company or payroll service (for example, a stunt coordinator hiring other stunt personnel or a special effects supervisor hiring his own effects crew), you should obtain a certificate of insurance from the employer (department head) to show evidence of workers compensation coverage for his employees.

Should a SAG-covered performer be injured in the course of employment with your company, the **Screen Actors Guild** requires that you send a copy of the accident report to them.

GUILD/UNION ACCIDENT COVERAGE

Employees traveling on company business are covered under a Travel Accident policy which provides coverage as specified in their governing guild or union bargaining agreements. If an employee is not a member of any union or guild, coverage is provided for a minimum amount. No employee, while on the company payroll is allowed to fly as a pilot or as a member of a flight crew unless specifically hired for that duty and scheduled on the insurance policy.

Under Guild/Union Travel Accident coverage, each production is required to keep track of: 1) the number of plane and/or helicopter flights taken by any guild/union member on each show; 2) number of hours each person may spend in a helicopter; 3) number of days each guild/union member may be exposed to hazardous conditions; and 4) number of days any DGA member may be exposed while filming underwater. This specific information may be requested from the insurance company at the completion of principal photography.

PRODUCTION PACKAGE, WHICH INCLUDES:

CAST INSURANCE

This coverage is placed on the director and a designated number of cast members—key components of your production not easily replaceable, if at all. If one of these individuals becomes ill or has an accident while working on your show and is unable to work for a matter of hours or days, the production company will be reimbursed for any extra expenses incurred in the completion of principal photography. (You will be required to present a thorough and complete substantiation of the company's extra costs incurred due to such an occurrence to the insurance company before a claim can be properly adjusted.)

Physical exams are required for those who are to be covered under Cast Insurance, and the insurance agency will furnish you with the name of a physician (or a choice of physicians) with whom you can set up appointments.

Cast Insurance usually starts three to four weeks prior to the commencement of principal photography, although additional prep coverage is often required. An example would be a key actor who is involved with the project from the very early stages of pre-production.

If at any point during pre-production or production, the director or one of the designated actors becomes ill, is injured or incapacitated in any way, call your insurance representative immediately. If one of them feels ill yet continues working; but you're not sure how he will be the following day or how the schedule may be affected later in the week, alert the insurance agency as to the possibility of an interruption in filming.

If you submit a claim, a doctor should examine the ill or injured person as soon as possible. The doctor's report is a necessary factor in substantiating the claim.

NEGATIVE FILM AND VIDEOTAPE DIRECT PHYSICAL LOSS

This coverage insures against all risks of direct physical loss, damage, or destruction of raw film or tape stock, exposed film, recorded video tape, sound tracks and tapes up to the amount of insured production costs.

FAULTY STOCK, CAMERA AND PROCESSING

This coverage insures against the loss, damage or destruction of raw film stock or tape stock, exposed film, recorded video tape and sound tracks caused by or resulting from fogging or the use of faulty equipment, faulty developing or faulty processing. It does not cover for losses due to mistakes made by the camera crew.

PROPS, SETS AND SCENERY, COSTUMES AND WARDROBE; MISCELLANEOUS RENTED EQUIPMENT; OFFICE CONTENTS

These provide coverage against all risks of direct physical loss, damage, or destruction to all property (contents, equipment, cameras, sets, wardrobe, lighting equipment, office furnishings, props, supplies, etc.) used in connection with the covered production.

Keep running inventories of all set dressing, props, wardrobe, equipment, etc., that is purchased and/or rented for each show. If anyone on your crew notices that something is missing or damaged—inform the insurance agency, make a note of it on the inventory log and on the back of the daily production report and file a police report if applicable. At the end of the show, the insurance company *may not* honor claims on lost or damaged equipment, props, set dressing or wardrobe without sufficient documentation.

Advise all your department heads to inform the Production Manager or Production Coordinator immediately of losses and damages. They should not wait until the completion of principal photography to submit invoices for repairs and replacement costs.

In specific cases of missing equipment, props, set dressing or wardrobe, a police report needs to be filed to substantiate the theft, otherwise the insurance company will not honor the claim. If at the end of principal photography, however, you discover you are short a few pieces of equipment, a few props or some pieces of wardrobe and have no idea when any of these items were taken, this is considered a "mysterious disappearance". Without a police report and documentation indicating when each item was discovered missing, who discovered it missing, etc.,—a claim of mysterious disappearance is difficult to substantiate and may not be covered.

No insurance reimbursements are issued for the loss of personal belongings such as purses or clothing. If an employee is using his personal computer or typewriter, you must have some documentation (deal memo/rental agreement) showing that the production company is renting the item— even at $1 a month—otherwise it is not covered under the company policy.

EXTRA EXPENSE

Claims of this type typically involve damage to sets, props, wardrobe or locations that actually delay production for some period of time. This insurance will cover expenditures over and above the total cost normally incurred to complete principal photography when any real and/or personal property is lost due to damage or the destruction of this property.

THIRD PARTY PROPERTY DAMAGE

This coverage pays all sums which the production company is legally obligated to pay as damages because of injury to or destruction of property of others while such property is in the care, custody or control of the production company.

Your insurance representative will advise you as to the specific limits and deductibles of the above coverages and any additional optional coverages you might require based on the needs of your production.

SUPPLEMENTAL (OR OPTIONAL) COVERAGES

UMBRELLA (EXCESS LIABILITY)

There will be times—with locations, for example— when higher limits than those provided under General Liability and/or Third Party Property Damage are mandatory. This coverage carries limits of liability in excess of $1,000,000.

AIRCRAFT

Inform the Insurance Agency as soon as you know you are planning to use any aircraft in your show at the earliest possible date prior to usage so that adequate Non-Owned Aircraft Liability and/or

hull coverages can be secured. To add protection for the possible negligence of the owner of the aircraft, it is also strongly advisable that the owner be asked to name your production company as Additional Insured under his owner's Hull and Liability Insurance policies. The production should secure a Hold Harmless and Waiver of Subrogation with respect to loss or damage to the hull of the aircraft, so that the production is not responsible for any damage to it. Request a Certificate of Insurance from the owner of the aircraft evidencing the Waiver of Subrogation and including the production company as an Additional Insured.

WATERCRAFT

If you are going to be using a boat (watercraft) for the purpose of filming or carrying a film crew and/or equipment, discuss the details with your insurance representative to determine if and what type of Marine coverages are necessary.

RAILROADS OR RAILROAD FACILITIES

For the use of railroads or railroad facilities, the production company is often required to indemnify the railroad for the production's negligence as well as the railroad's negligence. The insurance agency will need to review the contract provided by the railroad before proper coverage can be determined.

VALUABLES

Inform the insurance company as to the use of fine arts, jewelry, furs and expensive antiques and the values of each so that limits can be increased as required. Discuss with the insurance representative as to how these items are to be used with respect to the production, so appropriate coverage can be arranged.

LIVESTOCK OR ANIMALS

If insurance coverage is necessary for livestock or animals to be used in the production, it is arranged on a case by case basis depending on contractual obligations and the value of the animal(s). At no time would the limit of coverage be more than the value of the animal covered; and before coverage is issued, a veterinarian certificate on the animal would be necessary. Under certain circumstances, an animal may be insured under **Extra Expense**. This coverage would reimburse the production company for extra expenses incurred due to the unavailability of a covered animal.

Once you have filled out the appropriate applications and coverage is in place, you will be supplied with a copy of your insurance policy (and/or certificates) and the various accident and claim forms needed for each production. You should have a supply of the following in the production office and on the set at all times:

(1) Certificate of Insurance

(2) Automobile Loss Notice
(3) Property Loss Notice
(4) General Liability Notice of Occurrence/ Claim Notice
(5) Workers' Compensation—Employer's Report of Occupational Injury or Illness

Some you will use more frequently than others, but you should be familiar with all of them.

CLAIMS REPORTING PROCEDURES

If an accident, injury or theft occurs; if the director or a cast member becomes ill and unable to work; if you have a scratched negative or damage to equipment, props, set dressing or any of your sets; report it to the insurance agency as soon as possible. Back up each reported occurrence in writing by completing an appropriate claim form, noting such on the back of the daily production report for that particular day and/or by writing a letter to the insurance agency containing as much detail as possible—when the incident occurred (date of loss), where it occurred, how it happened, who was there at the time, etc. Report any major theft or major accident to the police, and attach a copy of the police report to your letter to the insurance agency. Even if you are not sure a loss would be covered, advise your insurance representative as to the possibility of a claim.

If a serious accident occurs, promptly record the names and phone numbers of witnesses (including staff/cast/crew members) so that an accurate description of the incident can be determined. Give statements or reports only to authorized representatives of the production company, and in turn, to your insurance representative.

SUBMITTING CLAIMS

When an incident occurs resulting in an insurance claim, the accounting department should begin to tag each related invoice indicating specific costs (or portions of) that were directly incurred as a result of the claim. When the claim is submitted, all related costs and overages should be presented budget-style starting with a budget top sheet indicating the exact impact to each account. Copies of invoices should be coded and placed behind the top sheet in the correct order of accounts.

In addition to applicable police and doctor reports and copies of invoices, backup should also include: call sheets; production reports; and both original and revised schedules, day-out-of-days, cast lists, etc,—anything to substantiate the changes created by the claim. Depending on the claim, copies of cast and crew deal memos, time cards, travel movement lists, equipment rental agreements and/or location agreements may also be required.

With regard to complicated or on-going claims,

it is a good idea for the producer or production manager to either maintain a log of events pertaining to the claim on a day-to-day basis or write memos to the file on a regular basis.

Begin each claim with a cover letter referencing the production, date of occurrence, claim number (if available), a description of the claim and a brief summary of the backup you are providing. [I suggest binding the backup with brads or in file folders secured with Acco fasteners.]

Start processing insurance claims as soon as they occur. Submit the full claim to the insurance agency as soon as costs can be assessed and backup provided. Do not wait until the end of principal photography to start processing your claims.

Once a claim is reported to your insurance representative, it is then turned over to an insurance agency claim representative. When all the information is in order, the claim is then submitted to the insurance company—who may or may not (depending on the claim) then assign it to an independent insurance auditor.

It is often advantageous for the production manager and production accountant to meet with the insurance auditor shortly after the incident occurs to better define the parameters of the claim and to know exactly what backup will be necessary.

The following are four **Insurance Claim Worksheets** which will be helpful in collecting needed information for the submission of insurance claims.

For further information regarding any aspect of insurance, contact your insurance agent.

FORMS INCLUDED IN THIS SECTION

Theft 16
Damage 17
Cast-Extra Expense-Faulty Stock 18
Automobile Accident 19-20

INSURANCE CLAIM WORKSHEET

(THEFT)

STOLEN   [ ] EQUIPMENT
            [ ] WARDROBE
            [ ] PROPS
            [✓] SET DRESSING
            [ ] VEHICLE

PRODUCTION ___THE WATCHER___

DATE ITEM(S) WERE DISCOVERED MISSING ___JUNE 29, 1993___

DESCRIPTION OF ITEM(S) STOLEN (Include I.D.#'s If Available) ___
MACINTOSH II si COMPUTER WITH MONITOR & KEYBOARD
I.D. # XSF23L276Z265

DEPARTMENT USED BY ___SET DRESSING___

PERSON USED BY ___USED AS SET DRESSING ONLY___

WHERE WERE ITEM(S) LAST SEEN ___"HERBY'S BEDROOM" SET___

WHO DISCOVERED ITEM(S) MISSING ___DARLENE DRESSER___

ITEM(S)   [ ] PURCHASED FOR SHOW -- PURCHASE PRICE $___
        [✓] RENTED FOR SHOW
        RENTED FROM ___CAL'S COMPUTER CENTER___
        ADDRESS ___9876 FLORES ST.___
        ___STUDIO VILLAGE, CA 90009___

        PHONE# ___818/ 555-9777___
        CONTACT ___CAL JONES___

        VALUE $ ___1,500___
        RENTAL PRICE $ ___50___   PER [ ] DAY
                                        [✓] WEEK
                                        [ ] MONTH

[✓] POLICE REPORT ATTACHED
[✓] OTHER ATTACHMENTS ___RENTAL AGREEMENT FROM CAL'S
COMPUTER CENTER___

SUBMITTED TO INSURANCE AGENCY ON ___JULY 2, 1993___
        ATTENTION ___SUSIE___
        CLAIM # ___005327___
INSURANCE COMPANY CLAIMS REP. ___CURTIS CLAIMS___

INSUR. CLAIM WORKSHEET COMPLETED BY ___CONNIE COORDINATES___
DATE ___JULY 2, 1993___   TITLE ___POC___

AMOUNT CREDITED TO AGGREGATE DEDUCTIBLE $ ___500___   DATE ___7-15-93___
REIMBURSEMENT CHECK PAID TO ___XYZ PRODUCTIONS___
        AMOUNT $ ___1,000___   DATE ___7-20-93___

INSURANCE CLAIM WORKSHEET

DAMAGE TO [✓] EQUIPMENT
[ ] WARDROBE
[ ] PROPS
[ ] SET DRESSING
[ ] LOCATION/PROPERTY

PRODUCTION _THE WATCHER_

DATE OF OCCURRENCE _6-24-93_   TIME _11 AM_

WHAT WAS DAMAGED _WALKIE-TALKIE_

LOCATION OF OCCURRENCE _HOLLYWOOD RIVER_

HOW DID DAMAGE OCCUR _SECOND ASSISTANT DIRECTOR ACCIDENTALLY_
DROPPED WALKIE-TALKIE IN RIVER WHILE ARRANGING
ATMOSPHERE FOR SCENE #25.

WITNESS _MIKE BOOM_   POSITION _SOUND MIXER_
PHONE# _213/555-9993_

DAMAGED ITEM(S)   [ ] PURCHASED FOR SHOW -- PURCHASE PRICE $_____
[✓] RENTED FROM/OWNER _XXX AUDIO SERVICES_
ADDRESS _123 MAIN STREET_
HOLLYWOOD, CA 91234
PHONE# _213/555-5311_
CONTACT _GEORGE_

RENTAL PRICE $ _30_   PER [ ] DAY
[✓] WEEK
[ ] MONTH

VALUE OF DAMAGED ITEM(S) $ _1,000_
ESTIMATE(S) TO REPAIR $ _600_

[✓] ATTACHMENTS _COPY OF DAILY PROD. REPORT (INCIDENT RECORDED)_
COPY OF REPAIR INVOICE

SUBMITTED TO INSURANCE AGENCY ON _6-29-93_
ATTENTION _SUSIE_
CLAIM # _005328_
INSURANCE COMPANY CLAIMS REP. _CURTIS CLAIMS_

INSURANCE CLAIM WORKSHEET COMPLETED BY _CONNIE COORDINATES_
DATE _6-28-93_   TITLE _POC_

AMOUNT CREDITED TO AGGREGATE DEDUCTIBLE $ _0_   DATE_____
REIMBURSEMENT CHECK PAID TO _XXX AUDIO SERVICES_
AMOUNT $ _600._   DATE _7-29-93_

INSURANCE CLAIM WORKSHEET

[✓] CAST
[ ] EXTRA EXPENSE
[ ] FAULTY STOCK

PRODUCTION _THE WATCHER_

DATE OF OCCURRENCE _July 2, 1993_   TIME _5PM_

DESCRIPTION OF INCIDENT _DIRECTOR'S CHAIR COLLAPSED_
WHILE ACTRESS WAS SITTING ON IT BETWEEN
TAKES. SHE INJURED HER RIGHT LEG AND
SPRAINED HER BACK

IF CAST CLAIM, WHICH ARTIST _SCARLET STARLET_

WAS A DOCTOR CALLED IN [✓] YES [ ] NO

NAME OF DOCTOR _A. PAINE, M.D._
ADDRESS _3327 INJECTION BLVD._
LOS ANGELES, CA 90000
PHONE# _(310) 555-1177_

COULD COMPANY SHOOT AROUND INCIDENT [ ] YES [✓] NO
IF YES, FOR HOW LONG _____

HOW MUCH DOWN TIME WAS INCURRED DUE TO THIS INCIDENT _1 DAY_

AVERAGE DAILY COST $ _50,000_

BACKUP TO CLAIM TO INCLUDE _COPY OF DAILY PROD. REPORT_
COPY OF DOCTOR'S REPORT
BACK-UP TO COSTS INCURRED DUE TO DOWN TIME

SUBMITTED TO INSURANCE AGENCY ON _JULY 12, 1993_
ATTENTION _SUSIE_
CLAIM # _005329_
INSURANCE COMPANY CLAIMS REP. _CURTIS CLAIMS_
INSURANCE AUDITOR _LAWRENCE LIABILITY_

INSURANCE CLAIM WORKSHEET COMPLETED BY _CONNIE COORDINATES_
DATE _7-11-93_   TITLE _POC_

AMOUNT CREDITED TO DEDUCTIBLE $ _0_   DATE _____
REIMBURSEMENT CHECK PAID TO _XYZ PRODUCTIONS, INC._
AMOUNT $ _65,000_   DATE _8-15-93_

© ELH Form #3

INSURANCE CLAIM WORKSHEET

AUTOMOBILE ACCIDENT

PRODUCTION ___THE WATCHER___

DATE OF OCCURRENCE __JUNE 25, 1993__ TIME __9:23 AM__

LOCATION OF OCCURRENCE __CORNER OF 4TH & MAPLE DR.__

HOW DID ACCIDENT OCCUR __DRIVER SHUTTLING CAST & CREW TO SET FROM PARKING AREA RAN INTO CAR IN FRONT OF HIM WHEN OTHER CAR STOPPED SHORT APPROACHING INTERSECTION.__

INSURED VEHICLE (Year, Make, Model) __1990 FORD AEROSTAR__
VEHICLE I.D.# __1234567X423__ LIC. PLATE# __XXX 2321__
OWNER OF VEHICLE __TINSELTOWN FORD__
ADDRESS __7503 CLUTCH DR.__ __BURBANK, CA 91503__
PHONE# __818/ 555-6000__ CONTACT __BUDDY__

DRIVER __TERRY TEAMSTER__
POSITION __TRANSPORTATION CAPTAIN__
DRIVER'S LIC.# __50030376__ USED W/PERMISSION [✓] YES [ ] NO
ADDRESS __523 N. BROADWAY #132__
__GLENDALE, CA__
PHONE# __818/ 555-2476__

WHERE CAN CAR BE SEEN __TINSELTOWN FORD__
WHEN __BETWEEN 9AM & 7PM__

DAMAGE TO CAR __DENTED FRONT FENDER, BUMPER, GRILL & HOOD FRONT END OUT OF ALIGNMENT DAMAGED RADIATOR__
ESTIMATE(S) TO REPAIR $ __2,600__ $ __3,000__

DAMAGE TO OTHER VEHICLE (Year, Make, Model) __1983 DODGE RAM PICK-UP__
LIC. PLATE# __237657322__
DRIVER OF OTHER VEHICLE __DENNIS DRIVER__
ADDRESS __7326 N. HILLTOP__
__LOS ANGELES, CA 90000__
PHONE(S)# __213/ 555-7676__ # _____

WHERE CAN CAR BE SEEN __AT MR. DRIVER'S HOME__
WHEN __EVENINGS BETWEEN 6PM & 8PM__

DAMAGE TO CAR __DENTED REAR BUMPER & TAILGATE BROKEN TRAILER HITCH__

ESTIMATE(S) TO REPAIR $ __1,500__ $ __1,750__

INSURANCE CLAIM WORKSHEET - AUTOMOBILE ACCIDENT
PAGE #2

INJURED _____ NO INJURIES _____   _____
ADDRESS _____   _____

PHONE# _____   _____
EXTENT OF INJURY _____   _____

WITNESS(ES) F. STOPP (DIR. OF PHOTOG)   PATRICK PEDESTRIAN
ADDRESS 3276 BELAIR PLACE   603 N. LUMBERJACK WAY
BELAIR, CA 90002   PASADENA, CA
PHONE# (310) 555-3131   (818) 555-'3652

☑ POLICE REPORT ATTACHED
☑ OTHER ATTACHMENTS ___ ESTIMATES TO REPAIR VEHICLES

SUBMITTED TO INSURANCE AGENCY ON ___ 6-30-93
ATTENTION ___ SUSIE
CLAIM # ___ 005330
INSURANCE COMPANY CLAIMS REP. ___ CURTIS CLAIMS

INSURANCE CLAIM WORKSHEET COMPLETED BY ___ ALEX AUTOS
DATE ___ 6-28-93 ___ TITLE ___ TRANSPORTATION COORDINATOR

INSURANCE ADJUSTER TO SEE INSURED VEHICLE ON ___ 7-7-93
TO SEE OTHER VEHICLE ON ___ 7-8-93

AMOUNT CREDITED TO DEDUCTIBLE $ ___ 4,100 — ___ DATE ___ 7-12-93
REIMBURSEMENT CHECK PAID TO _____
AMOUNT _____ DATE _____
TO _____
AMOUNT _____ DATE _____

NOTES: _____

  © ELH Form #4

CHAPTER 4

SETTING UP PRODUCTION FILES

This is a guide—delete or add files to fit the specific requirements of your show.

Type the name of the show in CAPS at the top of each file folder label—with the heading underneath. Secure each file with an Acco fastener so none of the papers falls out.

MOVIES FOR TV OR FEATURES
Art Dept/Set Construction
Budget
Budget/Cash Flow and Chart-of-Accounts
Budget/Cost Reports
Call Sheets
Camera
Cast List/SAG Contracts
Casting Submissions
Check Requests
Completion Bond Company
Contact List
Correspondence/Memos
Crew Lists/Deal Memos
Crew—Wrap Schedule
Day-out-of-Days
Director
Distribution Agreement
Equipment (Miscellaneous)
Extras
Hotel/Motel Accommodations
Grip/Electric
Insurance—General Policy Information Correspondence
Insurance—Workers Compensation
Insurance—Insurance Claims
Insurance—Certificates of Insurance
Inventory Logs
Locations/Location Agreements and Permits
Miscellaneous
Music
Network (or Cable) Format
Network Standards and Practices (if applicable)

Office (Equip, Furniture, Keys, etc.)
Payroll Information
Personal Releases
Post Production—Schedule and Delivery Requirements
Post Production—Contact List, Correspondence, etc.
Post Production—Screen Credits
Producer(s)
Production Reports
Property/Set Dressing
Publicity
Purchase Orders/P.O. Log
Research Report
Resumes
Script
Shooting Schedule/One-Liner
Transportation
Travel Arrangements/Movement Lists
Union/Guild Information
Wardrobe
Writer(s)

SERIES FILES
When setting up files for a television series, organize **General Production Files** with the name of the series in CAPS at the top of each file folder label, and the heading underneath. **Episode Files** should have the name of the episode in CAPS at the top of each file folder label, and the heading underneath.

GENERAL PRODUCTION FILES
Art Dept/Set Construction
Budget
Budget/Cash Flow and Chart-of-Accounts
Budget/Cost Reports
Camera
Cast List—Regulars
Check Requests
Contact List

Correspondence/Memos
Crew List/Deal Memos
Crew—Wrap Schedule
Director(s)
Episode Schedule (including writer, director and
    editor for each episode)
Equipment (Miscellaneous)
Extras
Hotel/Motel/Apartment Accommodations
Grip/Electric
Insurance—General Policy Information and
    Correspondence
Insurance—Workers Compensation
Insurance—Insurance Claims
Insurance—Certificates of Insurance/
    Vehicles and Equipment
Insurance—Certificates of Insurance/
    Locations
Inventory Logs
Locations—Miscellaneous Correspondence and
    Permits
Locations—Permanent Locations
Locations—One Location file for each episode
    (containing everything except permanent lo-
    cation information)
Miscellaneous
Music
Network Format
Network Standards and Practices
Office (Equipment, Furniture, Keys, etc.)
Payroll Information
Personal Releases
Post Production—Schedules and Delivery
    Requirements
Post Production—Contact List,
    Correspondence, etc.
Post Production—Screen Credits
Producer(s)
Property/Set Dressing
Publicity
Purchase Orders/P.O. Logs
Resumes
Transportation
Travel Arrangements/Movement Lists
Union/Guild Information
Wardrobe
Writer(s)

EPISODE FILES *(Three for each episode)*
    1. Complete script with all changes
    2. Call Sheets and Production Reports
    3. Cast List, Shooting Schedule, Day-out-of-
       Days, One-Liner, Research Report, etc.

CHAPTER 5

TALENT

FOLLOW-THROUGH AFTER AN ACTOR HAS BEEN SET

Once an actor has been set for a particular role, the Casting Office should send a **Booking Slip** to the actor's agent verifying the role, a minimum guaranteed number of days or weeks of employment and salary. (A booking slip should be provided no later than the day predceding the actor's first day of employment.) Casting will notify Production of the actor's name, address and phone number and the actor's agent's name and phone number.

Production then: 1) Notifies Wardrobe of actor's name and phone number; 2) Sends actor a script; 3) Arranges a physical for insurance purposes (if applicable).

A **Deal Memo** (which outlines the terms of the actor's employment on a particular film) is issued by the Casting Office and copies are sent to a pre-determined distribution list. When the entire cast has been set, the Casting Office will issue a final **Cast List**. Partial cast lists should be done prior to all roles being set. See Chapter 7 for a sample cast list.

Cast lists should also be sent to a pre-determined distribution list. (Make sure cast lists are given to your wardrobe, hair, makeup and transportation people.) Some cast lists may contain an additional column containing the actors' deals, but those are only to be given to a select few: Producer, Production Manager, Assistant Directors, Production Coordinator and Production Accountant. Actors' deals are not for general distribution.

Final casts lists detailed on the designated **SAG Final Cast List Information Sheets** are to be submitted to The Screen Actors Guild no later than 120 days afte the completion of principal photography or 90 days after the completion of post production, whichever is sooner. (If the Guild is holding a security deposit, the final cast list is submitted directly after the last performer's payroll has been processed.)

The Casting Office prepares the **SAG Contracts** (although sometimes the contracts are prepared and sent out from the Production Office) with all company-related riders and appropriate tax (W-4 and I-9) forms attached. **Weekly and Three-Day Player contracts** are sent directly to the respective agents with a cover letter instructing them as to where to return the contract once it has been signed by their client.

Be sure all lines, spaces, boxes, etc. that need to be signed or initialed by the actor are clearly indicated with red X's and/or paper clips to mark the spot.

The following is a sample of the **Cover Letter** which would be sent to agents with their client's SAG contract (also enclosed would be any applicable rider(s); all payroll forms and a self-addressed, stamped, return envelope):

```
Today's Date

Agent's Name
Address
City, State, Zip

Dear [Agent's Name]:

Enclosed is an agreement for (Actor's
Name)'s services on (Name of Project).
Please have (him) sign the contract
where indicated and complete the at-
tached payroll start slip, W-4 and I-9
forms. We would appreciate it if you
would send I-9 verification at the time
you return the signed agreement (a copy
of a driver's license and social secu-
rity card or passport.)

Enclosed is a self-addressed, stamped
```

envelope for your convenience. In addition to the contract and payroll forms, please return a check authorization form if you wish (Name of Actor)'s checks to be sent directly to your office.

Once the contract is fully-executed, a copy will be returned to you for your files.

If you have any questions, please do not hesitate to call me at [production office phone number.]

Sincerely yours,

If an actor does not have an agent, the contract should be sent directly to the actor, and the cover letter should read:

Today's Date

Actor's Name
Actor's Address
City, State, Zip

Dear [Actor's Name]:

Enclosed is an agreement for your services on [Name of Project.] Please sign the contract where indicated and complete the attached payroll start slip, W-4 and I-9 forms. We would appreciate it if you would send I-9 verification at the time you return the signed agreement (a copy of a driver's license and social security card or passport.)

Enclosed is a self-addressed, stamped envelope for your convenience.

Once the contract is fully-executed, a copy will be returned to you for your files.

If you have any questions, please do not hesitate to call me at [production office phone number.]

Sincerely yours,

Day-Player contracts are often prepared with the work date left off and given to the Production Coordinator. The date may be filled in the evening before an actor works, the contract sent to the set the next day for signature.

Standard employment contracts myst be available for signature not later than the first day of employment.

Be careful when communicating with a Day Player if there is a chance that the part may be cancelled. Sending an actor a script (or "sides") and having Wardrobe contact the actor constitutes a "booking" even if a firm work date has not yet been given and a contract has not yet been drawn-up.

Stunt Performer contracts are generally prepared and sent out from the Production Office. Specific SAG contracts exist for the employment of stunt players.

STUNT PERFORMER CATEGORIES:

STUNT DOUBLE: (Daily Performer Contract) may perform only for the character he agreed to double. Any other stunt work performed on any given day requires an additional contract.

UTILITY STUNT: (Weekly Performer Contract) may double more than one character during a single day and may perform any other stunt work that might be required without an additional contract(s) for these additional services. This type of employment is permitted only when hired under a weekly stunt contract.

ND STUNT: (non-descript stunt or general stunt work) is designated on a daily contract. Such performer may not double a specific character wihout an additional contract for that day.

The Casting Office will **Station 12** each actor (a SAG procedure to make sure the actor is in good standing with the Guild) prior to his reporting for work. The Production Office should Station 12 all actors (such as stunt performers) whose contracts originate from the Production Office and have not already been checked through the Casting Office.

The burden is on the production company (and not the actor) to notify the Guild of all SAG performers it is employing prior to their start dates. Not only should calls be made to the Guild to Station 12 actors, but verification calls from the Guild back to the Casting and Production Offices clearing each performer should be monitored to make sure that all are okayed to work.

Reasons that a performer may not be cleared through Station 12 might be that he is: delinquent in his Guild dues and must pay-up before he can work; that he must be Taft/Hartleyed or that he (after being Taft/Hartleyed once before) must join the Guild. It is therefore advantageous to clear a performer through Station 12 as soon as he is set so these additional steps (if necessary) can be taken. The fine for not clearing a performer who is not in good standing with the Guild presently is $500.

Once the actor signs his contract, it should be returned to the Production Coordinator. A copy of each contract, all accompanying W-4's and I-9's and a copy of the **Actors Production Time Report** (containing the actors' signatures) for each day of filming is to be turned in to the Production Accountant.

Make sure the actors' work times listed on the **Time Report** are the same as the times listed on the Daily Production Report and that the actors' signatures on the report are in ink. The top (original) copies of the SAG Time Sheets should be sent to SAG approximately once a week (to the attention of their Production Department.) A photocopy of each time sheet should be attached to the corresponding Daily Production Report.

The Production Coordinator will have the Producer sign the SAG contracts after they have been signed by the actors and will then distribute all fully-executed copies. The white (original) copy should be sent to your production executive for the company's legal files. Subsequent copies are for the production files, the Production Accountant and a copy is sent to the actor's agent (or directly to the actor if he has no agent.)

The following is a sample of a short letter that would accompany a copy of a **Fully-Executed Contract** that is returned to each respective agent:

```
Today's Date

Agent's Name
Agent's Address
City/State/Zip Code

Dear [Agent's Name]:

Enclosed is a fully-executed copy of
[Actor's Name]'s contract for his
services on "[Name of Project]".

If you have any questions, please do
not hesitate to call me.

Sincerely,
```

Again, if the performer has no agent, the letter should read:

```
Today's Date

Actor
Actor's Address
City/State/Zip code

Dear [Actor's Name]:

Enclosed is a fully-executed copy of
your contract for your services on
"[Name of Project]".
```

```
If you have any questions, please do
not hesitate to call me.

Sincerely,
```

Send all **Script Revisions** are to be sent to actors via the Production Office.

WORK CALLS

The Assistant Director will give all **"First" Work Calls** to the Casting Office. They, in turn, will call all respective agents with detailed information as to time, location and scenes to be shot the following day. The Assistant Director will usually follow-through and call the actors that evening to confirm that they have received calls from their agents and have been given the proper information. The Assistant Director will also handle all other work calls other than first calls.

If any of the actors calls the Production or Casting Office to find out her call for the next day, she should be informed as to what the call sheet reads, but it must be made clear that this is not a final call and is **Subject to Change**. Remind all actors that the Assistant Director will call them each evening with a definite work call for the next day.

Production should make sure Casting gets a call sheet each day and is kept up to date on all schedule changes.

THE WORK WEEK

The performer's workweek consists of any five consecutive days out of seven consecutive days, or on an overnight location—any six consecutive days out of seven consecutive, as designated by the Producer on each production unit. Any performer or extra employed on a theatrical motion picture who works on the designated sixth or seventh day of the work week is not entitled to **premium pay** unless such a day is the performer's sixth or seventh consecutive day worked.

CONSECUTIVE EMPLOYMENT

Performers are to be paid on a consecutive day's basis from the first day they are instructed to report for work, or when shooting on an overnight location, beginning with the **travel day**, which constitutes the first day of employment. For example, if a weekly freelance player is scheduled to work on a Monday and Tuesday, is *on hold* Wednesday and Thursday, and works again on Friday, she is to paid for the entire week, even though she was not given a call to report to work on Wednesday and Thursday. Additionally, because she is employed by the production company for the entire week, she is subject to being called in for work on Wednesday or Thursday, should there be a change in schedule.

Weekly performers who are on hold for several days during the schedule and are then called back to work for another day or two cannot be taken off payroll as a weekly performer and converted to a daily performer when called back for those additional days. That performer must be compensated on a weekly basis until her services on the film are completed.

A day performer, on the other hand, can be converted to a weekly performer if at the time of original engagement, the performer is given a firm pick-up date which is more than ten calendar days for films produced in the United States, and 14 calendar days for films produced outside the United States. Under these circumstances, compensation need not be given for the intervening time.

Performers employed on a day basis may also be returned on a weekly basis with an on or after pick-up date, (which refers to a specific date or the following day), thus allowing the Producer a 24-hour leeway.

One such break in employment is allowed for each performer per production.

Consecutive employment does not apply to stunt performers, unless the stunt performer has dialogue, which consitutes a role.

PERFORMER CATEGORIES

SAG members are classified by category as follows:

SCHEDULE A: Day Performers

SCHEDULES B and C: Freelance weekly performers (determined by the amount of compensation paid to the performer)

SCHEDULE D: Multiple-picture performers

SCHEDULE E and F: Contract performers (determined by the amount of compensation

SCHEDULE G-I: Professional singers employed by the day

SCHEDULE G-II: Professional singers employed by the week. (A professional singer is a person who is employed primarily to sing a set piece of music on a given pitch either as a solo or in a group requiring unison, melody and harmony.)

SCHEDULE H-I: Stunt performers employed by the day.

SCHEDULE H-II and H-III: Stunt performers employed by the week (depending on their salary)

SCHEDULE H-IV: Stunt performers under term contracts.

SCHEDULE I: Airline pilots—a pilot who is employed to fly or taxi aircraft— including helicopters—before the camera in the photographing of motion pictures.

SCHEDULE J: Extra Performers

All categories are determined by the amount of compensation received by the performer. Compensation rates are determined during contract year's end, adjusted yearly.

There are rules and rates that pertain to all SAG performers and those that are exclusive to performers who fit into a specific "schedule."

The following are a few basic regulations that apply to all SAG members and those that are exclusive to performers who fit into a specific schedule If in doublt of any rate or regulation, always check your SAG contract or call your SAG representative if you need additional information on any of these or other Guild-related issues.

EMPLOYMENT OF MINORS

When finalizing a deal for the **Employment of a Minor**, make sure his work permit is up to date. Most importantly, you need to be aware of both the Child Labor Laws in the state in which the minor is being hired and SAG policies regarding the employment of minors and to know which set of regulations apply to your production. Before you can hire minors, many states will have you apply for a **Permit To Employ Minors** in addition to requiring you to supply them with a certificate of insurance to show proof of your Workers' Compensation coverage.

Note that California has some of the most stringent child labor laws in the country which apply to both minors hired in California and those hired in other states but brought to California to work. If a minor is hired in California by a California-based company and the production company shoots the film in another state, California regulations apply. And if a company based in another state shoots their film in California, the minors which they employ are also subject to California laws.

If, however, minors are being employed by a company based in and shooting in a state other than California where child labor laws are less stringent, then SAG regulations would take precedence.

Regulations regarding the employment of minors are very precise. Depending on the child's age, he is allowed a required number of hours in which to work, attend school and rest. They cannot work earlier than a specified time in the morning nor past a specified time at night; and if under sixteen years of age, must be accompanied by a parent or guardian. These regulations also cover the employment of teacher/welfare workers and the number of children each teacher may teach and/or supervise.

In addition, California and New York have procedures whereby a judge will both "confirm" a contract with a minor (to prevent the minor from changing his mind later), and, at the same time, require the production company to put a portion of the minor's compensation into a supervised bank account until the minor reaches the age of majority (the amount is generally 25% of the gross.) Discuss this with your legal department or attorney to determine if court approval should be sought. Parents should also be informed of this when making the deal and should agree to cooperate in obtaining proper approvals.

It is important to be aware of the time frame necessary to secure a court order and establish a trust account for the minor, because the production company is still bound by the terms of the agreement for the payment of compensation.

Whether you are governed under State or SAG guidelines, make sure you and your assistant directors are fully acquainted with all the policies pertaining to the employment of minors.

TAFT/HARTLEY

The Taft/Hartley is a Federal law which allows a non-member of a union or guild to work on a union show for 30 days. At the end of that time period, he or she must join the union to continue working on that particular show or for another signatory company.

A Producer will generally choose to hire a performer who is not a member of the Screen Actors Guild for a few different reasons. The first scenario is when a decision to hire a non-member is made after lengthy interviews to find a specific look or type or someone with very specific abilities that cannot be met by a SAG member. Another scenario happens on the set during filming, on the spur of the moment, when the Director decides an additional performer is needed to make a scene more complete and upgrades an Extra or Stand-In who happens to be there at the time. This situation may also apply to wekk-known or famous people brought in to portray themselves. (It is best to check with the Guild for a ruling when this situation arises.)

Whenever a non-member is hired to perform on a SAG signatory show, a Taft/Hartley form must be completed and submitted to the Screen Actors Guild.

A Taft/Hartley form submitted on a television or theatrical film must be received by the Guild within fifteen calendar days of the performer's first day of work. Submissions postmarked on the 15th day do not count and will be subject to a fine. Submissions from Commercials must be received by the Guild within fifteen business days.

Taft/Hartley forms require the performer's name, address, phone number, social security number, information on your production and *reason for hire*. If the reason for hire does not satisfactorily explain why this person was hired opposed to someone who is already a Guild member, the production may be subject to a fine.

Production companies are more apt to be fined for this type of violation when it Taft/Hartleys an excessive number of performers on one show, which automatically raises doubt as to the need for so many people with special abilities or qualities who can't be found from within the SAG membership.

Damages for the employment of a performer in violation of provisions that pertain to the Taft/Hartley law is $500.

Also requested along with a completed Taft/Hartley form is a professional resume and photograph of the performer. If the performer does not have a professional photograph, attach a Polaroid photo. An explanation is required if a professional resume and/or photo does not exist. As soon as a performer is Taft/Hartleyed, he can join the Guild. In all states (other than the right-to-work states), a performer can work for 30 days from his first date of employment (or any amount of days within that 30-day period) without having to join the Guild. Once their 30 days has lapsed, they must join before they can be employed on another SAG film.

In a right-to-work state (Alabama, Arizona, Arkansas, Florida, Georgia, Idaho, Iowa, Kansas, Louisiana, Mississippi, Nebraska, Nevada, North Carolina, North Dakota, South Carolina, South Dakota, Tennessee, Texas, Utah, Virginia and Wyoming), a performer may join, but is not required to. He may work union or non-union films; and the production cannot be fined for hiring a non-SAG member who has worked on other SAG productions. Performers working on a union show, even if they are not a Guild members, must be cleared through Station 12 and Taft/Harley letters must be submitted. In addition, Pension and Health benefits must be paid by the production company and performer's employment must be reported to the Guild.

SAG EXTRAS

The different categories of SAG extras are as follows:

GENERAL EXTRAS: A performer of atmospheric business which includes the normal actions, gestures and facial expessions of the Extra Performer's assignment.

STAND-IN: An extra used as a substitute for another actor for the purpose of focusing shots, setting lights., etc, but is not actually photographed. Stand-ins may also be used as General Extras.

PHOTO DOUBLE: An extra who is actually photographed as a substitute for another actor.

DAY PERFORMER: An extra who delivers a speech or line of dialogue. An Extra Performer must be upgraded to Day Performer if given a line, except in the case of Omnies.

OMNIES: Extras who produce indistinguishable background noise and chatter typically used in a party or restaurant scene.

Guidelines pertaining to the employment of extras are relatively new and not yet uniform throughout the country. Contact your local SAG office to obtain the guidelines pertaining to the number of SAG extras you are required to use, compensations rates and other conditions relating to the use of SAG extras on your production. There are specific voucher forms supplied by SAG and extra casting agencies to be used by SAG extras. Taft/Hartley rules are the same for SAG extras as they are for other SAG performers, but there are different Taft/Hartley forms to fill out in such cases. Examples of both forms can be found in Chapter 6.

NUDITY

The following rules apply when there is a possibility of nudity:

A. The Producer's representative is to notify the performer (or their representative) of any nudity or sex acts expected in the role (if known by management at the time) prior to the first interview or audition. The performer shall also have prior notification of any interview or audition requiring nudity and shall have the absolute right to have a person of the performer's choice present at the audition.

B. During any production involving nudity or sex scenes, the set shall be closed to all persons having no business purpose in connection with the production.

C. No still photography of nudity or sex acts will be authorized by the Producer to be made without the consent of the performer.

D. The appearance of a performer in a nude or sex scene or the doubling of a performer in such a scene shall be conditioned upon the performer's prior written consent. Such consent may be obtained by letter or other writing prior to a commitment or written contract being made or executed. Such consent must include a general description as to the extent of the nudity and the type of physical contact required in the scene. If a performer has agreed to appear in such scene and then withdraws consent, the Producer shall also have the right to double the performer. Consent may not be withdrawn as to film already photographed. Producer shall also have the right to double young children or infants in nude scenes (not in sex scenes).

WORKING WITH ANIMALS

There is an availability of trained animals that can perform with realism and without danger of injury or death. To assure the responsible, decent and humane treatment of animals, Producers are encouraged to work with the American Humane Association as it pertains to the use of animals in their films.

Producers cannot utilize any performer in a scene which an animal is intentionally mistreated or killed, except when the animals being killed are subject to the provision of a legal hunting season.

Producers need to notify the American Humane Association prior to the commencement of any work involving an animal(s) and advise them as to the nature of the work to be performed. Scripted scenes involving animals should be made available to the American Humane Association. Representatives of the Association may be present at any time during the filming of a motion picture where animals are used.

Rules pertaining to casting and the employment of actors are varied and many. Additions and revision are enacted every three years when the Screen Actors Guild negotiates a new contract with the Alliance of Motion Picture and Television Producers. In addition to the few guidelines outlined, you should have a good working knowledge of pay scales and specific rules pertaining to: interviews; engagement and cancellation; makeup, hairdressing, wardrobe and fitting calls; employment contract; billing/screen credit; consecutive employment; production time reports and overtime records; location and travel time; transportation and location expenses; rest periods; meal penalty violations; night work; looping; overtime; work weeks; time of payment and late payments; reuse of film; stunt work; safety and affirmative action. Also be aware of the specifics on the employment of extras, minors, stunt performers, dancers, etc.

Keep a copy of the latest SAG contract (and contract summary pamphlets) close at hand. When in doubt concerning specific rules, contact your legal department or attorney or call your local SAG representative.

Screen Actors Guild Offices

NATIONAL HEADQUARTERS
5757 Wilshire Boulavard
Los Angeles, California 90036

Main Switchboard	(213) 465-4600
(open 9 a.m. til 5 p.m.)	
Theatrical Contracts	(213) 856-6842
Television Contracts	(213) 856-6855
Station 12	(213) 856-6772
(open 9 a.m. til 6:30 p.m.)	
SAG Extras	(213) 856-6867
Singers' Representative	(213) 856-6864
Residuals Information	
and Claims	(213) 856-6700
Signatory Status	(213) 856-6861

ARIZONA
1616 E. Indian School Rd., Suite 330
Phoenix, Arizona 85016
(602) 265-2712

CALIFORNIA—Los Angeles
NATIONAL HEADQUARTERS
7065 Hollywood Boulevard
Hollywood, California 90028
(213) 465-4600

CALIFORNIA—San Diego
7827 Convoy Court, Suite 400
San Diego, California 92111
(619) 278-7695

CALIFORNIA—San Francisco
235 Pine Street, 11th Floor
San Francisco, California 94104
(415) 391-7510

COLORADO
*(Colorado, New Mexico, Nevada and Utah all use
the Colorado office)*
950 South Cherry Street, Suite 502
Denver, Colorado 80222
(303) 757-6226

FLORIDA
2299 Douglas Road, Suite 200
Miami, Florida 33145
(305) 444-7677

GEORGIA
1627 Peachtree Street, N.E., Suite 210
Atlanta, Georgia 30309
(404) 897-1335

HAWAII
949 Kapiolani Blvd., Suite 105
Honolulu, Hawaii 96814
(808) 538-6122

ILLINOIS
307 N. Michigan Ave., Suite 312
Chicago, Illinois 60601
(312) 372-8081

MARYLAND
5480 Wisconsin Ave., Suite 201
Chevy Chase, Maryland 20815
(301) 657-2560

MASSACHUSETTS
11 Beacon Street
Boston, Massachusetts 02108
(617) 742-2688

MICHIGAN
28690 Southfield Road
Lathrup Village, Michigan 48076
(313) 559-9540

MINNESOTA*
15 South Ninth Street, Suite 400
Minneapolis, Minnesota 55402
(612) 371-9120

MISSOURI *
906 Olive Street, Suite 1006
St. Louis, Missouri 63101
(314) 231-8410

NEVADA
*(Colorado, New Mexico, Nevada and Utah all use
the Colorado office)*
950 South Cherry Street, Suite 502
Denver, Colorado 80222
(303) 757-6226

NEW MEXICO
*(Colorado, New Mexico, Nevada and Utah all use
the Colorado office)*
950 South Cherry Street, Suite 502
Denver, Colorado 80222
(303) 757-6226

NEW YORK HEADQUARTERS
1515 Broadway, 44th Floor
New York, New York 10036
(212) 944-1030

OHIO *
1367 East Sixth Street, Suite 229
Cleveland, Ohio 44114
(218) 579-9305

PENNSYLVANIA
230 South Broad Street, 10th Floor
Philadelphia, Pennsylvania 19102
(215) 545-3150

TENNESSEE
PO Box 121087
Nashville, Tennessee 37212
(615) 327-2958

TEXAS—Dallas/Ft. Worth
6060 North Central Expressway
Suite 302, LB 604
Dallas, Texas 75206
(214) 363-8300

TEXAS—Houston
2650 Fountainview Dr., Suite 326
Houston, Texas 77057
(713) 972-1806

UTAH
(Colorado, New Mexico, Nevada and Utah all use
the Colorado office)
950 South Cherry Street, Suite 502
Denver, Colorado 80222
(303) 757-6226

WASHINGTON *
601 Valley Street, Suite 200
Seattle, Washington 98109
(206) 282-2506

WASHINGTON, D.C./MARYLAND
5480 Wisconsin Ave., Suite 201
Chevy Chase, Maryland 20815
(301) 657-2560

     * These are AFTRA offices that also adminis-
ter SAG contracts.

CHAPTER 6

FORMS AND REPORTS
SAG, DGA, WGA

Many films are now being shot using non-union crews, but most are signatory to the **Screen Actors Guild**, the **Directors Guild** and the **Writers Guild**. Each of these three guilds has its own forms, reports and guidelines that signatory companies are asked to adhere to.

As a signatory, you will have copies of each of the Guild contracts and should know the rules and rates associated with each.

The following is a sampling of the most often used Guild contracts and report forms. Note that: (1), DGA deal memos are not included in this section but can be found under **deal memos** and (2), there are no samples of pension, health and welfare reports or gross earning reports in the following pages. The reporting of such are functions of either your Production Accountant or the payroll company handling your show and are not generally prepared by production personnel.

NOTICE OF TENTATIVE WRITING CREDITS

TELEVISION

Before writing credits are finally determined, you are required to send a copy of the **Notice of Tentative Writing Credits—Television** to the Writer's Guild and all participating writers concurrently.

At the completion of principal photography, you are required to send two copies of the revised final shooting script to each participating writer. The notice should state the Company's choice of credit on a tentative basis.

THEATRICAL MOTION PICTURES

Before the writing credits are finally determined, you are required to file a copy of the **Notice of Tentative Writing Credits—Theatrical Motion Pictures** with the Writer's Guild Credits Department (within three days after completion of principal photography). The notice should state the Company's choice of credit on a tentative basis. Copies must be sent concurrently to all participating writers and to the Writer's Guild along with a copy of the final shooting script to each participant.

[Note: Samples of both Television and Theatrical Motion Picture Notice of Tentative Writing Credits forms are found at the end of this chapter.]

FORMS INCLUDED IN THIS SECTION

Screen Actors Guild Forms
Daily Contract for Television
   Motion Pictures or Videotapes.............. 33-34
Minimum Three-Day Contract for Television,
Motion Pictures or VIdeotape 35-36
Minimum Freelance Weekly Contract for Television, Motion Pictures or VIdeotape........ 37-38
Daily Stunt Performer
   Contract for Television, Motion Pictures or
   VIdeotape 39-40
Stunt Performer Minimum Freelance
   Weekly Contract for Television, Motion Pictures or VIdeotape 41-42
Daily Contract for
   Theatrical Motion Pictures 43-44
Minimum Freelance Contract
   for Theatrical Motion Pictures 45
Daily Stunt Performer
   Contract for Theatrical Motion Pictures 46
Stunt Performer Minimum Freelance
   Weekly Contract—Motion Pictures 47-48
Taft-Hartley Report 49
Taft-Hartley Report—SAG Extras 50
SAG Extra Voucher 51
Theatrical and Television Sign-In 52
Actors Production Time Report 53
Casting Data Report 55-56
Casting Data Report for
   Stunt Performers 57-58
Casting Data Report—
   Low Budget/Affirmative Action 59-60
Final Cast List Information Sheet 61-62
Member Report—
   ADR Theatrical/Television 63

Directors Guild of America Forms
Weekly Work List 64
Employment Data Reort 65-66

Writers Guild of America Forms
Notice of Tentative
   Screen Credits—Theatrical....................... 67
Notice of Tentative
   Screen Credits—Television 68

SCREEN ACTORS GUILD

DAILY CONTRACT
(DAY PLAYER)
FOR TELEVISION MOTION PICTURES OR VIDEOTAPES

Company _XYZ PRODUCTIONS_

Date Employment Starts_____

Role_____

Production Title_____

Production Number_____

Date _JUNE 1, 1993_

Actor Name _JOHN DOE_

Address: _123 ACTORS ALLEY RD._
HOLLYWOOD, CA 90028

Telephone No. _(213) 555-7737_

Social Security No. _124-76-2278_

** Daily Rate $ _485 + 10% AGENCY COMMISSION_

** Weekly Conversion Rate $ _1,685 + 10% AGENCY COMM._

Wardrobe supplied by Actor _____Yes __✔__No

If so, number of outfits _____ @ $ _____

(formal) _____ @ $ _____

Date of Actor's next engagement_____

Complete for "Drop-And-Pick-Up" Deals ONLY:

Firm recall date on _____ or

on or after* _JULY 13, 1993_

("On or after" recall only applies to pick-up as Weekly Player.)

As ☐ Day Player ☒ Weekly Player

*Means date specified or within 24 hours thereafter

THIS AGREEMENT covers the employment of the above-named Player by _XYZ PRODUCTIONS_ _____ in the production and at the rate of compensation set forth above and is subject to and shall include, for the benefit of the Player and the Producer, all of the applicable provisions and conditions contained or provided for in the 1986 Screen Actors Guild Television Agreement (herein called the "Television Agreement"). Player's employment shall include performance in non-commercial openings, bridges, etc., and no added compensation shall be payable to Player so long as such are used in the role and episode covered hereunder in which Player appears; for other use, Player shall be paid the added minimum compensation, if any, required under the provisions of the Screen Actors Guild agreements with Producer.

Producer shall have all the rights in and to the results and proceeds of the Player's services rendered hereunder, as are provided with respect to "photoplays" in Schedule A of the Producer-Screen Actors Guild Codified Basic Agreement and the right to supplemental market use as defined in the Television Agreement.

Producer shall have the unlimited right throughout the world to telecast the film and exhibit the film theatrically and in supplemental markets in accordance with the terms and conditions of the Television Agreement.

If the motion picture is rerun on television in the United States or Canada and contains any of the results and proceeds of the Player's services, the Player will be paid for each day of employment hereunder the additional compensation prescribed therefor by the Television Agreement, unless there is an agreement to pay an amount in excess thereof as follows:

SAG MINIMUM

_____

_____

If there is foreign telecasting of the motion picture as defined in the Television Agreement, and such motion picture contains any of the results and proceeds of the Player's services, the Player will be paid in the amount in the blank space below for each day of employment hereunder, or if such blank space is not filled in, then the Player will be paid the minimum additional compensation prescribed therefor by the Television Agreement.

If the motion picture is exhibited theatrically anywhere in the world and contains any of the results and proceeds of the Player's services, the Player will be paid $_____ SAG MIN. _____, or if this blank is not filled in, then the Player will be paid the minimum additional compensation prescribed therefor by the Television Agreement.

If the motion picture is exhibited in supplemental markets anywhere in the world and contains any of the results and proceeds of the Player's services, then Player will be paid the supplemental market fees prescribed by the applicable provisions of the Television Agreement.

If the Player places his or her initials in the box below, he or she thereby authorizes Producer to use portions of said television motion picture as a trailer to promote another episode or the series as a whole, upon payment to the Player of the additional compensation prescribed by the applicable provisions of the Television Agreement.

***
BILLING : END CREDITS. SHARED CARD. PLACEMENT AT
      PRODUCER'S DISCRETION

Initial

By _Swifty Deals_   Producer

John Doe   Player

Production time reports are available on the set at the end of each day, which reports shall be signed or initialed by the Player.

Attached hereto for your use are the following: (1) Declaration Regarding Income Tax Withholding ("Part Year Employment Method of Withholding") and (2) Declaration Regarding Income Tax Withholding. You may utilize the applicable form by delivering same to Producer. Only one of such forms may be used.

NOTICE TO ACTOR: IT IS IMPORTANT THAT YOU RETAIN A COPY OF THIS CONTRACT FOR YOUR PERMANENT RECORDS.

***
INCLUDING THE "BILLING" (SCREEN CREDIT) IS NOT REQUIRED —
BUT IS AN IMPORTANT PART OF THE PERFORMER'S DEAL
WORTH ADDING TO THE SIGNED CONTRACT.

**
AS AGENTS DO NOT COLLECT COMMISSION ON "SCALE", 10% IS ADDED TO THE
COMPENSATION RATE FOR THOSE ACTORS WHO HAVE AGENTS & ARE RECEIVING "SCALE"
FOR THEIR PERFORMANCE

SCREEN ACTORS GUILD

**MINIMUM THREE-DAY CONTRACT
FOR TELEVISION MOTION PICTURES OR VIDEOTAPES
THREE-DAY MINIMUM EMPLOYMENT**

THIS AGREEMENT is made this __15th__ day of __MAY__, 19__93__, between __XYZ PRODUCTIONS__, a corporation, hereinafter called "Producer," and __RAYMOND BURRMAN__, hereinafter called "Performer."

WITNESSETH:

1. **Photoplay; Role and Guarantee.** Producer hereby engages Performer to render service as such in the role of __ELLIOT__, in a photoplay produced primarily for exhibition over free television, the working title of which is now __THE WATCHER__. Performer accepts such engagement upon the terms herein specified. Producer guarantees that it will furnish Performer not less than __THREE__ days' employment. (If this blank is not filled in, the guarantee shall be three (3) days.)

2. **Salary.** The Producer will pay to the Performer, and the Performer agrees to accept for three (3) days (and pro rata for each additional day beyond three (3) days) the following salary rate: $ __1,500__.

3. Producer shall have the unlimited right throughout the world to telecast the film and exhibit the film theatrically and in Supplemental Markets in accordance with the terms and conditions of the applicable Screen Actors Guild Television Agreement (herein referred to as the "Television Agreement").

4. If the motion picture is rerun on television in the United States or Canada and contains any of the results and proceeds of the Performer's services, the Performer will be paid the additional compensation prescribed therefor by the Television Agreement, unless there is an agreement to pay an amount in excess thereof as follows:

__SAG MINIMUM__

5. If there is foreign telecasting of the motion picture as defined in the Television Agreement, and such motion picture contains any of the results and proceeds of the Performer's services, the Performer will be paid the amount in the blank space below plus an amount equal to one-third (1/3) thereof for each day of employment in excess of three (3) days, or, if such blank space is not filled in, then the Performer will be paid the minimum additional compensation prescribed therefor by the Television Agreement. $__SAG MIN__.

6. If the motion picture is exhibited theatrically anywhere in the world and contains any of the results and proceeds of the Performer's services, the Performer will be paid $__SAG MIN__, plus an amount equal to one-third (1/3) thereof for each day of employment in excess of three (3) days. If this blank is not filled in, the Performer will be paid the applicable minimum additional compensation prescribed therefor by the Television Agreement.

7. If the motion picture is exhibited in Supplemental Markets anywhere in the world and contains any of the results and proceeds of the Performer's services, the Performer will be paid the supplemental market fees prescribed by the applicable provisions of the Television Agreement.

8. **Term.** The term of employment hereunder shall begin on __JUNE 20, 1993__, on or about* _____ and shall continue thereafter until the completion of the photography and recordation of said role.

---

* The "on or about clause" may only be used when the contract is delivered to the Performer at least three (3) days before the starting date.

9. **Incorporation of Television Agreement.** The applicable provisions of the Television Agreement are incorporated herein by reference. Performer's employment shall include performance in non-commercial openings, closings, bridges, etc., and no added compensation shall be payable to Performer so long as such are used in the role and episode covered hereunder and in which Performer appears; for other use, Performer shall be paid the added minimum compensation, if any, required under the provisions of the Screen Actors Guild agreements with Producer. Performer's employment shall be upon the terms, conditions and exceptions of the provisions applicable to the rate of salary and guarantee specified in Paragraphs 1. and 2. hereof.

10. **Arbitration of Disputes.** Should any dispute or controversy arise between the parties hereto with reference to this contract, or the employment herein provided for, such dispute or controversy shall be settled and determined by conciliation and arbitration in accordance with and to the extent provided in the conciliation and arbitration provisions of the Television Agreement, and such provisions are hereby referred to and by such reference incorporated herein and made a part of this agreement with the same effect as though the same were set forth herein in detail.

11. **Performer's Address.** All notices which the Producer is required or may desire to give to the Performer may be given either by mailing the same addressed to the Performer at _123 ELM ST. — HOLLYWOOD CA 90028_ or such notice may be given to the Performer personally, either orally or in writing.

12. **Performer's Telephone.** The Performer must keep the Producer's casting office or the assistant director of said photoplay advised as to where the Performer may be reached by telephone without unreasonable delay. The current telephone number of the Performer is (_213_) _555 - 4376_ .

13. If Performer places his initials in the box, he thereby authorizes Producer to use portions of said television motion picture as a trailer to promote another episode or the series as a whole, upon payment to the Performer of the additional compensation prescribed by the Television Agreement.

X _PB_ ☐

14. **Furnishing of Wardrobe.** The Performer agrees to furnish all modern wardrobe and wearing apparel reasonably necessary for the portrayal of said role; it being agreed, however, that should so-called "character" or "period" costumes be required, the Producer shall supply the same. When Performer supplies any wardrobe, Performer shall receive the cleaning allowance and reimbursement specified in the Television Agreement.

15. **Next Starting Date.** The starting date of Performer's next engagement is

BILLING: END CREDITS - SHARED CARD - PLACEMENT @ PRODUCER'S DISCRETION

IN WITNESS WHEREOF, the parties have executed this agreement on the day and year first above written.

By _Swifty Deals_
_____
Producer

X _Raymond Burr_
_____
Performer

_173 - 21 - 6342_
_____
Social Security No.

Production time reports are available on the set at the end of each day. Such reports shall be signed or initialed by the performer.

Attached hereto for your use is a Declaration Regarding Income Tax Withholding ("Part Year Employment Method of Withholding"). You may utilize such form by delivering same to Producer.

NOTICE TO PERFORMER: IT IS IMPORTANT THAT YOU RETAIN A COPY OF THIS CONTRACT FOR YOUR PERMANENT RECORDS.

SCREEN ACTORS GUILD

MINIMUM FREE LANCE WEEKLY CONTRACT
FOR TELEVISION MOTION PICTURES OR VIDEOTAPES

Continuous Employment - Weekly Basis - Weekly Salary
One Week Minimum Employment

THIS AGREEMENT is made this __28 th__ day of __MAY__, 19__93__,
between __XYZ PRODUCTIONS__, a corporation, hereinafter called
"Producer," and __Nancy Nicely__ hereinafter called "Performer."

WITNESSETH:

1. **Photoplay; Role and Guarantee.** Producer hereby engages Performer to render services as such, in the role of __MOM__, in a photoplay produced primarily for exhibition over free television, the working title of which is now __THE WATCHER__. Performer accepts such engagement upon the terms herein specified. Producer guarantees that it will furnish Performer not less than __Two (2)__ weeks employment. (If this blank is not filled in, the guarantee shall be one week).

2. **Salary.** The Producer will pay to the Performer, and the Performer agrees to accept weekly (and _pro rata_ for each additional day beyond guarantee) the following salary rate: $ __2,000__ per "studio week." (Schedule B Performers must receive an additional overtime payment of four (4) hours at straight time rate for each overnight location sixth day).

3. Producer shall have the unlimited right throughout the world to telecast the film and exhibit the film theatrically and in Supplemental Markets, in accordance with the terms and conditions of the applicable Screen Actors Guild Television Agreement (herein referred to as the "Television Agreement").

4. If the motion picture is rerun on television in the United States or Canada and contains any of the results and proceeds of the Performer's services, the Performer will be paid the additional compensation prescribed therefor by the Television Agreement, unless there is an agreement to pay an amount in excess thereof as follows:

_____

__SAG MINIMUM__

_____

5. If there is foreign telecasting of the motion picture, as defined in the Television Agreement, and such motion picture contains any of the results and proceeds of the Performer's services, the Performer will be paid $ __SAG MIN.__ plus _pro_ _rata_ thereof for each additional day of employment in excess of one week, or, if this blank is not filled in, the Performer will be paid the minimum additional compensation prescribed therefor by the Television Agreement.

6. If the motion picture is exhibited theatrically anywhere in the world and contains any of the results and proceeds of the Performer's services, the Performer will be paid $ __SAG MIN.__ plus _pro_ _rata_ thereof for each additional day of employment in excess of one week, or, if this blank is not filled in, the Performer will be paid the minimum additional compensation prescribed therefor by the Television Agreement.

7. If the motion picture is exhibited in Supplemental Markets anywhere in the world and contains any of the results and proceeds of the Performer's services, the Performer will be paid the supplemental market fees prescribed by the applicable provisions of the Television Agreement.

8. **Term.** The term of employment hereunder shall begin on JUNE 21, 1993 , on or about* _____ and shall continue thereafter until the completion of the photography and recordation of said role.

9. **Incorporation of Television Agreement.** The applicable provisions of the Television Agreement are incorporated herein by reference. Performer's employment shall include performance in non-commercial openings, closings, bridges, etc., and no added compensation shall be payable to Performer so long as such are used in the role and episode covered hereunder and in which Performer appears; for other use, Performer shall be paid the added minimum compensation, if any, required under the provisions of the Screen Actors Guild agreements with Producer. Performer's employment shall be upon the terms, conditions and exceptions of said provisions applicable to the rate of salary and guarantee specified in Paragraphs 1. and 2. hereof.

10. **Arbitration of Disputes.** Should any dispute or controversy arise between the parties hereto with reference to this contract, or the employment herein provided for, such dispute or controversy shall be settled and determined by conciliation and arbitration in accordance with and to the extent provided in the conciliation and arbitration provisions of the Television Agreement, and such provisions are hereby referred to and by such reference incorporated herein and made a part of this agreement with the same effect as though the same were set forth herein in detail.

11. **Performer's Address.** All notices which the Producer is required or may desire to give to the Performer may be given either by mailing the same addressed to the Performer at 4321 ORANGE RD - LOS ANGELES CA, 90068 or such notice may be given to the Performer personally, either orally or in writing.

12. **Performer's Telephone.** The Performer must keep the Producer's casting office or the assistant director of said photoplay advised as to where the Performer may be reached by telephone without unreasonable delay. The current telephone number of the Performer is (213) 555-5251 .

13. If the Performer places his initials in the box, he thereby authorizes Producer to use portions of said television motion picture as a trailer to promote another episode or the series as a whole, upon payment to the Performer of the additional compensation prescribed by the Television Agreement.

X〰〰

14. **Furnishing of Wardrobe.** The Performer agrees to furnish all modern wardrobe and wearing apparel reasonably necessary for the portrayal of said role; it being agreed, however, that should so-called "character" or "period" costumes be required, the Producer shall supply the same. When Performer supplies any wardrobe, Performer shall receive the cleaning allowance and reimbursement specified in the Television Agreement.

15. **Next Starting Date.** The starting date of Performer's next engagement is

BILLING: MAIN TITLES · SINGLE CARD · 3RD POSITION

IN WITNESS WHEREOF, the parties have executed this contract on the day and year first above written.

By _Swifty Deals_
                          Producer
X _Nancy Nicely_
                          Performer
372-46-2232
                   Social Security No.

Production time reports are available on the set at the end of each day. Such reports shall be signed or initialed by the performer.

NOTICE TO PERFORMER: IT IS IMPORTANT THAT YOU RETAIN A COPY OF THIS CONTRACT FOR YOUR PERMANENT RECORDS.

---

* The "on or about clause" may only be used when the contract is delivered to the performer at least three (3) days before the starting date.

28

SCREEN ACTORS GUILD
STUNT PERFORMER
DAILY STUNT PERFORMER CONTRACT
FOR TELEVISION MOTION PICTURES AND VIDEOTAPES

Company __XYZ PRODUCTIONS__

Date Employment Starts __JUNE 25, 1993__

Role __STUNT DOUBLE__ , or

Stunt Double for* _____ , or

Other (description) _____

Production Title __THE WATCHER__

Date __JUNE 24, 1993__

Stunt Performer Name __Johnny Rockett__

Address __123 HOLLYWOOD HILLS RD__
__HOLLYWOOD, CA 90028__

Telephone No. __213 / 555 - 1007__

Social Security No. __552 - 11 - 7627__

Daily Rate $ __485__

Weekly Conversion Rate $ _____

Stunt Adjustment(s):

$ __1,000__ for __HIGH FALL__ No. of takes __3__

$ _____ for _____ No. of takes _____

Wardrobe supplied by Stunt Performer _____ Yes __✓__ No

If so, number of outfits _____ @ $ _____

(formal) _____ @ $ _____

Date of Stunt Performer's next engagement: _____

COMPLETE FOR "DROP & PICK-UP" DEALS ONLY:

Firm recall date on _____ , or

on or after** _____

("On or after" recall only applies to pick-up as
Weekly Performer.)

As _____ Day Player _____ Weekly Player

**Means date specified or within 24 hours thereafter.

WITNESSETH:

1. THIS AGREEMENT covers the employment of the above-named Performer by __XYZ PRODUCTIONS__
in the production and at the rate of compensation set forth above and conditions contained or provided for in the Screen Actors Guild Television Agreement (herein called the "Television Agreement"). Performer's employment shall include performance in non-commercial openings, bridges, etc., and no added compensation shall be payable to Performer so long as such are used in the role and episode covered hereunder in which Performer appears.

2. Producer shall have the unlimited right throughout the world to telecast the film and exhibit the film theatrically and in supplemental markets in accordance with the terms and conditions of the Television Agreement.

3. If the motion picture is rerun on television in the United States or Canada and contains any of the results and proceeds of the Performer's services, the Performer will be paid for each day of employment hereunder the additional compensation prescribed therefor by the Television Agreement, unless there is an agreement to pay an amount in excess thereof as follows: __SAG MINIMUM__

4. If there is foreign telecasting of the motion picture as defined in the Television Agreement, and such motion picture contains any of the results and proceeds of the Performer's services, the Performer will be paid in the amount in the blank space below for each day of employment hereunder, or if such blank space is not filled in, then the Performer will be paid the minimum additional compensation prescribed therefor by the Television Agreement. __SAG MINIMUM__

*NOTE: STUNT DAY PERFORMERS MUST RECEIVE A SEPARATE DAY'S PAY AND CONTRACT FOR EACH PERSON DOUBLED.

5. If the motion picture is exhibited theatrically anywhere in the world and contains any of the results and proceeds of the Performer's services, the Performer will be paid $ _____ SAG MIN. _____ , or if this blank is not filled in, then the Performer will be paid the minimum additional compensation prescribed therefor by the Television Agreement.

6. If the motion picture is exhibited in supplemental markets anywhere in the world and contains any of the results and proceeds of the Performer's services, then Performer will be paid the supplemental market fees prescribed by the applicable provisions of the Television Agreement.

By _____

_____ Producer

_____

_____ Stunt Performer

Production time reports and/or time cards are available on the set at the end of each day, which reports shall be signed or initialed by the Performer and must indicate any agreed stunt adjustments.

Attached hereto for your use are the following: (1) Declaration Regarding Income Tax Withholding ("Part Year Employment Method of Withholding") and (2) Declaration Regarding Income Tax Withholding. You may utilize the applicable form by delivering same to Producer. Only one of such forms may be used.

NOTICE TO STUNT PERFORMER: IT IS IMPORTANT THAT YOU RETAIN A COPY OF THIS CONTRACT FOR YOUR PERMANENT RECORDS.

SCREEN ACTORS GUILD

STUNT PERFORMER

MINIMUM FREE LANCE WEEKLY CONTRACT
FOR TELEVISION MOTION PICTURES OR VIDEOTAPES

Weekly Basis — Weekly Salary
One Week Minimum Employment

THIS AGREEMENT, made this _____ __19TH__ _____ day of __JULY__ _____, 19 __93__, between

_____ __XYZ PRODUCTIONS__ _____, a corporation, hereinafter called "Producer,"

and _____ __CLIFF HANGERR__ _____, hereinafter called "Performer."

WITNESSETH:

1. PHOTOPLAY, ROLE AND GUARANTEE. Producer hereby engages Performer to render services as such,

   Check One:

   ☐ in the Role of _____, or

   ☐ as Stunt Double for_____, or

   ☒ as Utility Stunt Performer, or

   ☐ other (describe work)_____

   in a photoplay produced primarily for exhibition over free television, the working title of which is now _____ __THE WATCHER__
   _____ . Performer accepts such engagement upon the terms herein specified. Producer guarantees that it will furnish Performer
   not less than _____ weeks employment. (If this blank is not filled in, the guarantee shall be one week).

2. SALARY. The Producer will pay to the Performer, and the Performer agrees to accept weekly (and pro rata for each additional day beyond guarantee)
   the following salary rate: $ __1,808—__ per "studio week." (Schedule H-II Performers must receive an additional overtime payment
   for four (4) hours at straight time rate for each overnight location Saturday.)

3. STUNT ADJUSTMENTS. It is understood between the parties that the salary rate specified above may require adjustment depending upon the
   nature of the stunt activities Producer requires. If so, a Stunt Adjustment will be agreed upon between the parties through good faith bargaining
   and said adjustment shall be noted on the Performer's daily time sheet or time card. Such adjustment shall increase the Performer's compensation
   for the week in the manner prescribed in Schedule H of the Screen Actors Guild Codified Basic Agreement.

4. Producer shall have the unlimited right throughout the world to telecast the film and exhibit the film theatrically and in supplemental markets,
   in accordance with the terms and conditions of the Screen Actors Guild Television Agreement (herein referred to as the "Television Agreement").

5. If the motion picture is rerun on television in the United States or Canada and contains any of the results and proceeds of the Performer's services,
   the Performer will be paid the additional compensation prescribed therefor by the Television Agreement unless there is an agreement to pay an
   amount in excess thereof as follows:_____ __SAG MINIMUN__

6. If there is foreign telecasting of the motion picture as defined in the Television Agreement, and such motion picture contains any of the results
   and proceeds of the Performer's services, the Performer will be paid $ _____ __SAG MIN.__ _____ plus pro rata thereof for each day of
   employment in excess of one week, or, if this blank is not filled in, then the Performer will be paid the minimum additional compensation
   prescribed therefor by the Television Agreement.

7. If the motion picture is exhibited theatrically anywhere in the world and contains any of the results and proceeds of the Performer's services,
   the Performer will be paid $ _____ __SAG MIN.__ _____ plus pro rata thereof for each day of employment in excess of one week, or, if
   this blank is not filled in, the Performer will be paid the minimum additional compensation prescribed therefor by the Television Agreement.

8. If the motion picture is exhibited in supplemental markets anywhere in the world and contains any of the results and proceeds of the Performer's services, then Performer will be paid the supplemental market fees prescribed by the applicable provisions of the Television Agreement.

9. TERM. The term of employment hereunder shall begin

on _____ , OR on or about* ___JULY 20, 1993_____

10. CONTINUOUS EMPLOYMENT AND RIGHT TO ROLE. If the Stunt Performer portrays a role or has dialogue, such Performer shall be entitled to continuous employment and "right to role" and shall receive payment for the entire period from the Performer's first call to work on the picture until completion of the photography and recordation of said role.

11. INCORPORATION OF TELEVISION AGREEMENT. The applicable provisions of the Television Agreement are incorporated herein by reference. Performer's employment shall include performance in non-commercial openings, closings, bridges, etc., and no added compensation shall be payable to Performer so long as such are used in the role(s) and episode(s) covered hereunder and in which Performer appears. Performer's employment shall be upon the terms, conditions and exceptions of said provisions applicable to the rate of salary and guarantee specified in Paragraphs 1 and 2 hereof.

12. PERFORMER'S ADDRESS. All notices which the Producer is required or may desire to give to the Performer may be given either by mailing the same addressed to the Performer at___702 MAIN AVE. / SAN DIEGO, CA___ or such notice may be given to the Performer personally, either orally or in writing.   92021

13. PERFORMER'S TELEPHONE. The Performer must keep the Producer's casting office or the assistant director of said photoplay advised as to where the Performer may be reached by telephone without unreasonable delay. The current telephone number of the Performer is _(609) 555- 9879_____ .

14. NEXT STARTING DATE. The starting date of the Performer's next engagement is _____ .

IN WITNESS WHEREOF, the parties have executed this agreement on the day and year first above written.

PRODUCER _Swifty Deals_____

BY _SWIFTY DEALS_____

STUNT PERFORMER X _Cliff Hanger_____

SOCIAL SECURITY # _932- 76 - 4376_____

*The "on or about" clause may only be used when the contract is delivered to the Performer at least three (3) days before the starting date.

The Production time reports are available on the set at the end of each day, which reports shall be signed or initialed by the Performer and must indicate any agreed stunt adjustments.

Attached hereto for your use is a Declaration Regarding Income Tax Withholding.

NOTICE TO STUNT PERFORMER: IT IS IMPORTANT THAT YOU RETAIN A COPY OF THIS CONTRACT FOR YOUR PERMANENT RECORDS.

**SCREEN ACTORS GUILD
MINIMUM FREE LANCE CONTRACT
FOR THEATRICAL MOTION PICTURES**

Continuous Employment—Weekly Basis—Weekly Salary
One Week Minimum Employment

THIS AGREEEMENT, made this ___2ND___ day of ___MAY___, 19_93_, between_____
_____XYZ PRODUCTIONS_____, hereafter called "Producer", and
_____CLARK GRABLE_____, hereafter called "Player".

W I T N E S S E T H :

1. PHOTOPLAY, ROLE, SALARY AND GUARANTEE. Producer hereby engages Player to render services as such in the role of ___HERBY_____, in a photoplay, the working title of which is now ___THE WATCHER_____, at the salary of $ _2,000—_ per "studio week" (Schedule B Players must receive an additional overtime payment of four (4) hours at straight time rate for each overnight location Saturday). Player accepts such engagement upon the terms herein specified. Producer guarantees that it will furnish Player not less than ___SIX (6)___ week's employment (if this blank is not filled in, the guarantee shall be one week). Player shall be paid pro rata for each additional day beyond guarantee until dismissal.

2. TERM: The term of employment hereunder shall begin on

   on ___JUNE 1, 1993___

   on or about* _____
   and shall continue thereafter until the completion of the photography and recordation of said role.

3. BASIC CONTRACT. All provisions of the collective bargaining agreement between Screen Actors Guild, Inc. and Producer, relating to theatrical motion pictures, which are applicable to the employment of the Player hereunder, shall be deemed incorporated herein.

4. PLAYER'S ADDRESS. All notices which the Producer is required or may desire to give to the Player may be given either by mailing the same addressed to the Player at _1234 FIRST ST — MALIBU, CA_ _90272_ or such notice may be given to the Player personally, either orally or in writing.

5. PLAYER'S TELEPHONE. The Player must keep the Producer's casting office or the assistant director of said photoplay advised as to where the Player may be reached by telephone without unreasonable delay. The current telephone number of the Player is ___(310) 555 – 7332___

6. MOTION PICTURE AND TELEVISION RELIEF FUND. The Player ((does)) (does not) hereby authorize the Producer to deduct from the compensation hereinabove specified an amount equal to ___1 (ONE)___ per cent of each installment of compensation due the Player hereunder, and to pay the amount so deducted to the Motion Picture and Television Relief Fund of America, Inc.

7. FURNISHING OF WARDROBE. The (Producer) (Player) agrees to furnish all modern wardrobe and wearing apparel reasonably necessary for the portrayal of said role; it being agreed, however, that should so-called "character" or "period" costumes be required, the Producer shall supply the same. When Player furnishes any wardrobe, Player shall receive the cleaning allowance and reimbursement, if any, specified in the basic contract.

   Number of outfits furnished by Player ___2___ @ $ _11.50 ea._
   (formal) _____ @ $ _____

8. ARBITRATION OF DISPUTES. Should any dispute or controversy arise between the parties hereto with reference to this contract, or the employment herein provided for, such dispute or controversy shall be settled and determined by conciliation and arbitration in accordance with the conciliation and arbitration provisions of the collective bargaining agreement between the Producer and Screen Actors Guild relating to theatrical motion pictures, and such provisions are hereby referred to and by such reference incorporated herein and made a part of this Agreement with the same effect as though the same were set forth herein in detail.

9. NEXT STARTING DATE. The starting date of Player's next engagement is_____

10. The Player may not waive any provision of this contract without the written consent of Screen Actors Guild, Inc.

BILLING: *MAIN TITLES — SINGLE CARD — LAST POSITION*
"AND INTRODUCING CLARK GRABLE AS HERBY"

11. Producer makes the material representation that either it is presently a signatory to the Screen Actors Guild collective bargaining agreement covering the employment contracted for herein, or that the above-referred-to photoplay is covered by such collective bargaining agreement under the Independent Production provisions of the General Provisions of the Producer-Screen Actors Guild Codified Basic Agreement of 1983 as the same may be supplmented and/or amended.

IN WITNESS WHEREOF, the parties have executed this agreement on the day and year first above written.

PRODUCER *Swifty Deals*   PLAYER *Clark Grable*

BY *SWIFTY DEALS*   Social Security No. *332-62-7749*

*The "on or about" clause may only be used when the contract is delivered to the Player at least seven days before the starting date. See Codified Basic Agreement of 1983, Schedule B, Schedule C, otherwise a specific starting date must be stated.

Production time reports are available on the set at the end of each day, which reports shall be signed or initialed by the Player.

Attached hereto for your use are the following: (1) Declaration Regarding Income Tax Withholding ("Part Year Employment Method of Withholding") and (2) Declaration Regarding Income Tax Withholding. You may utilize the applicable form by delivering same to Producer. Only one of such forms may be used.

NOTICE TO ACTOR: IT IS IMPORTANT THAT YOU RETAIN A COPY OF THIS CONTRACT FOR YOUR PERMANENT RECORDS.

**THE ARTIST MAY NOT WAIVE ANY PROVISION OF THIS CONTRACT
WITHOUT THE WRITTEN CONSENT OF SCREEN ACTORS GUILD, INC.**

SCREEN ACTORS GUILD
DAILY CONTRACT
(DAY PLAYER)
FOR THEATRICAL MOTION PICTURES

Company _XYZ PRODUCTIONS_

Date Employment Starts _JUNE 23, 1993_

Production Title _THE WATCHER_

Production Number _0100_

Role _GEORGE_

Daily Rate $ _500_

Weekly Conversion Rate $ _____

Date _JUNE 10, 1993_

Actor Name _HOLLYWOOD MANN_

Address _3465 HORTENSE ST. WONDERLAND, CA 90000_

Telephone No. _(818) 555-1000_

Social Security No. _123-45-6789_

Date of Birth _10-21-52_

Legal Resident of (State) _CALIFORNIA_

Citizen of U.S. _✓_ Yes _____ No

Wardrobe supplied by Actor _✓_ Yes _____ No

If so, number of outfits _____ @ $ _____

(formal) _____ @ $ _____

Date of Actor's next engagement _____

BILLING: END CREDITS - CO-STARRING FIRST POSITION

Complete for "Drop-And-Pick-Up" Deals ONLY:

Firm recall date on _____ or

on or after* _____

("On or after" recall only applies to pick-up as Weekly Player.)

As ☐ Day Player   ☐ Weekly Player

*Means date specified or within 24 hours thereafter

The employment is subject to all of the provisions and conditions applicable to the employment of DAY PLAYERS contained or provided for in the Producer-Screen Actors Guild Codified Basic Agreement of 1986 as the same may be supplemented and/or amended.

The Player (does) (does not) hereby authorize the Producer to deduct from the compensation hereinabove specified an amount equal to _____.5_____ per cent of each installment of compensation due the Player hereunder, and to pay the amount of so deducted to the Motion Picture and Televison Relief Fund of America, Inc.

Special Provisions:

PRODUCER _Swifty Deals_   PLAYER X _Hollywood Mann_

BY _SWIFTY DEALS_

Production time reports are available on the set at the end of each day.
Such reports shall be signed or initialed by the Player.

Attached hereto for your use is Declaration Regarding Income Tax Withholding.

NOTICE TO ACTOR: IT IS IMPORTANT THAT YOU RETAIN A COPY OF THIS CONTRACT FOR YOUR PERMANENT RECORDS.

MOTION PICTURE DAILY

SCREEN ACTORS GUILD
STUNT PERFORMER
DAILY STUNT PERFORMER CONTRACT
FOR THEATRICAL MOTION PICTURES

Company __XYZ PRODUCTIONS__

Date Employment Starts __JUNE 29, 1993__

Production Title __THE WATCHER__

Production No. __0100__

Role __NO STUNTS__ , or

Stunt Double for* _____, or

Other (description) _____

Daily Rate $ __485__

Weekly Conversion Rate $ _____

Stunt Adjustment(s):

$ __500__ for __HIGH SPEED CHASE__ No. of takes __2__

$ _____ for _____ No. of takes _____

Date __JUNE 29, 1993__

Stunt Performer Name __DARREN DEVIL__

Address __1763 VINE AVE. HOLLYWOOD, CA 90028__

Telephone No. (__213__) __555 - 7000__

Social Security No. __532 - 28 - 4476__

Date of birth __9 - 14 - 58__

Legal Resident of (State) __CALIFORNIA__

Citizen of U.S. __✓__ Yes _____ No

Wardrobe supplied by Stunt Performer _____ Yes __✓__ No

If so, number of outfits_____ @ $ _____

(formal) _____ @ $ _____

Date of Stunt Performer's next engagement: _____

COMPLETE FOR "DROP & PICK-UP" DEALS ONLY:

Firm recall date on _____ , or

on or after** _____

("On or after" recall only applies to pick-up as
Weekly Player.)

As _____ Day Player _____ Weekly Player

**Means date specified or within 24 Hours thereafter.

WITNESSETH:

1. The employment is subject to all of the provisions and conditions applicable to the employment of Stunt Performers contained or provided for in the Producers-Screen Actors Guild Codified Basic Agreement as the same may be supplemented and/or amended. Refer to Schedule H.

2. The Stunt Performer (does) (does not) hereby authorize the Producer to deduct from the compensation hereinabove specified an amount equal to __½__ per cent of each installment of compensation due the Stunt Performer hereunder, and to pay the amount so deducted to the Motion Picture and Television Relief Fund of America, Inc.

3. Special Provisions: _____

_____

PRODUCER __Swifty Deals__ STUNT PERFORMER X __Darren Devil__

Production time reports and/or time cards are available on the set at the end of each day. Such reports shall be signed or initialed by the Stunt Performer and must indicate any agreed stunt adjustments.

Attached hereto for your use is Declaration Regarding Income Tax Withholding.

TO STUNT PERFORMER: IT IS IMPORTANT THAT YOU RETAIN A COPY OF THIS CONTRACT FOR YOUR PERMANENT RECORDS.

*NOTE: STUNT DAY PERFORMERS MUST RECEIVE A SEPARATE DAY'S PAY AND CONTRACT FOR EACH PERSON DOUBLED.

MOTION PICTURE WEEKLY

SCREEN ACTORS GUILD

STUNT PERFORMER

MINIMUM FREE LANCE WEEKLY CONTRACT
FOR THEATRICAL MOTION PICTURES

Weekly Basis — Weekly Salary
One Week Minimum Employment

THIS AGREEMENT, made this _____5TH_____ day of _____JULY_____, 19 _93_, between

_____X YZ PRODUCTIONS_____, hereafter called "Producer," and

_____DANGEROUS DANN_____, hereafter called "Performer."

WITNESSETH:

1. PHOTOPLAY, ROLE, SALARY AND GUARANTEE. Producer hereby engages Performer to render services as such,

    Check One:

    ☐ in the Role of _____ , or

    ☐ as Stunt Double for _____ , or

    ☒ as Utility Stunt Performer, or

    ☐ other (describe work) _____

    in a photoplay, the working title of which is now _____THE WATCHER_____ , at the
    salary of $ _1,808–_ per "studio week" (Schedule H-II Performers must receive an additional overtime payment of four (4) hours
    at straight time rate for each overnight location Saturday). Performer accepts such engagement upon the terms herein specified. Producer guarantees
    that it will furnish Performer not less than _ONE (1)_ weeks employment (if this blank is not filled in, the guarantee shall be one week).
    Performer shall be paid pro rata for each additional day beyond the guarantee until dismissal.

2. TERM. The term of employment hereunder shall begin on _____ OR on or about* _JULY 6, 1993_

3. STUNT ADJUSTMENTS. It is understood between the parties that the salary rate specified above may require adjustment depending upon the
    nature of the stunt activities Producer requires. If so, a Stunt Adjustment will be agreed upon between the parties through good faith bargaining
    and said adjustment shall be noted on the Performer's daily time sheet or time card. Such adjustment shall increase the Performer's compensation
    for the week in the manner prescribed in Schedule H of the Screen Actors Guild Codified Basic Agreement.

4. CONTINUOUS EMPLOYMENT AND RIGHT TO ROLE. If the Stunt Performer portrays a role or has dialogue, such Performer shall be
    entitled to continuous employment and "right to role" and shall receive payment for the entire period from the Performer's first call to work
    on the picture until completion of the photography and recordation of said role.

5. BASIC CONTRACT. All provisions of the collective bargaining agreement between Screen Actors Guild, Inc. and Producer, relating to theatrical
    motion pictures, which are applicable to the employment of the Performer hereunder, shall be deemed incorporated herein.

6. PERFORMER'S ADDRESS. All notices which the Producer is required or may desire to give to the Performer may be given either by mailing
    same addressed to the Performer at _P.O. BOX 456 / LOS ANGELES, CA 90000_ , or such notice may be given
    to the Performer personally, either orally or in writing.

* The "on or about" clause may only be used when the contract is delivered to the Performer at least seven (7) days before the starting date. See
    Codified Basic Agreement of 1983, Schedule B or Schedule C, otherwise a specific starting date must be stated.

7. PERFORMER'S TELEPHONE. The Performer must keep the Producer's casting office or the assistant director of said photoplay advised as to where the Performer may be reached by telephone without unreasonable delay. The current telephone number of the Performer is _(213) 555 - 5552_____ .

8. MOTION PICTURE AND TELEVISION RELIEF FUND. The Performer (does) (does not) hereby authorize the Producer to deduct from the compensation hereinabove specified an amount equal to ___1 (ONE)___ per cent of each installment of compensation due the Performer hereunder, and to pay the amount so deducted to the Motion Picture and Television Relief Fund of America, Inc.

9. ARBITRATION OF DISPUTES. Should any dispute or controversy arise between the parties hereto with reference to this contract, or the employment herein provided for, such dispute or controversy shall be settled and determined by conciliation and arbitration in accordance with the conciliation and arbitration provisions of the collective bargaining agreement between the Producer and Screen Actors Guild relating to theatrical motion pictures, and such provisions are hereby referred to and by such reference incorporated herein and made a part of this Agreement with the same effect as though the same were set forth herein in detail.

10. NEXT STARTING DATE. The starting date of the Performer's next engagement is _____ .

11. The Performer may not waive any provision of this contract without the written consent of Screen Actors Guild, Inc.

12. Producer makes the material representation that either it is presently a signatory to the Screen Actors Guild collective bargaining agreement covering the employment contracted for herein, or that the photoplay is covered by such collective bargaining agreement under the Independent Production provisions of the General Provisions of the Producer-Screen Actors Guild Codified Basic Agreement as the same may be supplemented and/or amended to date.

IN WITNESS WHEREOF, the parties have executed this agreement on the day and year first above written.

PRODUCER _Swifty Deals_____ PERFORMER _Dangerous Dann_____

BY _SWIFTY DEALS_____ SOCIAL SECURITY # _332 - 42 - 9758_____

Production time reports and/or time cards are available on the set at the beginning and end of each day, which reports shall be signed or initialed by the Performer and must indicate any agreed stunt adjustments.

Attached hereto for your use are the following: (1) Declaration Regarding Income Tax Withholding ("Part Year Employment Method of Withholding") and (2) Declaration Regarding Income Tax Withholding. You may utilize the applicable form by delivering same to Producer. Only one of such forms may be used.

NOTICE TO STUNT PERFORMER: IT IS IMPORTANT THAT YOU RETAIN A COPY OF THIS CONTRACT FOR YOUR PERMANENT RECORDS.

SCREEN ACTORS GUILD

TAFT/HARTLEY REPORT

ATTENTION: (CURRENT ADMINISTRATOR OF UNION SECURITY DEPT.) ATTACHED?: ✓ RESUME* ✓ PHOTO

EMPLOYEE INFORMATION

NAME __GOLDIE LOCKS__   SS# 111-22-3333

ADDRESS __433 BEARHOUSE LANE__   AGE (IF MINOR) 21

CITY/STATE __WOODLAND HILLS, CA__   ZIP 91364 PHONE (818) 555-6226

EMPLOYER INFORMATION

NAME __XYZ PRODUCTIONS__   Check ___ AD AGENCY
one: ___ STUDIO

ADDRESS __1234 FLICK DR.__   ✓ PRODUCTION COMPANY

CITY/STATE __HOLLYWOOD, CA__   ZIP 90038 PHONE (213) 555-3331

EMPLOYMENT INFORMATION

Check CONTRACT: __X__ DAILY   CATEGORY: __X__ ACTOR
one: ___ 3-DAY   ___ SINGER   ___ OTHER ___
     ___ WEEKLY   ___ STUNT

WORK DATE(S) __JULY 26, 1993__   SALARY __$485—__

PRODUCTION TITLE __THE WATCHER__   PROD'N/COM'L # ___

SHOOTING LOCATION (City & State) __VENICE BEACH, CALIFORNIA__

REASON FOR HIRE (be specific) __WHILE SHOOTING A SCENE ON THE STRAND AT VENICE BEACH. DIRECTOR DECIDED THAT MORE "LOCAL COLOR" WAS NEEDED TO MAKE THE SCENE MORE COMPLETE. MS. LOCKS, A ROLLER SKATING STREET PERFORMER OF EXCEPTIONAL ABILITY WHO WAS PERFORMING ON THE STRAND AT THE TIME, WAS ASKED TO PARTICIPATE IN THE SCENE AND TO INTERACT W/ FILM'S ACTORS.__

Employer is aware of General Provision, Section 14 of the Basic Agreement that applies to Theatrical and Television production, and Schedule B of the Commercials Contract, wherein Preference of Employment shall be given to qualified professional actors (except as otherwise stated). Employer will pay to the Guild as liquidated damages, the sums indicated for each breach by the Employer of any provision of those sections.

SIGNATURE __Swifty Deals__   DATE __7-26-93__
Producer or Casting Director - Indicate which

PRINT NAME __SWIFTY DEALS, PRODUCER__   PHONE (213) 555-3331

*PLEASE BE CERTAIN RESUME LISTS ALL TRAINING AND/OR EXPERIENCE IN THE ENTERTAINMENT INDUSTRY.

SAG EXTRA

SCREEN ACTORS GUILD

TAFT/HARTLEY REPORT

ATTENTION: (CURRENT ADMINISTRATOR OF UNION SECURITY DEPT.) ATTACHED?: ✓ RESUME ✓ PHOTO

EMPLOYEE INFORMATION

NAME CARY GOOPER   SS# 433-27-6327

ADDRESS 103 YORK BLVD   AGE (IF MINOR) 43

CITY/STATE LOS ANGELES, CA   ZIP 90026   PHONE (213) 555-6533

EMPLOYER INFORMATION

NAME XYZ PRODUCTIONS   Check ___ CASTING OFFICE
                                              one: ___ STUDIO
ADDRESS 1234 FLICK DR.   ✓ PRODUCTION
                                                       COMPANY
CITY/STATE HOLLYWOOD, CALIF.   ZIP 90038   PHONE (213) 555-3331

EMPLOYMENT INFORMATION

Check
one: General Extra ____   Special Ability Extra ✓   Dancer ____

WORK DATE(S) JULY 22, 1993   SALARY $75.00

PRODUCTION TITLE THE WATCHER

SHOOTING LOCATION (City & State) DOWNTOWN (5TH & BROADWAY) LOS ANGELES, CA

REASON FOR HIRE (be specific) MR. GOOPER WAS HIRED TO PLAY A
CARD SHARK STREET HUSTLER BECAUSE OF HIS SPECIAL
ABILITY IN "TRICK" CARD DEALING

Employer is aware of General Provision, Section 45 of the Producer-Screen Actors Guild Extra Player Agreement that applies to Theatrical and Television production, wherein Preference of Employment shall be given to qualified professional extras (except as otherwise stated). Employer will pay to the Guild as liquidated damages, a sum which shall be determined by binding arbitration for each breach by the Employer of any provision of those sections.

SIGNATURE *Swifty Deals*   DATE 7-22-93
        Producer or Casting Director - Indicate which

PRINT NAME SWIFTY DEALS, PRODUCER   PHONE (213) 555-3331

PLEASE PRESS
YOU ARE MAKING FOUR COPIES

PRODUCER: **XYZ PRODUCTIONS**

DATE 6-7-93	NAME (PRINT) ADAM DARK	PRODUCTION NO. OR TITLE THE WATCHER #100		DISMISSAL TIME 6P

SAG NO.	SOCIAL SECURITY NO. MUST BE PROVIDED TO MAKE PAYMENT	TYPE OF CALL	STARTING TIME 7A

☒ SINGLE ☐ MARRIED ☐ MARRIED but withheld at higher single rate

Total number of allowances you are claiming: _____ 0

Additional amount, if any, you want deducted $ _____

	BASIC WAGE RATE $65	TRAVEL TIME ARRIVE LOCATION: / LEAVE LOCATION:	PENALTIES	HOURS WORKED 10.5	MEAL PERIODS 1:30P / 2 / 1P / 1:10

ASST. DIR.-APPROVED FOR PAYMENT *A Dark*

		FITTING ☐	MEALS B ☐ L ☒ D ☐	INTERVIEW ☐

If claiming exemption from withholding, write exempt and year in box _____ 19_____

WARDROBE	PROPS	VEHICLE $27	MILEAGE 40 Mi RT x .30 = $18

EMPLOYEE: PLEASE PRINT INFORMATION LISTED ABOVE AND SIGN WHERE INDICATED

"I, the undersigned, certify that the number of income tax withholding exemptions claimed on this certificate does not exceed the number of which I am entitled.

"I agree to accept the sum properly computed based upon the times and the basic wage rate shown as payment in full for all services heretofore rendered by me for said employer.

"I further agree that the said sum, less all deduction required by law, may be paid to me by negotiable check issued by said company, said check to be addressed to me at my last reported address and deposited in the United States mail within the time periods provided by law.

"I hereby give and grant to the company named all rights of every kind and character whatsoever in and to all work heretofore done, and all poses, acts, plays and appearances heretofore made by me for you and in to all of the results and proceeds of my services heretofore rendered for you, as well as in and to the right to use my name, likeness and photographs, either still or moving for commercial and advertising purposes. I further give and grant to the said company the right to reproduce in any manner whatsoever any recordations heretofore made by said company of my voice and all instrumental, musical, or other sound effects produced by me. I further agree that in the event of a retake of all or any of the scenes in which I participate, or if additional scenes are required (whether originally contemplated or not) I will return to work and render my services in such scenes at the same basic rate of compensations as that paid me for the original taking.

"By signing this form, I hereby agree that said employer may take deductions from my earnings to adjust previous overpayments if and when said overpayments may occur."

Signature _Adam Dark_ Date 6/7/93

Address 124 RIVERSIDE ST. Apt # #304

City STUDIO VILLAGE, CA 91603 State / Zip

Phone Number (818) 555-7633

BACK OF WHITE COPY MUST BE COMPLETED

YOUR EMPLOYER OF RECORD IS __ABC PAYROLL CO.__
IF OTHER THAN A PAYROLL COMPANY, EMPLOYER'S FEDERAL I.D. NUMBER IS

DO NOT WRITE IN THIS SPACE ▶

TYPE OF WORK	PAY CODE	HOURS		AMOUNT	BASIC RATE $65
		WORK	PAY		
DAY		·	·	·	
NIGHT		·	·	·	ADJUSTMENTS $14 (SMOKE)
O/T		·	·	·	OVERTIME
WET		·	·	·	
SMOKE		·	·	·	ALLOWANCES
OTHER		·	·	·	
OTHER		·	·	·	GROSS
OTHER		·	·	·	
OTHER		·	·	·	

Screen Actors Guild
Kenmar Printing 357
Form No. 451

white—PAYROLL COPY
yellow—PRODUCTION COPY
pink—SAG COPY
golden rod—EXTRAS COPY

SCREEN ACTORS GUILD
THEATRICAL & TELEVISION SIGN-IN

PLEASE PRINT
ALL INFORMATION

AUDITION DATE 5-10-93

Prod'n Co. __XYZ PRODUCTIONS__   Casting Rep. __SHELDON SCOUT__ Phone __555-3334__
Prod'n Title __THE WATCHER__   Director __SID CELLULOID__   Phone __555-3331__
Episode Title/# __BOYS NIGHT OUT__   Producer __SWIFTY DEALS__   Phone __555-3331__

| | FILM
| | TV-MOW
| | TV-OTHER

PLAYER'S NAME	SOCIAL SECURITY	NAME OF ROLE	AGENT	VIDEO TAPED?	PROVIDED? PARKING	PROVIDED? SCRIPT	PLAYER'S ACTUAL CALL	TIME IN	TIME OUT	INITIALS
CLARK GRABLE	332-62-7749	HERBY	JOE COOL		✓	✓	9A	9A	9:25	CG
CARY GOOPER	523-76-5351	HERBY	ALICE AJINT		✓	✓	9:30A	9:33	10:05	CG
JAMES BONDD	237-61-2377	HERBY	RON REPPS		✓	✓	10A	9:55	10:30	JB
MARTY MELROSE	176-50-6104	HERBY	JOE COOL		✓	✓	10:30A	10:30	11:10	MM
SCARLET STARLET	823-76-7737	LAURA	RON REPPS		✓	✓	11A	11:05	11:20	SS
MARY MARVELOUS	437-96-2276	LAURA	JOE COOL		✓	✓	11:30A	11:40	11:50	M
GOLDIE LOCKS	338-42-9752	LAURA	HOLLY WOODS		✓	✓	12N	12N	12:45	GL
BEVERLY FAIRFAX	579-36-2173	LAURA	HOLLY WOODS		✓	✓	12:30	12:35	1:15	BF

_____
SIGNATURE OF AUTHORIZED REPRESENTATIVE

PRODUCER
1. Complete top half of form.
2. Sign your name.
3. Designate person to whom correspondence
   concerning this form shall be sent.

SCREEN ACTORS GUILD
ACTORS PRODUCTION TIME REPORT

PICTURE TITLE: _THE WATCHER_   PROD. # _0100_   DATE _MON, 6/7/93_   IS TODAY A DESIGNATED DAY OFF? * YES___ NO _X_

CAST - WEEKLY & DAY PLAYERS
Worked - W   Rehearsal - R   Finished - F
Started - S   Hold - H   Test - T
Travel - TR

CAST	CHARACTER	W/H/S/R/T (TR)	MAKEUP W/DBE.	WORKTIME REPORT ON SET	WORKTIME DISMISS ON SET	BKFST	1ST MEAL	2ND MEAL	TRAVEL TIME LEAVE FOR LOCATION	ARRIVE ON LOCATION	LEAVE LOCATION	ARRIVE AT STUDIO	STUNT ADJUST.	WARDROBE NO. OF OUTFITS PROVIDED	ACTORS SIGNATURE
CLARK GRABLE	HERBY	W	8A	8:30A	6P		1:30P	2P	7A	8A	6:15P	7:15P			_Clark Grable_
SCARLET STARLET	LAURA	W	7:30A	10A	8P	ND	1:30P	2P	6:45A	7:30A	8:15P	9P			_Scarlet Starlet_
HOLLYWOOD MANN	GEORGE	SW	9A	10A	8P		1:30P	2P							_signature_
KENNY SMILES	MARC	W	8A	8:30A	6P		1:30P	2P							_signature_
WIL PERFORMER	JED	W	8A	8:30A	6P		1:30P	2P							_signature_
DARREN DEVIL	ND STUNTS	SW	9A	10A	7P		1:30P	2P					$500		_signature_

* This refers to the 2 days (1 day on overnight location) which producer can designate as day(s) off for the production.

SCREEN ACTORS GUILD

Casting Data Report

See Reverse For Instructions

THIS FORM MUST BE COMPLETED FOR EACH MOTION PICTURE AND EACH EPISODE OF EACH SERIES PRODUCED FOR THE QUARTER IN WHICH PRINCIPAL PHOTOGRAPHY WAS COMPLETED.

1) PRODUCTION COMPANY XYZ PRODUCTIONS

2) QUARTER and YEAR 3RD QUARTER – 1993

3) PROJECT (Title, Prod. No., etc.) THE WATCHER – PROD. # 0100

4) DESCRIPTION (Feature, M.O.W., TV Series, etc.) FEATURE

5) TOTAL NO. OF DAYS OF PRODUCTION (Principal Photography Only) 58

6) DATA SUBMITTED BY CONNIE COORDINATES NAME

   TELEPHONE NUMBER (213) 555-3331

7) CHECK IF APPROPRIATE [✓] NO STUNTS

PART I

CATEGORY		FORM OF HIRING — DAILY	WEEKLY	SERIES	9) CAST TOTALS	10) NO. OF DAYS WORKED	11) AGE — UNDER 40	40 and OVER	UNKNOWN
MALE	LEAD		3		3	170	2	1	1
	SUPPORT	21			21	84	11	9	
FEMALE	LEAD		2		2	100	2	2	
	SUPPORT	16			16	48	11	5	

PART II

CATEGORY		12) DAILY M	DAILY F	WEEKLY M	WEEKLY F	SERIES M	SERIES F	13) DAYS WORKED M	DAYS WORKED F	14) UNDER 40 M	UNDER 40 F	40 and OVER M	40 and OVER F	UNKNOWN M	UNKNOWN F
ASIAN / PACIFIC	LEAD			1				58		1					
	SUPPORT	2			3			10	15	2	3				
BLACK	LEAD			1	1			58	50	1	1				
	SUPPORT	3			3			17	18	3	3				
CAUCASIAN	LEAD			1	1			54	50	1			5		
	SUPPORT	9			10			50	15	9	5				
LATINO / HISPANIC	LEAD														
	SUPPORT	5						5					4		1
N. AMERICAN INDIAN	LEAD														
	SUPPORT														
UNKNOWN/OTHER	LEAD														
	SUPPORT	2						2			2				

INSTRUCTIONS

1. Indicate the Production Company (e.g. "THE ABC COMPANY").

2. Indicate the quarter/year (e.g. "1st quarter 1981").

   The quarters consist of:
January — March	(1st)
April — June	(2nd)
July — September	(3rd)
October — December	(4th)

3. Indicate the name of the film for which you are reporting.

4. Indicate the type of project (feature, television movie, television pilot, television series, animation).

5. Use a number to respond to this question.

6. Indicate the name of person completing this form and the telephone number for same.

7. Two separate reports are required, one for Performers only and one for Stunt Performers only. If there were no Stunt Performers employed on the film, check the "No Stunt" box. If Stunt Performers were employed, complete the casting data report form for Stunt Performers.

8. Part I. Indicate the total number of lead and supporting Performers in each of the applicable categories.

9. Use numbers only to indicate the total number of Performers in the category.

10. Use numbers only to indicate the total number of days worked by ALL Performers in the category.

11. Use numbers only to indicate how many Performers were in each age group.

12. Part II. Indicate the total number of males and females in each category.

13. Use number only to indicate the total number of days worked by ALL the Performers in male and female category.

14. Use numbers only to indicate how many performers were in each age group.

NOTE: PLEASE MAKE EVERY EFFORT TO INSURE THAT YOUR NUMBERS CORRESPOND ACROSS AND AMONG PART I AND PART II.

SCREEN ACTORS GUILD

Casting Data Report for Stunt Performers Only

THIS FORM MUST BE COMPLETED FOR EACH MOTION PICTURE AND EACH EPISODE OF EACH SERIES PRODUCED FOR THE QUARTER IN WHICH PRINCIPAL PHOTOGRAPHY WAS COMPLETED.

See Reverse For Instructions

1) PRODUCTION COMPANY _XYZ PRODUCTIONS_
2) QUARTER and YEAR _3RD QUARTER - 1993_
3) PROJECT (Title, Prod. No., etc.) _THE WATCHER - PROD # 0100_
4) DESCRIPTION (Feature, M.O.W., TV Series, etc.) _MOW_
5) TOTAL NO. OF DAYS OF PRODUCTION (Principal Photography Only) _30_

6) DATA SUBMITTED BY _CONNIE COORDINATES_ NAME
   TELEPHONE NUMBER _(213) 555-3331_
7) NAME OF STUNT COORDINATOR _CLIFF HANGER_

PART I

CATEGORY	FORM OF HIRING DAILY	FORM OF HIRING WEEKLY	FORM OF HIRING SERIES	9) PERFORMER TOTALS	10) NUMBER DAYS WORKED	11) AGE UNDER 40	AGE 40 and OVER	AGE UNKNOWN	12) STUNT SUMMARY DESCRIPT	STUNT SUMMARY NON-DESCRIPT
MALE	6	2		8	31	3	4	1	4	4
FEMALE	2	1		3	13	2	1		2	1

PART II

CATEGORY	DAILY M	DAILY F	WEEKLY M	WEEKLY F	SERIES M	SERIES F	NDW M	NDW F	U40 M	U40 F	40+ M	40+ F	UNK M	UNK F	DESC M	DESC F	NON-DESC M	NON-DESC F
ASIAN/PACIFIC	1						1		1						1			
BLACK	1	1	1	1			17	2	1	1				1	1	1	1	1
CAUCASIAN	3	1	1	1			11	1	3						2	1	2	
HISPANIC				1			2	10				1						1
N. AMERICAN INDIAN	1																1	
OTHER/UNKNOWN																		

FORMS AND REPORTS 57

INSTRUCTIONS

**There are two separate report forms required.
Complete one report for Performers and one report for Stunt Performers.

1. Indicate the Production Company (e.g. "THE ABC COMPANY").

2. Indicate the quarter/year (e.g. "1st quarter 1981").

    The quarters consist of:

January — March	(1st)
April — June	(2nd)
July — September	(3rd)
October — December	(4th)

3. Indicate the <u>name</u> of the film for which you are reporting.

4. Indicate the <u>type</u> of project (feature, television movie, television series).

5. Use a number to respond to this question.

6. Provide the name and telephone number of the person who completes this form.

7. Provide the name of the stunt coordinator for the film.

Part I

8. Indicate the total number of males and females in each category.

9. Use numbers only to indicate the total number of stunt performers in the category.

10. Use numbers only to indicate the total amount of days worked by all stunt performers in the category.

11. Use numbers only to indicate how many stunt performers are in a certain age group.

12. Use numbers only to indicate the stunts as descript or non-descript.

Part II

13. Indicate the total number of males and females in each category.

14. Use numbers only to indicate the total number of days worked by <u>all</u> the Performers in each category.

15. Use numbers only to indicate how many performers were in each age group.

16. Indicate the stunts as descript or non-descript.

NOTE: Please make every effort to insure that your numbers correspond across categories and among Part I and Part II.

SCREEN ACTORS GUILD

LOW-BUDGET
AFFIRMATIVE ACTION

Casting Data Report

See Reverse
For Instructions

THIS FORM MUST BE COMPLETED FOR EACH MOTION PICTURE AND EACH EPISODE OF EACH SERIES PRODUCED FOR THE QUARTER IN WHICH PRINCIPAL PHOTOGRAPHY WAS COMPLETED.

1) PRODUCTION COMPANY ___XYZ PRODUCTIONS___

2) QUARTER and YEAR ___4TH QUARTER - 1993___

3) PROJECT (Title, Prod. No., etc.) ___THE WATCHER - PROD. #0100___

4) DESCRIPTION (Feature, M.O.W., TV Series, etc.) ___FEATURE___

5) TOTAL NO. OF DAYS OF PRODUCTION (Principal Photography Only) ___36___

6) DATA SUBMITTED BY ___CONNIE COORDINATES___ NAME

   TELEPHONE NUMBER ___(213) 555-3331___

7) CHECK IF APPROPRIATE ☑ NO STUNTS

PART I

CATEGORY		DAILY	WEEKLY	SERIES	CAST TOTALS	NO. OF DAYS WORKED	UNDER 40	40 to 60	60 & Over
MALE	LEAD		1		1	36	1		
	SUPPORT	6	1		7	37	4	1	2
FEMALE	LEAD		2		2	68	2	2	
	SUPPORT	4	1		5	18	2	2	1

PART II

CATEGORY		DAILY M	DAILY F	WEEKLY M	WEEKLY F	SERIES M	SERIES F	DAYS WORKED M	DAYS WORKED F	UNDER 40 M	UNDER 40 F	40 to 60 M	40 to 60 F	60 & Over M	60 & Over F
ASIAN / PACIFIC	LEAD														
	SUPPORT	1	1					3	2	1					
BLACK	LEAD			1					32				1		
	SUPPORT	2	1					3	2	1	1				
CAUCASIAN	LEAD	1	1					36	36	1	1	1	1		
	SUPPORT	3	2					6	11	2		1			1
LATINO / HISPANIC	LEAD														
	SUPPORT	1	1					25	3	1	1		1	1	
N. AMERICAN INDIAN	LEAD														
	SUPPORT														
UNKNOWN / OTHER	LEAD														
	SUPPORT														

INSTRUCTIONS

1. Indicate the Production Company (e.g. "THE ABC COMPANY").

2. Indicate the quarter/year (e.g. "1st quarter 1981").

   The quarters consist of:

January — March	(1st)
April — June	(2nd)
July — September	(3rd)
October — December	(4th)

3. Indicate the name of the film for which you are reporting.

4. Indicate the type of project (feature, television movie, television pilot, television series, animation).

5. Use a number to respond to this question.

6. Indicate the name of person completing this form and the telephone number for same.

7. Two separate reports are required, one for Performers only and one for Stunt Performers only. If there were no Stunt Performers employed on the film, check the "No Stunt" box. If Stunt Performers were employed, complete the casting data report form for Stunt Performers.

8. Part I. Indicate the total number of lead and supporting Performers in each of the applicable categories.

9. Use numbers only to indicate the total number of Performers in the category.

10. Use numbers only to indicate the total number of days worked by ALL Performers in the category.

11. Use numbers only to indicate how many Performers were in each age group.

12. Part II. Indicate the total number of males and females in each category.

13. Use number only to indicate the total number of days worked by ALL the Performers in male and female category.

14. Use numbers only to indicate how many performers were in each age group.

NOTE: PLEASE MAKE EVERY EFFORT TO INSURE THAT YOUR NUMBERS CORRESPOND ACROSS AND AMONG PART I AND PART II.

SCREEN ACTORS GUILD
7065 Hollywood Blvd.
Hollywood, CA 90028-7594

FINAL CAST LIST INFORMATION SHEET

DATE FILED: **8 - 2 - 93**   # 10

PICTURE TITLE _THE WATCHER_

PRODUCTION COMPANY _XYZ PRODUCTIONS_

ADDRESS _1234 FLICK DR. HOLLYWOOD, CA 90038_

PHONE _213-555-3331_   CONTACT _____

DISTRIBUTOR _XYZ INTERNATIONAL_

SHOOTING LOCATION _LOS ANGELES_

START DATE _JUNE 1, 1993_   COMPLETION DATE _JULY 30, 1993_

FEDERAL I.D. # _____   STATE I.D. # _____

PICTURE # _0100_

Check One: MP ___   MOW ✓   OTHER TV ___   INDUSTRIAL ___   OTHER ___

To establish Residual payments, see Section 5.2 of the 1980 Basic Agreement.

PLAYER NAME & SOCIAL SECURITY NUMBER	PLAYER ADDRESS INCLUDING ZIP	PERIOD WORKED (1) #WKS	PERIOD WORKED (1) #DYS	(1) Start Date	(1) Finish Date	(2) Contract Type	(3) Player Type	(4) TOTAL GROSS SALARY	(5) BASE SALARY	Time Units	Salary Units	Total Units	FOR SAG USE ONLY
CLARK GRABLE 332-62-7749	1234 FIRST ST MALIBU, CA 90272	6		6/1	7/12	W	A	$14,325	$2,000 PER WK.				
SCARLET STARLETT 823-76-7737	2024 RADFORD AVE STUDIO CITY, CA 91604	3		6/1	6/19	W	A	$5,860	$1,853.50 PER WK.				
GOLDIE LOCKS 111-22-3333	433 ICEHEHOUSE LANE WOODLAND HILLS, CA 91364		1	7/16	7/16	D	A	$485	$485 PER DAY				
DANGEROUS DANN 332-42-9758	P.O. BOX 456 LOS ANGELES, CA 90000	1		7/6	7/10	W	ST	$2,158	$1,808 PER WK.				
JOHNNY ROCKETT 552-11-7627	125 HOLLYWOOD HILLS RD. HOLLYWOOD, CA 90028		3	6/15	6/29	D	ST	$2,655	$485 PER DAY				

(1) Include days not worked, but considered worked under continuous employment provisions.
    Report contractually guaranteed work period or actual time worked, whichever is longer.

(2) Insert D for Daily or W for Weekly type of contract.

(3) Insert: A = Actor; ST = Stunt; P = Pilot; SG = Singer; ADR = Automated Dialogue Replacement.

(4) Include all salary, Overtime, Premium, and Stunt Adjustments. Do not include any Penalties paid (i.e. Meal Penalties, forced Calls, etc.).

(5) List base contractual salary (i.e. $1,500.00/week or $500.00/day).

To establish Residual payments, see Section 5.2 of the 1980 Basic Agreement.

PLAYER NAME & SOCIAL SECURITY NUMBER	PLAYER ADDRESS INCLUDING ZIP	(1) PERIOD WORKED # DYS	# WKS	(1) Start Date	(1) Finish Date	(2) Contract Type	(3) Player Type	(4) TOTAL GROSS SALARY	(5) BASE SALARY	Time Units	Salary Units	Total Units	FOR SAG USE ONLY

(1) Include days not worked, but considered worked under continuous employment provisions. Report contractually guaranteed work period or actual time worked, whichever is longer.

(2) Insert D for Daily or W for Weekly type of contract.

(3) Insert: A = Actor; ST = Stunt; P = Pilot; SG = Singer; ADR = Automated Dialogue Replacement.

(4) Include all salary, Overtime, Premium, and Stunt Adjustments. Do not include any Penalties paid (i.e. Meal Penalties, forced Calls, etc.).

(5) List base contractual salary (i.e. $1,500.00/week or $500.00/day).

(THIS FORM IS USED FOR THOSE PERFORMERS NOT EMPLOYED DURING PRINCIPAL PRODUCTION OR FOR THOSE NOT "LOOPING" THEIR OWN ROLE.)

SCREEN ACTORS GUILD
MEMBER REPORT
ADR THEATRICAL/TELEVISION

EXHIBIT I

It is the responsibility of the reporting member to file a copy of this report with the Screen Actors Guild within forty-eight (48) hours of each session and to deliver a copy to the employer or the employer's representative at the conclusion of each session. If there is a contractor, he shall assume these responsibilities with respect to each session.

Work Date __8/20/93__ Title __THE WATCHER__

Episode Title __BOYS NIGHT OUT__ Prod. No. __0100__

Production Co./Employer __XYZ PRODUCTIONS__ Studio Facility __ABC SOUND STUDIOS__ Sound Supervisor Editor __SELMA HIGHLAND__

Address __1234 FLICK DR.__ __HOLLYWOOD, CA__ __90038__ Address __9123 VINE ST__ __HOLLYWOOD, CA__ __90028__ Sound Engineer/Mixer __DAN DUBBER__ ADR Supervisor __LARRY LOOPER__

Phone # __(213)555-3331__ Phone # __(213)555-9000__ Employer Rep. __PAULA POST__

Type of Film: Theatrical _____ TV Series _X_ TV MOW _____ TV Pilot _____ Other _____

Performer's Name	Performer's Social Security #	Character of 6+ Lines (sync)	Additional sets of up to 3 characters under 5 sync lines each	Hours Employed Studio Time Report/Dismiss	Meal Period From/To	Performer's Initials
BOB HOPEFULL	332-62-7749	BALL GAME ANNOUNCER	—	7A – 11A	—	BH
ROBERT BLUFORD	432-76-7737	—	BALL GAME SPECTATOR	10A – 4P	1–1:30P	RB
LORETTA OLDER	372-44-2232	—	"	10A – 4P	1–1:30P	LO
RICKY MOONEY	173-21-6342	—	"	10A – 4P	1–1:30P	RM
BRANDON MARLOW	519-36-2173	PITCHER	—	3P – 6P	—	BM

Reel #s Recorded: __#4__

NOTES: _____

This engagement shall be governed by and be subject to the applicable terms of the Screen Actors Guild Codified Basic or Television Agreement.

Production Co./EMPLOYER __XYZ PRODUCTIONS__

Signature of Employer or Employer Representative __Paula Post__, __POST PRODUCTION SUPERVISOR__

SAG Reporter _____ (Print name) _____

SAG Reporter's Phone # ( ) _____ Date _____ **EXHIBIT I**

DIRECTORS GUILD OF AMERICA
WEEKLY WORK LIST

From: __XYZ PRODUCTIONS__
(signatory company)
__1234 FLICK DR.__
(address)
__HOLLYWOOD, CA 90038__

Return to:
Directors Guild of America, Inc.

Week Ending: __6-12-93__

Name	Soc. Sec.#	Cat.	Project
SID CELLULOID	123-45-6789	DIRECTOR	THE WATCHER
FRED FILMER	234-56-7890	UPM	
ALICE DEES	456-78-9012	1ST A.D	
R.D. DURHAM	567-89-0123	KEY 2ND A.D.	
LAURA LAS PALMAS	678-90-1234	2ND 2ND A.D	

Prepared by

Phone #
RC314/031489

DGA EMPLOYMENT DATA REPORT

DATE: __8-2-93__ PREPARED BY: __FRED FILMER__ PHONE NO: __(213) 555-3331__

SIGNATORY COMPANY: __XYZ PRODUCTIONS__

QUARTER COVERED: __3RD__

PROJECT: __THE WATCHER__

DIRECTOR

	C	B	H	A	AI	UNKNOWN
MALE		/				
FEMALE						

UNIT PRODUCTION MANAGER

	C	B	H	A	AI	UNKNOWN
MALE	/					
FEMALE						

FIRST ASSISTANT DIRECTOR

	C	B	H	A	AI	UNKNOWN
MALE						
FEMALE		/				

SECOND ASSISTANT DIRECTOR

	C	B	H	A	AI	UNKNOWN
MALE	/					
FEMALE			/			

FIRST TIME DIRECTOR

	C	B	H	A	AI	UNKNOWN
MALE						
FEMALE						

INSTRUCTIONS

The minority codes utilized in this report represent the following:

C	—	CAUCASIAN
B	—	BLACK
H	—	HISPANIC
A	—	ASIAN
AI	—	AMERICAN INDIAN

When completing this report, the employment statistics must be reported in order that two (2) types of statistics can be obtained. The first statistic will indicate the number of persons employed in the respective category (referenced above) during that quarter. The second statistic will indicate the number of days worked or guaranteed in the respective categories for that quarter. Therefore in each category, there will be two separate sets of statistics: one of top of the other separated by a horizontal slash (example below). The top statistic will represent the number of employees working, the bottom statistic will be the number of days worked or guaranteed during the same quarter.

Example:

DIRECTOR

	C	B	H	A	AI	UNKNOWN
MALE	1/56					
FEMALE		1/25				

In the above example, there was one (1) male Caucasian Director working during the quarter for a total of fifty-six (56) days worked or guaranteed. There was one (1) female Black Director working for a total of twenty-five (25) days worked or guaranteed.

This report is to be submitted on a per-production basis not on a per episode basis. In instances where the same DGA employee is employed for multiple episodes in a continuing series, such employee shall only be counted once in the number of employees statistics, but such employee's cumulative days worked shall be included in that statistic.

<u>NOTICE OF TENTATIVE WRITING CREDITS - THEATRICAL</u>

DATE <u>5/29/93</u>

TO: Writers Guild of America
        <u>AND</u>
    All Participating Writers (or to the current agent if that participant so elects)

<u>NAMES OF PARTICIPATING WRITERS</u>   ADDRESS

F. SCOTT RYDER   *9336 W. BALBOA BLVD.*
                                    LOS ANGELES, CA

Title of Photoplay *THE WATCHER*
Executive Producer *HARRY HONCHO*
Producer *SWIFTY DEALS*
Director *SID CELLULOID*
Other Production Executives, including their titles, if
    Participating Writers

According to the provisions of Schedule A of the Writers Guild of America Theatrical and Television Basic Agreement of 1985 credits are now being determined on the above entitle production.

ON SCREEN, the tentative writing credits are as follows:

      SCREEN PLAY BY F. SCOTT RYDER

SOURCE MATERIAL upon which the photoplay is based, if any:

ON SCREEN, <u>FORM</u> of Source Material credit, if any:

PRESENTATION or PRODUCTION credits, if any, which are intended for use in advertising and/or on-screen: *XYZ PRODUCTIONS PRESENTS*
                                 A
               SID CELLULOID FILM

The above tentative writing credits will become final unless a protest is* communicated to the undersigned not later than 6:00 P.M. on <u>6/15/93</u> *

                             XYZ PRODUTIONS
                             (Signatory Company)

*(NO FEWER THAN 10 WORKING   BY *Swifty Deals*
DAYS AFTER THIS FORM IS   NAME *SWIFTY DEALS*
SUBMITTED TO THE WGA)   ADDRESS *1234 FLICK DR. HOLLYWOOD*
                               PHONE *(213) 555-3331* *CA 90038*

NOTICE OF TENTATIVE WRITING CREDITS - TELEVISION

DATE _5/14/93_

TO: Writers Guild of America
            AND
        Participating Writers

NAMES OF PARTICIPATING WRITERS   ADDRESS
_____J. MILLER_____   _1723 MADISON DR., LOS ANGELES, CA_
_____R. MILLER_____   _20086 DIAMOND LN., CULVER CITY, CA_
_____   _____

Title of Episode___BOYS NIGHT OUT_____   Prod. No. _0100___
              (If Pilot or MOW or other special or unit program,
               indicate Network and length.)
Series Title___THE WATCHER_____
Producing Company___XYZ PRODUCTIONS_____
Executive Producer___HARRY HONCHO_____
Producer___SWIFTY DEALS_____   Assoc. Producer_____
Director___SID CELLULOID_____   Story Editor_____
                                    (or Consultant)

Other Production Executives, if
    Participating Writers_____

Writing credits on this episode are tentatively determined as follows:

ON SCREEN:

            SCREEN PLAY BY J. MILLER AND R. MILLER

Source Material credit ON THIS EPISODE (on separate card, unless otherwise
indicated) if any:

Continuing source material or Created By credit APPEARING ON ALL EPISODES
OF SERIES   (on separate card):

Revised final script was sent to participating writers on _5/21/93_____

The above tentative writing credits will become final unless a protest is
communicated to the undersigned not later than 6:00 P.M. on _5/28/93____

                            _XYZ PRODUCTIONS_____
                                    (Company)
                            BY _Swifty Deals_____

CHAPTER **7**

STANDARD PRODUCTION FORMS AND FORMATS

The following are examples of some the most frequently used standard production forms and samples of "how to" do a: shooting schedule, one-line schedule, crew list and contact list, all of which are used on every show.

As stated in the introduction, there are computer software programs that will breakdown your script and automatically produce a day-out-of-days, a shooting schedule and a one-liner; but if you wish to do them manually, the information is here.

Not included in this section are certain accounting forms—blank **budget** and related **cash flow** and **cost report** formats. Whereas not all production managers and assistant directors use breakdown software programs, almost all production accountants use one of a few excellent production accounting software programs that contain built-in budgeting formats. I highly recommend using one of these programs for budgeting and cost analysis.

SCRIPT REVISIONS

The term **final draft** almost never means final. It would be ideal if all script changes could be made in the early stages of pre-production, but reality is that changes (even if they're small ones) are often made not only up to, but also throughout, principal photography.

Script revisions need to be indicated in a precise manner in order for everyone to know if and how each change will effect them or their department.

It is not necessary to run off entire new scripts every time there are changes. The accepted standard is to distribute colored change pages. For example, the first set of change pages are copied onto blue paper; the second set, onto pink, and so forth. The color progression usually runs: blue, pink, yellow, green, goldenrod, buff, salmon, cherry, tan, gray, and ivory. Some productions choose to stop aat goldenrod and others run through ivory before beginning again with white, if necessary.

Just as important as the various colors are to differentiating between sets of changes, it's also very important to indicate the changes by typing *Revised/(date)* at the top left-hand corner of every change page and by indicating the individual changes with asterisks (*) in the right-hand margin next to the specific line where the change occurs.

When a scene is omitted, the scene number remains in the script with the word *omitted* typed next to it and an asterisk in the right margin.

Once a show has been scheduled, you should not change the scene numbers. If you wish to add a scene, for example, between scenes 4 and 5, you would number the new scene, *4A* An addition to that would be scene 4B, and so on. In the same vein, you also do not want to change the page numbers. So if you want to lengthen a scene that appears on page 20 and now runs a page and-a-half, you would not disturb page 21, but would instead type the additional half page onto a new page that would be numbered *21A*. All new pages and scene numbers are also to be indicated with asterisks.

Your **Script Supervisor** will keep track of all revised page counts and revised number of scenes on her daily log which will in turn be transferred to the daily production report.

With each set of new pages, members of the cast and crew will insert each of the latest pages into his/her script, replacing the original white or out-dated colored change page. By the time most shows have completed filming, the scripts are rainbow-colored.

When change pages are generated, it's imperative that they are distributed to the people who need them immediately. In addition to the Producer(s), Director and Production Manager; the First Assistant Director will need to know if and how these changes will affect his/her schedule; the Casting Director and/or specific cast members will need to know if there are changes in their dialogue; the Location Manager will need to know if any location has been deleted or a new one added. The same will be true for each department head. Will new equipment or props have to be ordered? Will more or less extras be needed? Again, changes need to be distributed to those who need them as soon as possible.

Once a show has finished filming and post production is completed, a truly *final* script is generated. It's called a **Continuity Script** and contains the exact (word-for-word) dialogue and action as it appears in the final cut version of the picture.

Continuity scripts are for purposes of distribution and are required as part of your delivery requirements.

FORMS AND FORMATS INCLUDED IN

THIS SECTION

Breakdown Sheet 71
Day-out-of-Day 72
Call Sheet (2 pages) 73-74
Production Report (2 pages) 75-76
Check Request 77
Purchase Order 78
Petty Cash Accounting 79
Received of Petty Cash Slip 80
Shooting Schedule 81
One-Line Schedule 82
Crew List 83
Cast List 84
Executive Staff List 85
Contact List 86

BREAKDOWN SHEET

SHOW __THE WATCHER__

EPISODE __"BOYS NIGHT OUT"__

LOCATION __SWEETWATER ROAD — HOLLYWOOD LAKE__

BREAKDOWN PAGE # __3__

PRODUCTION # __0100__

DATE __5/17/93__

SCENE #'S	DESCRIPTION	NO. OF PAGES
	(INT) (EXT) ROAD LEADING TO LAKE (DAY) (NIGHT)	
6	THE BOYS WALK TO THE LAKE	1/8
7	THE BOYS SPOT LAURA SUNBATHING	1/8
8 & 9	THE BOYS HIDE & WATCH LAURA	5/8
	TOTAL	7/8

NO.	CAST	BITS/DOUBLES	ATMOSPHERE
1. 3. 6. 7.	HERBY LAURA MARC JED		6 SUNBATHERS MAN WALKING DOG 2 KIDS PLAYING BALL
		WARDROBE	**PROPS/SET DRESSING**
		BOYS IN T-SHIRTS & SHORTS LAURA IN WHITE BIKINI	BEACH CHAIRS UMBRELLAS / BALL SUNTAN LOTION SUNGLASSES
		SPEC. EFFECTS	**TRANS/PIC VEHICLES**
			LAURA'S CAR PARKED ON SIDE OF ROAD

STUNTS	MUSIC/SOUND/CAMERA	WRANGLERS/LIVESTOCK
		N.D. DOG

HAIR/MAKE-UP	SPECIAL REQUIREMENTS
CUT ON HERBY'S HAND	DOG WRANGLER

DAY-OUT-OF-DAYS

PRODUCTION COMPANY __XYZ PRODUCTIONS__
PRODUCTION TITLE __THE WATCHER__
EPISODE TITLE __"BOYS NIGHT OUT"__
PRODUCTION # __0100__
SCRIPT DATED __FEB 16, 1993__

DATE __JUNE 1, 1993__
PRODUCER __SWIFTY DEALS__
DIRECTOR __SID CELLULOID__
UNIT PRODUCTION MGR. __FRED FILMER__
FIRST ASST. DIRECTOR __A. DEES__

NAME	CHARACTER	Jun 18 F (1)	19 S (2)	20 S	21 M (3)	22 T (4)	23 W (5)	24 TH (6)	25 F (7)	26 S (8)	27 S	28 M (9)	29 T (10)	30 W (11)	Jul 1 TH (12)	2 F (13)	3 S (14)	TRAVEL	START	FINISH	WORK	IDLE	TOTAL
CLARK GRABLE	HERBY	TRS	W		W	W	W	W	H			W	W	H	W	W	TRF	2	6/18	7/3	10	2	14
ROCKY RIZZO	JAKE	TRS	W		W	W	W	W	H			H	H	H	W	W	TRF	2	6/18	7/3	7	5	14
SCARLET STARLET	LAURA				TRS	W	W	H	W			W	W	TRF				3	6/21	6/30	6	1	9
NANCY NICELY	MOM				TRS	W	W	H	H			W	H	W	W	TRF		2	6/21	7/2	5	4	11
HOLLYWOOD MANN	GEORGE				TRS	W	H	H	TRF									2	6/22	6/26	3	1	5
KENNY SMILES	MARC				TRS	W	W	H	W			W	TRF					2	6/21	6/29	4	2	8
LLOYD LOCAL	POLICE SGT.						SWF													6/24	1	1	1

CALL SHEET

PRODUCTION COMPANY __XYZ PRODUCTIONS, INC.__	DATE __7-2-93 FRIDAY__
SHOW __THE WATCHER__	DIRECTOR __SID CELLULOID__
SERIES EPISODE __"BOY'S NIGHT OUT"__	PRODUCER __SWIFTY DEALS__
PROD# __0100__ DAY# __6__ OUT OF __8__	LOCATION __SWEETWATER RD - HOLLYWOOD LAKE__
	SUNRISE __6:20A__ SUNSET __7:40P__
IS TODAY A DESIGNATED DAY OFF? [ ] YES [ ] NO	ANTICIPATED WEATHER __85°__

CREW CALL __7A__

LEAVING CALL _____

SHOOTING CALL __8:30A__

[ ] Weather Permitting   [✓] See Attached Map

[✓] Report to Location   [ ] Bus to Location

Set Description	Scene Nos.	Cast	D/N	Pages	Location
EXT. ROAD TO LAKE (BOYS ON WAY TO LAKE)	6	1,6,7	D	1/8	HOLLYWOOD LAKE
EXT BUSHES (BOYS WATCH LAURA)	7,8,9	1,3,6,7	D	6/8	
EXT LAKE (GEORGE JOINS LAURA)	10,11	3,5	D	3 2/8	
		TOTAL -		4 1/8 PG.	

Cast	Part Of	Leave	Makeup	Set Call	Remarks
CLARK GRABLE	HERBY (1)	7:15A	8A	8:30A	TO BE PICKED-UP @ 7A
SCARLET STARLET	LAURA (3)	6:30A	7A	9:30A	TO BE PICKED-UP @ 6:15A
HOLLYWOOD MANN (NEW)	GEORGE (5)	—	9A	10A	REPORT TO LOC.
KENNY SMILES	MARC (6)	—	8A	8:30A	REPORT TO LOC.
WIL PERFORMER	JED (7)	—	8A	8:30A	REPORT TO LOC.

Atmosphere & Stand-ins	
3 STANDINS	REPORT TO LOC @ 7:30A
6 SUNBATHERS	
1 MAN WALKING DOG	
2 KIDS PLAYING BALL	

NOTE: No forced calls without previous approval of unit production manager or assistant director.   All calls subject to change.

Advance Schedule Or Changes

MONDAY - 7-5-93
INT. HERBY'S BEDROOM (N) SCS. 5, 8, 115 THRU 123   STG. 14
INT. HERBY'S KITCHEN (N) SCS. 7, 14, 15, 22
INT. HERBY'S FRONT DOOR (N) SC. 73

Assistant Director __A. Dees__

Production Manager __Fred Filmer__

PRODUCTION REQUIREMENT

SHOW: THE WATCHER PROD#: 0100 DATE: 7-2-93

NO.	STAFF & CREW	TIME	NO.	STAFF & CREW	TIME	NO.	EQUIPMENT	
1	Production Mgr. F. FILMER	7A	1	Gaffer	7A	2	Cameras PANAFLEX	
1	1st Asst. Dir. A. DEES	7A	1	Best Boy			ARRI	
1	2nd Asst. Dir. R. DURHAM	6:30A	1	Lamp Oper.		1	Dolly CHAPMAN	
	2nd 2nd Asst. Dir.			Lamp Oper.			Crane	
	DGA Trainee			Lamp Oper.			Condor	
1	Script Supervisor K. KANDU	8A		Local 40 Man				
	Dialogue Coach						Sound Channel	
1	Prod. Coordinator C. COORDINATES	8A	1	Prod. Designer				
1	Prod. Sect'y G. AIDES	7A		Art Director			Video	
1	Prod. Accountant C. FIGURESS	8A		Asst. Art Dir.				
1	Asst. Accountant L. TRAINER	8A		Set Designer			Radio Mikes	
1	Location Manager B. SCOUT	6:30A		Sketch Artist		8	Walkie/talkies	
1	Asst. Location Mgr. T. FINDER	6:30A						
1	Teacher/Welfare Worker S. MARM	8:30A		Const. Coord.		5	Dressing Rooms	
3	Production Assts. JONES, SMITH	6:30A	1	Const. Foreman			Schoolrooms	
	MILLER			Paint Foreman		1	Rm. for Parents	
1	Dir. of Photography F. STOPP	7:30A		Labor Foremen				
1	Camera Operator S. SHUTTER	7:30A		Const. First Aid			Projector	
1	Camera Operator						Moviola	
	SteadyCam Operator		1	Set Decorator				
1	Asst. Cameraman		1	Lead Person			Air Conditioners	
1	Asst. Cameraman		1	Swing Crew			Heaters	
	Asst. Cameraman		1	Swing Crew			Wind Machines	
1	Still Photographer			Swing Crew				
	Cameraman-Process		1	Drapery				
	Projectionist							
				Technical Advisor			SUPPORT PERSONNEL	TIME
1	Mixer			Publicist			Policemen	
1	Boomman			MEALS			Motorcycles	
1	Cableman			Caterer			Fireman	
	Playback		25	Breakfasts ND READY @ 7A			Guard	
	Video Oper.			Wlkg. Breakfasts rdy @			Night Watchman	
			10	Gals. Coffee				
1	Key Grip		75	Lunches rdy @ 12N Crew @ 1P				
1	2nd Grip			Box Lunches				
1	Dolly Grip			Second Meal				
1	Grip							
1	Grip						VEHICLES	
	Grip			DRIVERS		1	Prod. Van	
			1	Trans. Coord.	6A		Camera	
	Greensman		1	Trans. Capt.	6A	1	Grip	
			1	Driver	6:30A		Electric	
	S/By Painter		1	Driver			Effects	
1	Craftservice		1	Driver		1	Props	
1	First Aid		1	Driver		1	Wardrobe	
			1	Driver		1	Makeup	
	Spec. Efx		1	Driver		1	Set Dressing	
	Spec. Efx		1	Driver			Crew Bus	
			1	Driver			Honeywagon	
1	Propmaster		1	Driver		2	Motorhomes	
1	Asst. Props		1	Driver			Station Wagons	
1	Asst. Props		1	Driver		2	Mini-buses	
			1	Driver			Standby Cars	
1	Costume Designer		1	Driver			Crew Cabs	
	Costume Supervisor		1	Driver			Insert Cars	
1	Costumer		1	Driver			Generators	
1	Costumer		1	Driver			Water Wagon	
			1	Driver		1	Picture Cars LAURA'S CAR	
1	Makeup Artist	6:30A	1	Driver				
	Makeup Artist		1	Driver				
	Body Makeup							
1	Hairstylist			Stunt Coord.				
	Hairstylist			Wranglers				
			1	Animal Handlers	8A		Livestock	
1	Editor	O/C				1	Animals ND DOG	
1	Asst. Editor							
	Apprentice Editor							

DEPARTMENT	SPECIAL INSTRUCTIONS
PROPS / SET DRESSING	BEACH CHAIRS, UMBRELLAS, BALL, SUNTAN LOTION SUNGLASSES
MAKEUP	BODY MAKEUP FOR "LAURA"

© ELH Form #7A

DAILY PRODUCTION REPORT

	1st Unit	2nd Unit	Reh.	Test	Travel	Holidays	Change Over	Retakes & Add. Scs.	Total	Schedule	
No.Days Sched.	30	4			2				36	Ahead	
No.Days Actual	6				1				7	Behind	

Title **THE WATCHER**   Prod# **0100**   Date **MON, JUNE 7, 1993**
Producer **SWIFTY DEALS**   Director **SID CELLULOID**
Date Started **6-1-93**   Scheduled Finish Date **7-16-93**   Est. Finish Date **7-16-93**

Sets **(EXT) ROAD & FENCE ALONG LAURA'S HOUSE - (EXT) LAKE SHORE**
Location **SWEETWATER ROAD — HOLLYWOOD LAKE**
Crew Call **7A**   Shooting Call **8:30A**   First Shot **9:30A**   Lunch **1:30**   Til **2P**
1st Shot After Lunch **2:35P**   2nd Meal ___   Til ___   Camera Wrap **8P**   Last Man Out **9P**
Company dismissed at [ ] Studio [✔] Location [ ] Headquarters   Round Trip Mileage **18 MI.**   Is Today A Designated Day Off? [ ] YES [✔] NO

SCRIPT SCENES AND PAGES			MINUTES		SETUPS		ADDED SCENES		RETAKES		
	SCENES	PAGES								PAGES	SCENES
			Prev.	31:37	Prev.	83	Prev.	4	Prev.	4 1/8	3
			Today	2:15	Today	23	Today	0	Today	4/8	1
Script	215	117 6/8	Total	33:52	Total	106	Total	4	Total	4 5/8	4
Taken Prev.	76	35 3/8	Scene No.	3, 4, 5, 26, 27, 30							
Taken Today	6	5 3/8									
Total to Date	82	40 5/8	Added Scenes								
To be Taken	133	77 1/8	Retakes Sc. 15				Sound Tracks				

FILM STOCK	FILM USE	GROSS	PRINT	NO GOOD	WASTE	1/4" ROLLS	FILM INVENTORY 5296	
5296	Prev.					10	Starting Inv.	20,000
	Today					2	Additional Rec'd.	0
	To Date					12	Today	0
							Total	20,000

FILM STOCK	FILM USE	GROSS	PRINT	NO GOOD	WASTE		FILM INVENTORY 5293	
5293	Prev.	21,386	12,860	5536	2990		Starting Inv.	10,260
	Today	4730	1850	1150	610		Additional Rec'd.	0
	To Date	26,116	14,710	6686	3600		Today	3,610
							Total	6,650

FILM STOCK	FILM USE	GROSS	PRINT	NO GOOD	WASTE		FILM INVENTORY 5247	
5247	Prev.						Starting Inv.	18,250
	Today						Additional Rec'd.	0
	To Date						Today	0
							Total	18,250

CAST - WEEKLY & DAY PLAYERS
Worked - W   Rehearsal - R   Finished - F
Started - S   Hold - H   Test - T
Travel - TR

CAST	CHARACTER	W H S F R TR	MAKEUP WDBE.	REPORT ON SET	DISMISS ON SET	MEALS OUT	MEALS IN	LEAVE FOR LOC.	ARRIVE ON LOC.	LEAVE LOCATION	ARRIVE AT HDQ.	STUNT ADJ.
CLARK GRABLE	HERBY	W	8A	8:30A	6P	1:30P	2P	7A	8A	6:15P	7:15P	
SCARLET STARLET	LAURA (XX)	W	7:30A	10A	8P	1:30P	2P	6:45A	7:30A	8:15P	4P	
HOLLYWOOD MANN	GEORGE	SW	9A	10A	8P	1:30P	2P					
KENNY SMILES	MARC	W	8A	8:30A	6P	1:30P	2P					
WILL PERFORMER	JED	W	8A	8:30A	6P	1:30P	2P					

XX = N.D. BREAKFAST   * = DISMISS TIME INCLUDES 15 MIN. MAKEUP / WARD. REMOVAL
X = NOT PHOTOGRAPHED   S = SCHOOL ONLY

EXTRA TALENT

No	Rate	1st Call	Set Dismiss	Final Dismiss	Adj.	MPV	No.	Rate	1st Call	Set Dismiss	Final Dismiss	Adj.	MPV
3	@ $90	7:30A	8P										
6	@ 40	7:30A	8P		+WARD								
3	@ 65	8A	8P		+WARD								

Assistant Director _G. Dees_   Production Manager _____

© ELH Form #8

SHOW: **THE WATCHER** PROD#: *0100* DATE: *6-7-93*

NO.	STAFF & CREW	TIME	NO.	STAFF & CREW	TIME	NO.	EQUIPMENT	
1	Production Mgr. *F. FILMER*	*7A*		Gaffer			Cameras *PANAFLEX*	
1	1st Asst. Dir. *A. DEES*	*7A*	1	Best Boy			*ARRI*	
1	2nd Asst. Dir. *R. D. DURHAM*	*6:30A*	1	Lamp Oper.		1	Dolly *CHAPMAN*	
1	2nd 2nd Asst. Dir. *K. GALLO*	*6:30A*	1	Lamp Oper.			Crane	
	DGA Trainee		1	Lamp Oper.			Condor	
1	Script Supervisor *K. KANDU*	*7:30A*	1	Local 40 Man				
1	Dialogue Coach *A. WILKES*	*9A*					Sound Channel	
1	Prod. Coordinator *C. COORDINATES*	*7:30A*		Prod. Designer				
1	Prod. Sect'y *K. TYPES*	*8A*		Art Director			Video	
1	Prod. Accountant *I. COUNTS*	*9A*		Asst. Art Dir.				
1	Asst. Accountant *R. AIDE*	*9A*		Set Designer			Radio Mikes	
1	Location Manager *B. SCOUT*	*6:30A*		Sketch Artist		8	Walkie/talkies	
1	Asst. Location Mgr. *A. BRIGHT*	*7A*						
1	Teacher/Welfare Worker *S. MARM*	*8A*		Const. Coord.		5	Dressing Rooms	
3	Production Assts *SMITH,*	*6:30A*		Const. Foreman		1	Schoolrooms	
	JONES, MILLER			Paint Foreman		1	Rm. for Parents	
1	Dir. of Photography *F. STOPP*	*8A*		Labor Foremen				
1	Camera Operator			Const. First Aid			Projector	
	Camera Operator						Moviola	
	SteadiCam Operator			Set Decorator				
1	Asst. Cameraman			Lead Person			Air Conditioners	
1	Asst. Cameraman			Swing Crew			Heaters	
1	Asst. Cameraman			Swing Crew			Wind Machines	
1	Still Photographer			Swing Crew				
	Cameraman-Process			Drapery				
	Projectionist							
				Technical Advisor			SUPPORT PERSONNEL	TIME
1	Mixer			Publicist		2	Policemen	*6:30A*
1	Boomman			**MEALS**		2	Motorcycles	*6:30A*
	Cableman			Caterer	*6:30A*		Fireman	
	Playback		25	Breakfasts		1	Guard	
	Video Oper.		120	Wlkg. Breakfasts rdy @		1	Night Watchman	
			15	Gals. Coffee				
1	Key Grip			Lunches rdy @ *1P* Crew @ *1:30*				
1	2nd Grip			Box Lunches				
1	Dolly Grip			Second Meal				
1	Grip							
1	Grip						**VEHICLES**	
1	Grip			**DRIVERS**		1	Prod. Van	
			1	Trans. Coord.		1	Camera	
1	Greensman		1	Trans. Capt.		1	Grip	
			1	Driver			Electric	
	S/By Painter		1	Driver			Effects	
1	Craftservice		1	Driver		1	Props	
1	First Aid		1	Driver		1	Wardrobe	
			1	Driver			Makeup	
	Spec. Efx		1	Driver		1	Set Dressing	
	Spec. Efx		1	Driver			Crew Bus	
			1	Driver		1	Honeywagon	
1	Propmaster		1	Driver		2	Motorhomes	
1	Asst. Props		1	Driver		1	Station Wagons	
1	Asst. Props		1	Driver		2	Mini-buses	
			1	Driver		2	Standby Cars	
	Costume Designer		1	Driver			Crew Cabs	
	Costume Supervisor		1	Driver			Insert Cars	
	Costumer		1	Driver		2	Generators	
	Costumer		1	Driver		1	Water Wagon	
				Driver		2	Picture Cars *LAURA'S CAR*	
	Makeup Artist			Driver			*GEORGE'S CAR*	
	Makeup Artist			Driver				
	Body Makeup							
1	Hairstylist			Stunt Coord.				
1	Hairstylist			Wranglers				
			1	Animal Handlers			Livestock	
1	Editor					1	Animals *NO DOG*	
1	Asst. Editor							
	Apprentice Editor							

COMMENTS - DELAYS (EXPLANATION) - CAST, STAFF & CREW ABSENCE

- *SCARLET STARLET 30 MIN. LATE TO SET*
- *KATIE KANDU (SCRIPT SUPV'R.) TOOK ILL ON SET. REPLACED @ NOON.*
- *WILLIE WYKES (ELECTRICIAN) BURNED HAND - TREATED ON SET*
- *MACINTOSH II SI COMPUTER W/ MONITOR & KEYBOARD DISCOVERED MISSING FROM "HERBY'S BEDROOM" SET. POLICE REPORT FORTHCOMING.*

☐ NO ACCIDENTS REPORTED TODAY

© ELH Form #8A

CHECK REQUEST

SHOW ___THE WATCHER___   PROD# ___0100___

COMPANY ___XYZ PRODUCTIONS___

ADDRESS ___1234 FLICK DR.___   PHONE# ___213/555-3331___

___HOLLYWOOD, CA 90001___   FAX# ___213/555-3332___

DATE ___6-10-93___   AMOUNT $ ___180⁻___

CHECK PAYEE ___CAL'S COMPUTER CENTER___

ADDRESS ___9876 FLORES ST___

___STUDIO VILLAGE, CA 90009___

PHONE# ___818/555-1000___   FAX # ___818/555-1001___

ATTN: ___CAL___

PAYEE SS# OR FED. ID# _____

DESCRIPTION	CODING	AMOUNT
2 MONTH-RENTAL OF	865-55	$90 PER MO.
HP LASER JET PRINTER		
(STARTS 6-15-93) FOR		
USE BY ACCNTG. DEPT		

TOTAL: $180⁻

[ ] PURCHASE
[✓] RENTAL   CHECK NEEDED: [ ] IMMEDIATELY
[ ] DEPOSIT   [✓] WITHIN NEXT DAY OR TWO
[ ] ADVANCE   [ ] WITHIN NORMAL PROCESSING TIME
[ ] 1099
[ ] INVENTORY

WHEN READY: [ ] PLEASE MAIL CHECK
                [✓] PLEASE GIVE CHECK TO ___CINDY FIGURES___

CHECK REQUESTED BY ___ADAM ACCOUNTANT___   DEPT. ___ACCOUNTING___

APPROVED BY ___Fred Filmer___   DATE ___6-12-93___

(INVOICE SUBSTANTIATION MUST FOLLOW THIS REQUEST)

PAID BY CHECK # ___1327___   DATE ___6-15-93___

PURCHASE ORDER

DATE _JUNE 14, 1993_   P.O.# _0125_

SHOW _THE WATCHER_   PROD# _0100_

COMPANY _XYZ PRODUCTIONS, INC._

ADDRESS _1234 FLICK DR._   PHONE# _213/555-3331_

HOLLYWOOD, CA 90038   FAX# _213/555-3332_

VENDOR _EASTERN COSTUME CO._

ADDRESS _123 HOLLYWOOD WAY_   PHONE# _213/555-2137_

HOLLYWOOD, CA 90028   FAX# _213/555-2130_

CONTACT _LULU_

[ ] PURCHASE   [✓] RENTAL   [ ] SERVICE

DESCRIPTION	CODING	AMOUNT
ASSORTED T-SHIRTS & SHORTS FOR HERBY, MARC & JED	831-56	$75—
TATTERED CLOTHES FOR JAKE	831-56	$25—

SET #(s) _____

TOTAL COST: $ _100—_   Per Show [ ]
                       Day [ ]
IF TOTAL COST CANNOT BE DETERMINED   Week [✓]
AT THIS DATE, ESTIMATE OF COSTS WILL Month [ ]
NOT EXCEED $ _____

IF P.O. IS FOR A <u>RENTAL</u>, PLEASE ESTIMATE DATE OF RETURN _7-10-93_

ORDER PLACED BY _FRIEDA FITTER_   DEPT. _WARDROBE_

APPROVED BY _Fred Gilmer_   DATE _6-15-93_

cc: Vendor (Orig)
       Production Manager
       Accounting Dept.
       Department Head

© ELH Form #10

PETTY CASH ACCOUNTING

NAME PAULA PROPPS   SHOW THEWATCHER   AMOUNT RECEIVED $ 500 —   ENVELOPE # 1

DEPARTMENT PROPERTY   FROM 6/1 19 93 TO 6/8 19 93   * DATE 6/9/93   CHECK # 0037

DATE	NO.	PAID TO	FOR	ACCOUNT	AMOUNT	
6/1	1	AWE SPORTING GOODS	BASKETBALL		$ 23.50	Inv
6/2	2	JOE'S MARKET	CANNED FOOD		15.37	
6/2	3	SHADES INC.	SUNGLASSES		62.05	
6/3	4	FOOD·TO·GO	COOKED DINNER		130.63	
6/4	5	JOE'S MARKET	SOFT DRINKS		37.09	
6/4	6	AL'S DRUGS	SUNTAN LOTION		6.52	
6/5	7	APE DEPT STORE	MAKEUP KIT		53.17	
6/5	8	BED & BATH SHOP	BEACH TOWELS		33.64	
6/5	9	JAY'S NEWSSTAND	NEWSPAPERS		6.51	
6/6	10	AL'S DRUGS	CIGARETTES		10.36	
6/7	11	HORIZON ELECTRONICS	WALKMAN		25.17	Inv
6/7	12	JOE'S MARKET	MISC. GROCERIES		69.77	
6/8	13	AWE SPORTING GOODS	BAT/BALL		28.39	Inv
6/8	14	ROLAH'S OPTICAL CO.	LAURA'S GLASSES		150.06	Inv
				TOTAL: ***	$ 652.73	

FOR ACCOUNTING USE ONLY

ACCOUNT	AMOUNT

AMOUNT ADVANCED * $ 500 —
TOTAL ACCOUNTED FOR ** 652.73
CASH ON HAND
    -OR-
AMT. TO BE REIMBURSED / 152.73

NOTE: EACH RECEIPT SHOULD BE CLEARLY LABELED WITH A DATE AND DESCRIPTION AS TO WHAT THEY ARE FOR AND ATTACHED IN THE SAME ORDER IN WHICH THEY APPEAR ON THE ENVELOPE.

APPROVED Fred Gilmer

AUDITED Adam Accountant   ENTERED 6/10/93

PETTY CASH ADVANCE/REIMBURSEMENT	SIGNATURE
RECEIVED IN CASH $ 652.73 ON 6/10 , 19 93	Paula Propps

© ELH Form #11

FORMS AND REPORTS   79

AMOUNT $ _400_   NO. _27_

RECEIVED OF PETTY CASH

DATE _5-25-93_

NAME _____ FRIEDA FITTER _____

DEPARTMENT _____ WARDROBE _____

DESCRIPTION _____
_____
_____
_____

☑ *PETTY CASH TO BE ACCOUNTED FOR*

APPROVED BY   RECEIVED BY
Fred Felmer, UPM   _Frieda Fitter_

© ELH Form #12

"THE WATCHER" - PROD# 0100

SHOOTING SCHEDULE

PRODUCER:	SWIFTY DEALS	FILM SHOOTS - 36 DAYS:	
DIRECTOR:	SID CELLULOID	TUESDAY, JUNE 1, 1993	
PRODUCTION MANAGER:	FRED FILMER	THROUGH	
1ST ASST. DIRECTOR:	A. DEES	FRIDAY, JULY 17, 1993	

DATE	SET/SCENES	CAST	LOCATION
1ST DAY TUESDAY 6/1/93	EXT. LAUREL ROAD - D D-1 1 1/8 Pg. Scs. 6,7,8 The boys discover a hole in the fence and look through to the other side. NOTES:	1. HERBY 3. JED 4. MARC ATMOS 2 elderly ladies (passers-by) VEHICLES old truck next to fence	SWEETWATER ROAD PACIFIC PALISADES PROPS Marc's ball WARDROBE/MAKEUP Herby's cut hand

----

| | EXT. LAURA'S BACKYARD
D-1 1 4/8 Pgs.
Scs. 9 & 10

The boys see Laura
sunbathing by her
pool.

NOTES: | 1. HERBY
2. LAURA
3. JED
4. MARC

VEHICLES
Laura's Mercedes
(in driveway) | (SAME AS ABOVE)

PROPS
Towel
Makeup bag
Laura's sunglasses

WARDROBE/MAKEUP
Laura's white bikini

SPEC. EFX
Light steam off pool |

| | EXT. LAURA'S BACKYARD
D-1 2 4/8 Pgs.
Sc. 11

Steve joins Laura and
chases the boys away
from the fence.

NOTES: | 1. HERBY
2. LAURA
3. JED
4. MARC
7. STEVE

VEHICLES
Laura's Mercedes
Steve's BMW | (SAME AS ABOVE)

PROPS
Same as above

WARDROBE/MAKEUP
Steve in sport shirt
and jacket |

END OF DAY #1 -	TOTAL PAGES:	5 1/8

ONE-LINE SCHEDULE

PRODUCER: SWIFTY DEALS   FILM SHOOTS - 36 DAYS:
DIRECTOR: SID CELLULOID   TUESDAY, JUNE 1, 1993
PRODUCTION MANAGER: FRED FILMER   THROUGH
1ST ASST. DIRECTOR: A. DEES   FRIDAY, JULY 16, 1993

FIRST DAY - TUESDAY, JUNE. 1, 1993

Sc.	1	EXT. PIER AT SUNRISE - D Sunrise over pier and Venice Beach	1/8 pg.
Scs.	2 - 13	EXT. VENICE BEACH - D Steve jogs	1 6/8 pgs.
Sc.	23	EXT. FRONT OF HOTEL - D Steve jogs up to front of hotel	1/8 pg.
Scs.	46 - 52	EXT. STRAND VENICE - D Steve greets friends on way out to jog. He smiles at Laura	2 3/8 pgs.
Scs.	87 - 90	EXT. VENICE STRAND - D Nick and Cory walk together	6/8 pg.
Sc.	95	EXT. VENICE STRAND - D Steve & Laura talk to Herby	4/8 pg.
Sc.	101	INT. VENICE RESTAURANT - D Inside - people wave hello to Steve & Laura	1/8 pg.
Sc.	91	EXT. STRAND AREA (NEAR PIER) - D Marc skates for them	6/8 pg.
		END OF FIRST DAY - TOTAL PAGES	**6 4/8 pgs.**

SECOND DAY - WEDNESDAY, JUNE, 2, 1993

Sc.	60	INT. GIFT SHOP - D George spots Steve & Laura outside	3/8 pg.
Sc.	61	EXT. BEACH - VENICE STRAND - D Steve gets dope on horse from Jake	4 3/8 pgs.
Scs.	63 & 64	EXT. BIKE PATH - VENICE - D Steve & Laura ride on bicycle- built-for-two	1 5/8 pgs.
Sc.	66	EXT. BIKE PATH - VENICE - D George's POV of Steve & Laura on bicycle - from high window	1/8 pg.
		END OF SECOND DAY - TOTAL PAGES	**6 4/8 pgs.**

CREW LIST

XYZ Productions
1234 Flick Drive
Hollywood, CA 90038
213/555-3331 • 213/555-3332 (FAX)

9/15/93

THE WATCHER—Production No. 0100

EXECUTIVE PRODUCER	MARVIN MOGUL	Office:	213/555-7250
	555 School Street	Home:	818/555-5554
	Los Angeles, CA 90001	Beeper:	213/555-1166
PRODUCER	SWIFTY DEALS	Office:	213/555-7254
	12353 Rhodes Ave.	Home:	714/555-0897
	Toluca lake, CA 91150	Car:	213/307-5687
DIRECTOR	SID CELLULOID		818/555-6033
	2764 Carson Street	Fax:	818/555-6031
	Valencia, CA 90477		

ASSOCIATE PRODUCER
PRODUCTION MANAGER
1ST ASSISTANT DIRECTOR
2ND ASSISTANT DIRECTOR
PRODUCTION COORDINATOR
PRODUCTION ACCOUNTANT
ASSISTANT ACCOUNTANT
SCRIPT SUPERVISOR
CASTING DIRECTOR
EXTRA CASTING DIR.
LOCATION MANAGER
TEACHER/WELFARE WORKER
PUBLICIST
PRODUCTION DESIGNER
ART DIRECTOR
SET DESIGNER
SET DECORATOR
LEAD PERSON
SWING PERSON
CONSTRUCTION COORDINATOR
PROPERTY MASTER
ASSISTANT PROPERTY MASTER
SPECIAL EFFECTS SUPERVISOR
DIRECTOR OF PHOTOGRAPHY
CAMERA OPERATOR
STEADICAM OPERATOR
EXECUTIVE PRODUCER
PRODUCER
DIRECTOR
ASSOCIATE PRODUCER
1ST ASSISTANT CAMERAMAN
PRODUCTION MANAGER
ASSISTANT DIRECTORS
PRODUCTION COORDINATOR
2ND ASSISTANT CAMERAMAN

(continue this column on a separte page. Put all the contact information in this second column, following the format above.)

STILL PHOTOGRAPHER
GAFFER
BEST BOY/ELECTRICIAN
ELECTRICIAN
KEY GRIP
BEST BOY/GRIP
DOLLY GRIP
GRIP
SOUND MIXER
BOOM OPERATOR
CABLE PERSON
COSTUME DESIGNER
WARDROBE SUPERVISOR
COSTUMER
HAIR STYLIST
MAKEUP ARTIST
POST PRODUCTION SUPERVISOR
FILM EDITOR
ASSISTANT EDITOR
APPRENTICE EDITOR
MUSIC EDITOR
STUNT COORDINATOR
SPECIAL EFFECTS
VISUAL EFFECTS
TRANSPORTATION COORDINATOR
TRANSPORTATION CAPTAIN
DRIVER
WRANGLER
CRAFT SERVICE
PRODUCTION ASSISTANT
SET SECURITY
CATERING

CAST LIST

XYZ Productions
1234 Flick Drive
Hollywood, CA 90038
213/555-3331 • 213/555-3332 (FAX)

THE WATCHER—Production No. 0100

ROLE	ACTOR	AGENT
GEORGE	HOLLYWOOD MANN	JOE COOL
	3465 Hortense Street	Talented Artists Agency
	Wonderland, CA 90000	1515 Sunset Blvd.
	Home: 818/555-1000	213/555-2345
	Service: 213/555-2000	FAX 213/555-7890
	SS#: 123-45-6789	

EXECUTIVE STAFF LIST

It's helpful to add the company's EXECUTIVE STAFF LIST to the end of your crew list.

9/15/93

XYZ Productions
1234 Flick Drive
Hollywood, CA 90038
213/555-3331 • 213/555-3332 (FAX)

THE WATCHER—Production No. 0100

PRESIDENT	HARRY HONCHO	Office:	Ext. 340
	5678 Constitution Place	Home:	818/555-8000
	Beverly Hill, CA 90222	Car:	818/555-8001
	Asst: Alice Abet		
	Sect'y: Terri Types		

VICE PRESIDENT, LEGAL AFFAIRS
VICE PRESIDENT, DEVELOPMENT
VICE PRESIDENT, BUSINESS AFFAIRS
VICE PRESIDENT, PRODUCTION
PRODUCTION, EXECUTIVE
VICE PRESIDEN, POST PRODUCTION
CONTROLLER
OFFICE MANAGER
and so forth.

CONTACT LIST

Supply your production staff with a listing of company contacts and services they will need in setting up and running their production.

List companies you have used in the past that have given you good service and good rates. (If you use many of the same suppliers on all your shows, you're more likely to be given discounted rates.)

Your contact list should look something like this:

XYZ Productions   9/15/93
1234 Flick Drive
Hollywood, CA 90038
213/555-3331 • 213/555-3332 (FAX)

THE WATCHER—Production No. 0100

ATTORNEY	CHARLES CHEATEM	213/555-7789
	DEWEY, CHEATEM & HOWE	Fax# 555-9000
	100 S. Whiskey Road	
	Los Angeles, CA 90004	
INSURANCE COMPANY	ABC INSURANCE COMPANY	818/555-2345
	4579 W. Frederick St.	Fax# 555-8090
	Burbank, CA 91502	
	CONTACT: Darryl Deductible	Dir# 555-5555

INSURANCE DOCTOR	*(continue this list down the left column with the*
COMPLETION BOND CO.	*contact information in the right column.)*
ACCOUNTING FIRM	EXPENDABLES
PAYROLL SERVICE	GENERATORS
BANK	OFFICE SUPPLIES
PUBLIC RELATIONS FIRM	STORAGE FACILITIES
TRAVEL AGENT	COPIER MACHINE, RENTAL/REPAIR
EXTRA CASTING AGENCY	TYPEWRITER, RENTAL/REPAIR
EXTRA PAYROLL SERVICE	COMPUTER, RENTAL/REPAIR
LAB	FAX MACHINE, RENTAL/REPAIR
SOUND TRANSFERS	TELEPHONE EQUIPMENT/SERVICING
SCRIPT RESEARCH CO.	PRODUCT PLACEMENT FIRMS
MUSIC CLEARANCE CO.	WARDROBE RENTAL HOUSES
FILM PERMIT SERVICE	PROP/SET DRESSING RENTAL HOUSES
FIRE/POLICE OFFICERS	BOTTLED WATER/REFRIGERATORS
VEHICLE RENTALS	COFFEE MACHINES/KITCHEN SUPPLIES
HONEYWAGON RENTAL	MESSENGER SERVICE
CATERING CO.	OVERNIGHT COURIER SERVICE
RAW STOCK	SCRIPT TYPING SERVICE
CAMERA EQUIPMENT	WEATHER REPORT(S)
SOUND EQUIPMENT/WALKIE-TALKIES	EDITING ROOMS
BULLHORNS/HEADSETS	POST PRODUCTION FACILITIES
BEEPERS	SCREENING ROOMS
GRIP/ELECTRIC EQUIPMENT	STRIKE/CLEANING SERVICE
DOLLYS	... and any other services you may need/use.
CRANES/CONDORS	

CHAPTER 8
DEAL MEMOS

Prepare a **deal memo** for each member of your shooting company.

With the exception of the Directors Guild of America (DGA) deal memos, the others included in this chapter are intended as basic guidelines. You or your legal advisor may want to incorporate specific provisions and conditions to the terms of employment encompassed by these agreements.

Give all employees a copy of their signed deal memo. Also give a copy to the production manager, production accountant and/or payroll service. Retain the original for the company's master files. Send a copy of any signed DGA deal memo to the DGA's Reports Compliance Department in care of the National Office of the Directors Guild at 7950 Sunset Blvd, Los Angeles, CA 90046. Their phone and fax are: 310/289-2000, FAX 310/289-2029.

[Note: as of July 1, 1993, the following will be added into the DGA Basic Agreement if ratified by the membership. "Upon commencement of principal photography or a theatrical motion picture, or of a television motion picture 90 minutes or longer, Employer shall furnish to the Director and to the Guild an addendum to the Director's deal memorandum containing the following information to the extent that it is then known to the employer: the dates scheduled for start and finish of the Director's cut; the dates for special photography and processes, if any; the date for delivery of answer print; and the date of release (for theatrical films) or date of network broadcast (if applicable.)" *At press time, the new form was unavailable from the DGA.]*

FORMS INCLUDED IN THIS SECTION

Cast Deal Memo 88
Crew Deal Memo 89
Writer's Deal Memo 90
Writing Team Deal Memo............................91
DGA Director Deal Memo............................92
DGA UPM and Assistant Director
    Film Deal Memo.......................................93
Extra Talent Voucher 94

CAST DEAL MEMO

PRODUCTION COMPANY __XYZ PRODUCTIONS, INC.__   DATE __MAY 11, 1993__

ADDRESS __1234 FLICK DR.__   PHONE# __213 / 555 - 3331__

__HOLLYWOOD, CA__   FAX# __213 / 555 - 3332__

SHOW __THE WATCHER__   EPISODE _____

CASTING DIRECTOR __SHELDON SCOUT__   PROD# __0100__

ARTIST __SCARLET STARLET__   SOC.SEC.# __555-55-5555__

ADDRESS __555 SCHOOL ST.__   PHONE# __213 / 555-6262__

__HOLLYWOOD, CA 90038__   MESSAGES __213 / 555-6000__

ROLE __"LAURA"__   START DATE __6-9-93__

[✓] ACTOR	[✓] THEATRICAL	[ ] DAY PLAYER
[ ] SINGER	[ ] TELEVISION	[ ] 3-DAY PLAYER
[ ] STUNT	[ ] OTHER _____	[✓] WEEKLY
[ ] OTHER _____		

COMPENSATION $ __30,000—__   PER   [ ] DAY   [ ] WEEK   [✓] SHOW

	#DAY/WEEKS	DATES
TRAVEL	2 DAYS	6/9/93 + 6/16/93
REHEARSAL/FITTINGS	1 DAY - FITTINGS	5/19/93
PRINCIPLE PHOTOGRAPHY	5 DAYS	6/10 - 15
ADDITIONAL SHOOT DAYS	ALLOW: 2	AS NECESSARY
POST PRODUCTION DAYS	ALLOW: 1	TBD

PER DIEM/EXPENSES __$100 PER DAY__

TRANSPORTATION/TRAVEL __ROUND-TRIP FIRST CLASS AIR TRAVEL & TRANSPORTATION TO & FROM AIRPORT__

ACCOMMODATIONS __1ST CLASS HOTEL ACCOMODATIONS__

OTHER __FIRST-CLASS DRESSING RM WHEN ON STAGE - MOBILE HOME WHEN ON LOCATION__

BILLING __SINGLE CARD - MAIN TITLES - 3RD POSITION__

[✓] PAID ADVERTISING

AGENT __JOE COOL__   HOME# __310 / 555-5663__

AGENCY __TALENTED ARTISTS AGENCY__   OFFICE# __213 / 555-2345__

ADDRESS __1515 SUNSET BLVD.__   FAX# __213 / 555-7890__

__L.A. 91111__

[✓] LOAN OUT

CORPORATION NAME __STARLET NIGHTS INC.__

Address __C/O TAA - 1515 SUNSET BLVD.__

__L.A. 91111__

Federal I.D.# __95 - 1234567__

CONTRACT PREPARED BY __BARBARA BUSINESS AFFAIRS__ DATE SENT OUT __5-15-93__

SENT: [ ] To Agent   [ ] To Artist   [ ] To Set

[✓] SENT SCRIPT   [✓] NOTIFIED WARDROBE   [✓] STATION 12   [✓] INSURANCE PHYSICAL

APPROVED BY __Swifty Deals__   TITLE __PRODUCER__

CREW DEAL MEMO

PRODUCTION CO. **XYZ PRODUCTIONS, INC.** DATE **5-31-93**

SHOW **THE WATCHER** PROD# **0100**

NAME **MIKE BOOM** SOC.SEC.# **123-45-6789**

ADDRESS **21735 BROADWAY #120** PHONE (Home) **818/555-4500**

ENCINO, CA 91322 (Beeper) _____

START DATE **JUNE 4, 1993** (Fax) _____

JOB TITLE **SOUND MIXER** ACCOUNT# **835-01**

UNION/GUILD _____ GUARANTEE **6** (wks.)

RATE (In Town) **$2500** Per [Hour] [Day] [Week] ✓ for a (5)[6] **5** -day week

(Distant Loc.) **$3,000** Per [Hour] [Day] [Week] ✓ for a [5] (6) **6** -day week

ADDITIONAL DAY(S) PRO-RATED @ **1/5** (th) Of a week

OVERTIME **X 1/2** After **8** hours **XX** After **14** hours

BOX RENTAL _____ Per Day/Week

EQUIPMENT/VEHICLE RENTAL **$1750** Per Day/(Week)

MILEAGE ALLOWANCE _____ Per Day/Week

> NOTE: Box & Equipment rental & mileage allowance are subject to 1099 reporting. -- Any equipment rented by the Production Co. from the employee must be listed or inventoried before rental can be paid.

TRAVEL/ACCOMODATIONS **ROUND-TRIP BUSINESS CLASS AIRFARE & TRANSPORTATION TO & FROM THE AIRPORT**

EXPENSES/PER DIEM **$50/DAY PER DIEM**

OTHER **USE OF A CAR WHILE ON LOCATION**

✓ LOAN OUT

CORP. NAME **BOOM AUDIO RENTALS** FED. ID# **95-1234567**

ADDRESS (If Different From Above) _____

AGENT **NONE** AGENCY _____

ADDRESS _____ PHONE# _____

  Fax# _____

EMPLOYER OF RECORD **PAULINE'S PAYROLL SER.**

ADDRESS **7325 RHODES LANE** PHONE# **818/555-4444**

STUDIO VILLAGE, CA FAX# **818/555-4443**

IF AWARDED SCREEN CREDIT, HOW WOULD YOU LIKE YOUR NAME TO READ _____

SOUND MIXER — MICHAEL R. BOOM

APPROVED BY **Fred Filmer** TITLE **UPM**

ACCEPTED **Mike Boom** DATE **6-3-93**

© ELH Form #14 FORMS AND REPORTS 89

WRITER'S DEAL MEMO

PRODUCTION COMPANY __XYZ PRODUCTIONS, INC.__ DATE __2-28-93__

ADDRESS __1234 FLICK DR.__ PHONE# __213/555-3331__

__HOLLYWOOD, CA 90038__ FAX# __213/555-3332__

SHOW __THE WATCHER__ PROD# __0100__

EPISODE _____

WRITER __F. SCOTT RYDER__ PHONE# __213/555-7662__

SOC. SEC.# __555-00-5500__ MESSAGES _____

ADDRESS __9336 W. BALBOA BLVD.__ FAX# __213/555-7660__

__LOS ANGELES, CA__

DATES OF EMPLOYMENT _____

COMPENSATION __$150,000 FOR ORIGINAL SCREENPLAY PLUS ONE__
__ADDT'L. REWRITE & ONE POLISH__

ADDITIONAL TERMS OF EMPLOYMENT __ONE 1ST CLASS, ROUND-TRIP AIR__
__FARE TO MILWAUKEE, WISCONSIN LOCATION__

BILLING __SCREENPLAY BY__
__F. SCOTT RYDER__

✓ PAID ADVERTISING

WRITER'S AGENT __JOE COOL__ DIRECT# __213/555-2367__

AGENCY __TALENTED ARTISTS AGENCY__ PHONE# __213/555-2345__

ADDRESS __1515 SUNSET BLVD.__ FAX# __213/555-7870__

__LOS ANGELES, CA 91111__

✓ LOAN OUT

CORPORATION NAME __GREAT RYDERS, INC.__

ADDRESS __(SAME AS ABOVE)__

FEDERAL I.D.# __95-3327543__

CONTRACT PREPARED BY __R. GREEN, BUSINESS AFFAIRS__

DATE SENT OUT __3-2-93__

APPROVED BY __Swifty Deals__

TITLE __PRODUCER__ DATE __2/28/93__

© ELH Form #15

WRITING TEAM DEAL MEMO

PRODUCTION COMPANY _XYZ PRODUCTIONS_   DATE _6-10-93_

ADDRESS _1234 FLICK DR._   PHONE# _213/555-3331_

HOLLYWOOD, CA 90038   FAX# _213/555-3332_

SHOW _THE WATCHER_   PROD# _0100_

EPISODE _"BOYS NIGHT OUT"_

WRITERS _J. MILLER_   _R. MILLER_

SOC.SEC# _555-03-2764_   _555-04-2765_

ADDRESS _1723 MADISON DR._   _20076 DIAMOND LN._

LOS ANGELES, CA   _CULVER CITY, CA_

PHONE# _213/555-0404_   _310/555-7772_

FAX# _213/555-0406_   _310/555-7773_

DATES OF EMPLOYMENT _6-12-93 THROUGH 8-31-93_

COMPENSATION _$50,000_

ADDITIONAL TERMS OF EMPLOYMENT_____

BILLING _SCREENPLAY BY_
J. MILLER and R. MILLER

[✓] PAID ADVERTISING

WRITER'S AGENTS _JOE COOL_   _(SAME)_

AGENCY _TALENTED ARTISTS AGENCY_

ADDRESS _1515 SUNSET BLVD._

LOS ANGELES, CA 91111

PHONE# _____

[✓] LOAN OUT   [✓] LOAN OUT

CORP. NAME _J. MILLER, INC._   _R. MILLER, INC._

ADDRESS _(SAME AS ABOVE)_   _(SAME AS ABOVE)_

FED. I.D.# _95-9764321_   _95-3627312_

CONTRACT PREPARED BY _R. GREEN, BUSINESS AFFAIRS_

DATE SENT OUT _6-15-93_

APPROVED BY _Swifty Deals_

TITLE _PRODUCER_   DATE _6/18/93_

DGA—DIRECTOR DEAL MEMORANDUM

Note: The dates in this form are for example only. Check with the DGA regarding each particular project.

DIRECTOR DEAL MEMORANDUM

This confirms our agreement to employ you to direct the project described as follows:

Name: _SID CELLULOID_   SS#: _999-88-7777_

Loanout (if applicable): _____   Tel. #: _(805) 555-6033_

Address: _2764 CARSON ST., VALENCIA, CA. 90477_

Salary: $ _150,000.—_   ☐ per week   ☐ per day   ☑ per show

Additional Time: $ _SCALE_   ☑ per week   ☐ per day

Start Date: _7-12-93_   Guaranteed Period: _13 WKS._   ☐ pro rata

Project Information:

Picture or Series Title: _THE WATCHER_

Episode/Segment Title: _____   Epsd.# _____

Length of Program: _2 HRS._   Is this a Pilot? ☐ Yes   ☑ No

Produced Primarily/Mainly for:

☑ Theatrical   ☐ Network   ☐ Syndication
☐ Basic Cable   ☐ Disc/Cassette   ☐ Pay/TV: _____
                                                   (service)

Theatrical Film Budget (check one)   Free Television/Pay Television
   ☐ A. Under $500,000   ☐ Network Prime Time (type)
   ☐ B. Between $500,000 and $1,500,000   ☐ Other than Network Prime Time (type)
   ☑ C. Over $1,500,000

Check one (if applicable): ☐ Segment   ☐ Second Unit

The **INDIVIDUAL** having final cutting authority over the film is : _SWIFTY DEALS, PRODUCER_

Other conditions (including credit above minimum): _$100 PER DIEM; 1ST CL. ROUND-TRIP AIRFARE;_ _HOTEL ACCOMMODATIONS; RENTAL CAR + (JET) MOTORHOME WHILE ON DISTANT LOCATION._

This employment is subject to the provisions of the Directors Guild of America Basic Agreement of 1993.

Accepted and Agreed: Signatory Co: _XYZ PRODUCTIONS_
Employee: _Sid Celluloid_   By: _Swifty Deals, Producer_
Date: _July 1, 1993_   Date: _July 1, 1993_

RC300/070193

ADDENDUM TO THE DIRECTOR'S DEAL MEMORANDUM POST PRODUCTION SCHEDULE
(FOR A THEATRICAL MOTION PICTURE OR A TELEVISION MOTION PICTURE 90 MINUTES OR LONGER)

Director's Name: _SID CELLULOID_

Project Title: _THE WATCHER_

Company Name: _XYZ PRODUCTIONS_

Directors Cut: Start Date: _10-18-93_

           Finish Date: _11-28-93_

PLEASE INDICATE DATES BELOW:

Special Photography
    & Processes (if any): _NONE_

Delivery of Answer Print: _JAN 10, 1994_

Release (Theatrical Film): _1-10-94_

Network Broadcast (if applicable): _2-11-94_

DGA—Unit Production Manager &
Assistant Director Film Deal Memorandum

Unit Production Manager &
Assistant Director Film Deal Memorandum

This confirms our agreement to employ you on the project described below as follows:

Name: __ALICE DEES__   SS#: __666-55-4444__

Loanout (if applicable): _____   Tel. #: __(818) 555-6546__

Address: __12353 AVE. OF THE STARS__
__HOLLYWOOD, CA 90028__

- ☐ Unit Production Manager
- ☑ First Assistant Director
- ☐ Key Second Assistant Director
- ☐ 2nd Second Assistant Director
- ☐ Additional Second Assistant Director
- ☐ Technical Coordinator

- ☑ Principal Photography
- ☐ Second Unit
- ☐ Both

Salary: $ __SCALE + $100.__ $ _____   ☑ per week   ☐ per day
    (STUDIO)   (LOCATION)

Production Fee: $ _____ $ __SCALE + $100.__
    (STUDIO)   (LOCATION)

Start Date: __7-12-93__   Guaranteed Period: __2 WEEKS__

Film or Series Title: __THE WATCHER__
Episode/Segment Title: __"BOYS NIGHT OUT"__
Length of Program: __1 HOUR__   Is this a Pilot? ☐ Yes   ☑ No

Intended Primary Market:
- ☐ Theatres
- ☐ Basic Cable
- ☑ Network
- ☐ Disc/Cassette
- ☐ Syndication
- ☐ Pay/TV: _____
      (service)

Other Terms (e.g., credit, suspension, per diem, etc.): __1ST CLASS ROUND-TRIP AIRFARE; $50 PER DIEM__
__AND $15. PER DAY INCIDENTAL ALLOWANCE WHILE ON DISTANT LOCATION.__

- ☐ Studio
- ☐ Distant Location
- ☑ Both

☐ Check if New York Area Amendment Applies

This employment is subject to the provisions of the Directors Guild of America Basic Agreement of 1993.

Accepted and Agreed: Signatory Co: __XYZ PRODUCTIONS__
Employee: __Alice Dees__   By: __Thrifty Deale, Producer__
Date: __7-12-93__   Date: __7-12-93__

RC301/070193

EXTRA TALENT VOUCHER

DATE WORKED _JUNE 10, 1993_

PRODUCTION _THE WATCHER_   PROD# _0100_

EXTRA CASTING AGENCY _RAZMATAZ EXTRA CASTING_

CONTACT _BAMBI_   PHONE# _555-8998_

EMPLOYER OF RECORD _PAULINE'S PAYROLL SERVICE_

ADDRESS _7327 HOLLYWOOD LANE_
HOLLYWOOD, CA

PHONE# _555-9990_

NAME (Please Print) _ALICE TULIPS_

ADDRESS _317 MAPLE DR._
PASADENA CA 41326

PHONE# _555-7777_

SOC. SEC.# _003-25-2507_

[ ] Married   [✓] Single   _O_ Exemptions   [✓] Completed I-9

			BASE RATE		
REPORTING TIME _7A_	_8_	HRS. of S.T.	@ _5.00_ per. hr.	$40 -
MEAL _1-1:30P_	_4_	HRS. of 1 1/2X	@ _7.50_ per. hr.	30 -
2ND MEAL	_1_	HRS. of 2X	@ _10.00_ per. hr.	10 -
DISMISSAL TIME _8:30 P_		ADJUSTMENT(S)		

TOTAL HRS. WORKED: _13_   GROSS TOTAL: $80 -

MILEAGE REIMBURSEMENT $12
WARDROBE REIMBURSEMENT $10
OTHER REIMBURSEMENT

I acknowledge receipt of the compensation stated herein as payment in full for all services rendered by me on the days indicated. I hereby grant to my employer permission to photograph me and to record my voice, performances, poses, acts, plays and appearances, and use my picture, photograph, silhouette and other reproductions of my physical likeness and sound in the above-named production and in the unlimited distribution, advertising, promotion, exhibition and exploitation of the production by any method or device now known or hereafter devised in which the same may be used. I agree that I will not assert or maintain against you, your successors, assigns and licensees, any claim, action, suit or demand of any kind or nature whatsoever in connection with your authorized use of my physical likeness and sound in the production as herein provided.

SIGNATURE _Alice Tulips_
(If minor, parent or guardian must sign)

APPROVED BY _R.D. Durham_

TITLE _2ND ASST. DIRECTOR_

     © ELH Form #17

CHAPTER 9

CLEARANCES AND RELEASE FORMS

Obtaining **clearances** is the process of getting permission to use someone's likeness, name, logo, photograph, product, premisses, publication, film clip, stock footage, music or song in your film—and in most circumstances, for a fee. Using stock footage and music is granted through a **license**. Other clearances are secured with a signed **release form**, each designed to grant permission for the use of that particular element (likeness, name, logo, photo, product, etc.)

Both your insurance agency and attorney will request that you have your script "researched" in order to find out what elements in the script need to be cleared or potentially licensed. When you send your script to a research service, they will send back a report. You will need to follow through to make sure all the items are cleared or licensed. The distributor of your film will insist on receiving copies of all license agreements and release forms. Releasing a picture without the proper clearances may result in costly law suits or insurance claims.

Your attorney, or the business affairs department, will most likely handle any complicated clearances. Music clearances are generally handled through a **music clearance service**, but you should be able to secure most routine clearances on your own. Many of the release forms found in this chapter can be used for this purpose. If you need a release form that is not here, your attorney or legal affairs department can prepare one for you. And, again, even though they've all been approved by an attorney, have your own attorney look them over before you use them. The following are some general rules pertaining to clearances.

LIKENESS

Permission to use a performer's likeness is incorporated into their SAG contract and extras grant permission by signing their extra voucher.

Occasionally, people who are not extras are filmed as "**background**. This may occur when the director decides that although there were no extras planned for the day, some **atmosphere** would make a scene more complete—or when the director doesn't have enough extras; and on the spur-of-the-moment, people walking down a street are recruited to participate in a scene. In this situation, each person filmed as background (whether being paid for their appearance or not) should sign a **Personal Release**; or if there are several people, a **Group Release** would be appropriate.

When a large group of people is recruited for an audience that will be filmed, post signs in easy-to-read locations stating that their presence as a member of this audience constitutes their permission for the production company to use their likenesses.

The same would apply to shooting a street scene within a confined location or filming in a specific "area" such as a shopping center. Signs would be posted indicating that filming is taking place—people entering the area may appear in the Picture, and by entering the area, they grant permission to the production company to use their likeness. (Exact wording for these signs is included in this chapter.)

Clearance would not be required if the passers-by being filmed are an incidental part of the background or if they will not be recognizable in the picture.

LOCATIONS

Permission to use a premises or property as a shooting location is obtained when the owner of the property signs a release form called a **Location Agreement**.

NAMES

Although a *fictional* character may share a common name with an actual person, the names of actual persons (printed or spoken) should not be used unless permission is granted by that person.

Public figures may be referenced, providing such references are not derogatory.

NAMES OF ACTUAL BUSINESS OR ORGANIZATIONS

The use of the actual name of a business, organization, building, etc., that is a shooting location is permissible, providing the location agreement grants the right to use such name. If the name of a business, organization or building is featured in your film but is not used as a shooting location, then permission for **Use of Name** or **Use of Trademark or Logo** would be necessary.

PHOTOGRAPH OR LIKENESS OF ACTUAL PERSON

If the person in the photograph is not the copyrighted owner of the photo, it is necessary to obtain permission from both the person in the photograph and the copyright owner.

TELEPHONE NUMBERS

Since it is difficult to clear references to identifiable phone numbers, most films use phone numbers that begin with the prefix *555* (a prefix which does not exist in any area code except for directory information.)

LICENSE PLATES

As it is also difficult to clear identifiable license plates, prop houses will manufacture fictitious plates for you.

DEPICTION OF PUBLIC AUTHORITIES

Clearance is required for the portrayal of police officers, firemen, prison guards and other public authorities of identifiable departments or locations, whether uniforms are used or not. Wardrobe and prop departments will supply *generic* uniforms and related paraphernalia if you cannot get clearances.

STREET ADDRESS

Referencing or identifying an actual street address must be cleared.

USE OF LITERARY MATERIAL

Clearance is required for the use of a book, manuscript, screenplay, magazine or newspaper—reference to a specific article, translation of, or quotation from contents. Even literary material that is public domain must be cleared as bindings and covers are protected by copyright.

DEPICTION OF IDENTIFICATION OF ACTUAL PRODUCTS

A depiction or reference to an actual product does not have to be cleared if the depiction or reference is *incidental* and not derogatory. Featuring a product or service trademark or logo does, however, require a clearance. A **Use of Trademark or Logo Release Form** would be appropriate in this situation.

Often, goods or services (such as wardrobe, food and soft drink products, plane tickets or the use of vehicles) are given to the production in exchange for using or referencing a product or service in the Picture. In most cases, the provider of the goods or services would also receive screen credit in the end titles of the film. A **Product Placement Release Form** would cover the necessary clearance associated with this type of arrangement.

FILM AND VIDEO CLIPS

Clearances are required for all film or video playback, film and audio clips *patched* over televisions or entire film clips depicted in the Picture.

MUSIC

See Chapter 11.

Copies of fully-executed release forms should be given to:

1. The person who signs the release
2. The Production Coordinator
3. The Production Accountant (when a payment is involved)
4. The Assistant Directors should receive copies of fully-executed **Location Agreements** to have on the set with them at each location. The original release should be given to your Production Executive to be stored in permanent company files.

FORMS INCLUDED IN THIS SECTION

Location Agreement 97-98
Personal Release 99
Personal Release—Payment 100
Group Release 101
Use of Name 102
Use of Trademark or Logo 103
Use of Literary Material 104
Use of Still Photographs (Copyrighted Owner, Not Person in Photo) 105
Use of Still Photographs (Person in Photo/Free) 106
Use of Still Photographs (Person in Photo/Payment) 107
Use of Still Photographs (Copyrighted Owner, Not Person in Photo/Free) 108
Wording for Multiple Signs 109
Film/Tape Clip for Promotional Uses 110
Product Placement Release 111-112
Film/Tape Footage Release 113-114
Request for Videocassette 115

LOCATION AGREEMENT

XYZ PRODUCTIONS
1234 Flick Drive
Hollywood, CA   90028

Gentlemen:

You have advised the undersigned that you are producing a **motion picture** tentatively entitled **"THE WATCHER"**, (the "Picture"). In consideration of your payment to the undersigned for the sum of **$2,000**, you and the undersigned hereby agree as follows:

1.   The undersigned hereby irrevocably grants you and your agents, employees, licensees, successors and assigns:

(a)   The right to enter and remain upon the property, which shall include not only real property but any fixtures, equipment or other personal property thereat or thereon, located at: **THE OFFICES OF DEWEY CHEATEM AND HOWE, 1000 ATLANTIC BLVD., SUITE 700, LOS ANGELES, CA 90067** (the "Property"), with personnel and equipment (including without limitations, props, temporary sets, lighting, camera and special effects equipment) for the purpose of photographing scenes and making recordings of said Property in connection with the production of the Picture on the following date(s): **PREP: JUNE 14, 1993; SHOOT: JUNE 15, 1993; STRIKE: JUNE 16, 1993.** If the weather or other conditions are not favorable for such purpose on such date(s), the date(s) shall be postponed to **TBD**.

(b)   The right to take motion pictures, videotapes, still photographs and/or sound recordings on and of any and all portions of the Property and all names associated therewith or which appear in, on or about the Property.

(c)   All rights of every nature whatsoever in and to all films and photographs taken and recordings made hereunder, including without limitation of all copyrights therein and renewals and extensions thereof, and the exclusive right to reproduce, exhibit, distribute, and otherwise exploit in perpetuity throughout the universe (in whole or in part) such films, photographs and recordings in any and all media, whether now known or hereafter devised, including without limitation in and in connection with the Picture and the advertising and other exploitation thereof.

2.   You agree to indemnify and to hold the undersigned harmless from and against all liability or loss which the undersigned may suffer or incur by reason of any injury to or death of any person, or damage to any property (ordinary wear and tear excepted), directly caused by any of your agents or employees when present on the Property or by reason of the use by any of your agents or employees or any equipment brought by them on to the property.

3.   The undersigned warrants and represents (as a condition to the payment of the compensation referred to above), that the undersigned has the full right and authority to enter into this agreement and grant the rights herein granted, and that the consent or permission of no other person, firm, or entity is necessary in order to enable you to exercise or enjoy the rights herein granted.

4.   The undersigned hereby releases you from, and covenants not to sue you for, any claim or cause of action, whether known or unknown, for defamation, invasion of

his privacy, right of publicity or any similar matter, or any other claim or cause of action, based upon or relating to the exercise of any of the rights referred to in Paragraph 1 hereof; provided, however, that the foregoing shall not affect your obligations to indemnify the undersigned pursuant to Paragraph 2 hereof.

5.   The undersigned further warrants neither he/she or anyone acting for him/her, gave or agreed to give anything of value, except for use of the Property, to anyone at **XYZ PRODUCTIONS** or anyone associated with the production for using the Property as a shooting location.

6.   This agreement shall inure to benefit of and shall be binding upon your and our respective successors, licensees, assigns, heirs and personal representatives. You shall not be obligated actually to exercise any of the rights granted to you hereunder; it being understood that your obligations shall be fully satisfied hereunder by payment of the compensation referred to above. The agreement constitutes the entire agreement between the parties with respect to the subject matter hereof and cannot be amended except by a written instrument signed by the parties.

Very truly yours,

ACCEPTED & AGREED TO:

_____
(Signature)

BY_____   _____
(Please Print Name)

_____
(Title)

_____
(Address)

_____
(Phone Number)

_____
(Business Phone)

PERSONAL RELEASE

XYZ PRODUCTIONS
1234 Flick Drive
Hollywood, CA   90028

Gentlemen:

I, the undersigned, hereby grant permission to **XYZ PRODUCTIONS** to photograph me and to record my voice, performances, poses, acts, plays and appearances, and use my picture, photograph, silhouette and other reproductions of my physical likeness and sound as part of the **motion picture** tentatively entitled **"THE WATCHER"** (the "Picture") and the unlimited distribution, advertising, promotion, exhibition and exploitation of the Picture by any method or device now known or hereafter devised in which the same may be used, and/or incorporated and/or exhibited and/or exploited.

I agree that I will not assert or maintain against you, your successors, assigns and licensees, any claim, action, suit or demand of any kind or nature whatsoever, including but not limited to, those grounded upon invasion of privacy, rights of publicity or other civil rights, or for any other reason in connection with your authorized use of my physical likeness and sound in the Picture as herein provided. I hereby release you, your successors, assigns and licensees, and each of them, from and against any and all claims, liabilities, demands, actions, causes of action(s), costs and expenses whatsoever, at law or in equity, known or unknown, anticipated or unanticipated, which I ever had, now have, or may, shall or hereafter have by reason, matter, cause or thing arising out of your use as herein provided.

I affirm that neither I, nor anyone acting for me, gave or agreed to give anything of value to any of your employees or any representative of any television station, network or production entity for arranging my appearance on the Picture.

I have read the foregoing and fully understand the meaning and effect thereof and, intending to be legally bound, I have signed this release

Very truly yours,

_____
(Signature)

_____
(Please print name)

_____

_____
(Address)

_____
(Phone number)

FORMS AND REPORTS   99

PERSONAL RELEASE—PAYMENT

JUNE 25, 1993

XYZ PRODUCTIONS
1234 Flick Drive
Hollywood, CA   90028

Gentlemen:

In consideration of payment to me of the sum of **$25.00**, receipt of which is hereby acknowledged, I, the undersigned, hereby grant permission to **XYZ PRODUCTIONS** to photograph me and to record my voice, performances, poses, acts, plays and appearances, and use my picture, photograph, silhouette and other reproductions of my physical likeness and sound as part of the **motion picture** tentatively entitled **"The Watcher"** (the "Picture") and the unlimited distribution, advertising, promotion, exhibition and exploitation of the Picture by any method or device now known or hereafter devised in which the same may be used, and/or incorporated and/or exhibited and/or exploited.

I agree that I will not assert or maintain against you, your successors, assigns and licensees, any claim, action, suit or demand of any kind or nature whatsoever, including but not limited to, those grounded upon invasion of privacy, rights of publicity or other civil rights, or for any other reason in connection with your authorized use of my physical likeness and sound in the Picture as herein provided. I hereby release you, your successors, assigns and licensees, and each of them, from and against any and all claims, liabilities, demands, actions, causes of action(s), costs and expenses whatsoever, at law or in equity, known or unknown, anticipated or unanticipated, which I ever had, now have, or may, shall or hereafter have by reason, matter, cause or thing arising out of your use as herein provided.

I affirm that neither I, nor anyone acting for me, gave or agreed to give anything of value to any of your employees or any representative of any television station, network or production entity for arranging my appearance on the Picture.

I have read the foregoing and fully understand the meaning and effect thereof and, intending to be legally bound, I have signed this release

Very truly yours,

_____
(Signature)

_____
(Please print name)

_____
(Address)

_____
(Phone number)

GROUP RELEASE

XYZ PRODUCTIONS
1234 Flick Drive
Hollywood, CA   90028

Gentlemen:

I, the undersigned, hereby grant permission to **XYZ PRODUCTIONS** to photograph me and to record my voice, performances, poses, acts, plays and appearances, and use my picture, photograph, silhouette and other reproductions of my physical likeness and sound as part of the **motion picture** tentatively entitled "**The Watcher**" (the "Picture") and the unlimited distribution, advertising, promotion, exhibition and exploitation of the Picture by any method or device now known or hereafter devised in which the same may be used, and/or incorporated and/or exhibited and/or exploited.

I agree that I will not assert or maintain against you, your successors, assigns and licensees, any claim, action, suit or demand of any kind or nature whatsoever, including but not limited to, those grounded upon invasion of privacy, rights of publicity or other civil rights, or for any other reason in connection with your authorized use of my physical likeness and sound in the Picture as herein provided. I hereby release you, your successors, assigns and licensees, and each of them, from and against any and all claims, liabilities, demands, actions, causes of action(s), costs and expenses whatsoever, at law or in equity, known or unknown, anticipated or unanticipated, which I ever had, now have, or may, shall or hereafter have by reason, matter, cause or thing arising out of your use as herein provided.

I affirm that neither I, nor anyone acting for me, gave or agreed to give anything of value to any of your employees or any representative of any television station, network or production entity for arranging my appearance on the Picture.

I have read the foregoing and fully understand the meaning and effect thereof and, intending to be legally bound, I have signed this release.

NAME	ADDRESS	SOC. SEC.#
_____	_____	_____
_____	_____	_____
_____	_____	_____
_____	_____	_____
_____	_____	_____
_____	_____	_____
_____	_____	_____

USE OF NAME

XYZ PRODUCTIONS
1234 Flick Drive
Hollywood, CA   90028

Gentlemen:

For good and valuable consideration, receipt of which I hereby acknowledge, I hereby grant to you and to your successors, assigns, distributees and licensees forever, throughout the universe, the sole, exclusive and unconditional right and license to use, simulate and portray my name to such extent and in such manner as you in your sole discretion may elect, in or in connection with your **television movie** tentatively entitled **"THE WATCHER"** (including reissues, remakes of and sequels to any such production) prepared by you or any successor to your interest therein, together with the right to publish synopses thereof, and to advertise, exploit, present, release, distribute, exhibit and/or otherwise utilize said productions and publications throughout the world.

I agree that I will not bring, institute or assert or consent that others bring, institute or assert any claim or action against you or your successors, licensees, distributees, or assigns, on the ground that anything performed in any such production or contained in the advertising or publicity issued in connection therewith is libelous, reflects adversely upon me, violates my right of privacy, or violates any other rights, and I hereby release, discharge, and acquit you and them of and from any and all such claims, actions, causes of action, suits and demands whatsoever that I may now or hereafter have against you or them.

In granting of the foregoing rights and licenses, I acknowledge that I have not been induced so to do by any representation or assurance by you or on your behalf relative to the manner in which any of the rights or licenses granted hereunder may be exercised; and I agree that you are under no obligation to exercise any of the rights or licenses granted hereunder.

Very truly yours,

ACCEPTED & AGREED TO: _____
                                         (Signature)
By _____

                                         _____
                                         (Please Print Name)

                                         _____

                                         _____
                                         (Address)

                                         _____
                                         (Phone Number)

USE OF TRADEMARK OR LOGO

JUNE 25, 1993

XYZ PRODUCTIONS
1234 Flick Drive
Hollywood, CA   90028

Gentlemen:

For good and valuable consideration, receipt of which is hereby acknowledged, the undersigned hereby grants to you, your successors, licensees and assigns, the non-exclusive right, but not the obligation to use and include all or part of our trademark(s), logo(s), and/or animated or identifiable characters (the Mark(s)) listed below in the **television series** tentatively entitled **"THE WATCHER"** (the "Picture"), and to utilize and reproduce the Mark(s) in connection with the Picture, without limitation as to time or number of runs, for reproduction, exhibition and exploitation, throughout the world, in any and all manner, methods and media, whether now known or hereafter known or devised, and in the advertising, publicizing, promotion, trailers and exploitation thereof.

The undersigned acknowledges, as does the company which he represents, that, under the Federal Communications Act, it is a federal offense to give or agree to give anything of value to promote any product, service or venture in connection with the Picture on the air, and warrants and represents that neither he nor they have done or will do so.

The undersigned and the company he represents, hereby warrant, represent and affirm that he and the company have the right to grant the rights granted herein, free of claims by any person or entity.

    Mark(s):

        COUNTRY ROADS COLLECTION — LOGO

Very truly yours,

_____
(Signature)

ACCEPTED & AGREED TO:

_____
(Please print name)

_____
(Title)

By_____

_____
(Address)

_____
(Phone #)

USE OF LITERARY MATERIAL

JUNE 25, 1993

XYZ PRODUCTIONS
1234 Flick Drive
Hollywood, CA   90028

Gentlemen:

I am informed that you are producing a **motion picture** presently entitled **"THE WATCHER"** (the "Picture") and that you have requested that I grant you the right to use the title and/or portions of the following literary material owned and published by the undersigned for inclusion in the Picture:

THE COMPLETE FILM PRODUCTION HANDBOOK

For good and valuable consideration, receipt of which is hereby acknowledged, I (the undersigned) do hereby confirm the consent hereby given you with respect to your use of the above title and/or literary material (the "Materials") in connection with the Picture, and I do hereby grant to you, your successors, assigns and licensees, the perpetual right to use the Materials in connection with the Picture. I agree that you may record the Materials on tape, film or otherwise and use the Materials and recordings in and in connection with the exhibition, advertising, promotion, exploitation, and any other use of the Picture as you may desire.

I hereby release you, your agents, successors, licensees and assigns, and each of them, from and against any and all claims, liabilities, demands, actions, causes of action, costs and expenses, whatsoever, at law or in equity, known or unknown, anticipated or unanticipated, suspected or unsuspected, with I ever had, now have, or may, shall or hereafter have by any reason, matter, cause or thing whatsoever, arising out of your use of the Materials as provided herein in connection with the Picture. I realize that in using the Materials, you are relying upon the rights granted to you hereunder.

Very truly yours,

_____
(Signature)

ACCEPTED & AGREED TO:

_____
(Please Print Name)

_____

_____
(Address)

By_____

_____
(Phone Number)

USE OF STILL PHOTOGRAPH(S)

(COPYRIGHTED OWNER—NOT PERSON IN PHOTO/PAYMENT)

JUNE 25, 1993

XYZ PRODUCTIONS
1234 Flick Drive
Hollywood, CA   90028

Gentlemen:

In consideration of the payment of the sum of **$300.00** and other good and valuable consideration, receipt of which is hereby acknowledged, the undersigned hereby grants to you, your successors, licensees and assigns, the non-exclusive right, but not the obligation to use and include the still photograph(s) (the Still(s)) as described below in the **motion picture** tentatively entitled **"THE WATCHER"** (the "Picture"), and to utilize and reproduce the Still(s) in connection with the Picture, without limitation as to time or number of runs, for reproduction, exhibition and exploitation, throughout the world, in any and all manner, methods and media, whether now known or hereafter known or devised, and in the advertising, publicizing, promotion, trailers and exploitation thereof.

The undersigned acknowledges, as does the company which he represents, that, under the Federal Communications Act, it is a federal offense to give or agree to give anything of value to promote any product, service or venture in connection with the Picture on the air, and warrants and represents that neither he nor they have done or will do so.

The undersigned and the company he represents, hereby warrant, represent and affirm that he and the company have the right to grant the rights granted herein, free of claims by any person or entity.

Description of the Still(s):

1985 HEAD SHOT OF WILL PERFORMER

Very truly yours,

_____
(Signature)

ACCEPTED & AGREED TO:
_____
(Please Print name)

_____
(Title)

By_____

_____
(Address)

_____
(Phone Number)

USE OF STILL PHOTOGRAPH(S)

(PERSON IN PHOTO/FREE)

JUNE 25, 1993

XYZ PRODUCTIONS
1234 Flick Drive
Hollywood, CA   90028

Gentlemen:

For good and valuable consideration, receipt of which is hereby acknowledged, I, the undersigned, hereby grant to you, your successors, licensees and assigns, the non-exclusive right, but not the obligation to use and include my physical likeness in the form of still photograph(s) (the Still(s)) as described below in the **television movie** tentatively entitled **"THE WATCHER"** (the "Picture"), and to utilize and reproduce the Still(s) in connection with the Picture, without limitation as to time or number of runs, for reproduction, exhibition and exploitation, throughout the world, in any and all manner, methods and media, whether now known or hereafter known or devised, and in the advertising, publicizing, promotion, trailers and exploitation thereof.

I agree that I will not assert or maintain against you, your successors, assigns and licensees, a claim, action, suit or demand of any kind or nature whatsoever, including but not limited to, those grounded upon invasion of privacy, rights of publicity or other civil rights, or for any other reason in connection with your authorized use of the Still(s) in the Picture as herein provided. I hereby release you, your successors, assigns and licensees from any and all such claims, actions, causes of action, suits and demands whatsoever that I may now or hereafter have against you or them.

In the granting of the foregoing rights and licenses, I acknowledge that I have not been induced to do so by any representative or assurance by you or on your behalf relative to the manner in which any of the rights or licenses granted hereunder may be exercised; and I agree that you are under no obligation to exercise any of the rights or licenses granted hereunder.

Description of the Still(s):

HEADSHOT OF SCARLET STARLET

Very truly yours,

ACCEPTED & AGREED TO:

_____
(Signature)

_____
(Please print name)

By_____

_____
(Address)

_____
(Phone Number)

USE OF STILL PHOTOGRAPH(S)

(PERSON IN PHOTO/PAYMENT)

JUNE 25, 1993

XYZ PRODUCTIONS
1234 Flick Drive
Hollywood, CA   90028

Gentlemen:

In consideration of the payment of the sum of **$300.00** and other good and valuable consideration, receipt of which is hereby acknowledged, I, the undersigned hereby grant to you, your successors, licensees and assigns, the non-exclusive right, but not the obligation to use and include my physical likeness in the form of the still photograph(s) (the Still(s)) as described below in the **motion picture** tentatively entitled **"THE WATCHER"** (the "Picture"), and to utilize and reproduce the Still(s) in connection with the Picture, without limitation as to the number of runs, for reproduction, exhibition and exploitation, throughout the world, in any and all manner, methods and media, whether now known or hereafter known or devised, and in the advertising, publicizing, promotion, trailers and exploitation thereof.

I agree that I will not assert or maintain against you, your successors, assigns and licensees, a claim, action, suit or demand of any kind or nature whatsoever, including but not limited to, those grounded upon invasion of privacy, rights of publicity or other civil rights, or for any other reason in connection with your authorized use of the Still(s) in the Picture as herein provided. I hereby release you, your successors, assigns and licensees from any and all such claims, actions, causes of action, suits and demands whatsoever that I may now or hereafter have against you or them.

In the granting of the foregoing rights and licenses, I acknowledge that I have not been induced to do so by any representative or assurance by you or on your behalf relative to the manner in which any of the rights or licenses granted hereunder may be exercised; and I agree that you are under no obligation to exercise any of the rights or licenses granted hereunder.

Description of the Still(s):

1985 HEADSHOT OF WILL PERFORMER

Very truly yours,

_____
(Signature)

ACCEPTED & AGREED TO:

_____
(Please Print Name)

By_____

_____

_____
(Address)

_____
(Phone Number)

USE OF STILL PHOTOGRAPH(S)

(COPYRIGHTED OWNER—NOT PERSON IN PHOTO/FREE)

JUNE 25, 1993

XYZ PRODUCTIONS
1234 Flick Drive
Hollywood, CA   90028

Gentlemen:

For good and valuable consideration, receipt of which is hereby acknowledged, the undersigned hereby grants to you, your successors, licensees and assigns, the non-exclusive right, but not the obligation to use and include the still photograph(s) (the Still(s)) as described below in the **television movie** tentatively entitled "**THE WATCHER**" (the "Picture"), and to utilize and reproduce the Still(s) in connection with the Picture, without limitation as to time or number of runs, for reproduction, exhibition and exploitation, throughout the world, in any and all manner, methods and media, whether now known or hereafter known or devised, and in the advertising, publicizing, promotion, trailers and exploitation thereof.

The undersigned acknowledges, as does the company which he represents, that, under the Federal Communications Act, it is a federal offense to give or agree to give anything of value to promote any product, service or venture in connection with the Picture on the air, and warrants and represents that neither he nor they have done or will do so.

The undersigned and the company he represents, hereby warrant, represent and affirm that he and the company have the right to grant the rights granted herein, free of claims by any person or entity.

Description of the Still(s):

HEADSHOT OF SCARLET STARLET

Very truly yours,

ACCEPTED & AGREED TO:

_____
(Signature)

_____
(Please print name)

_____
(Title)

By_____

_____
(Address)

_____
(Phone Number)

WORDING FOR MULTIPLE SIGNS

PLACE IN A STUDIO WHEN TAPING OR FILMING BEFORE A LIVE AUDIENCE:

Please be advised that your presence as a member of the studio audience during the **taping** of the program entitled **The Watcher** constitutes your permission to **XYZ Productions** to use your likeness on the air in any form and as often as they deem appropriate and desirable for promotional or broadcast purposes.

If for any reason you object to your likeness being so used, you should leave the studio at this time. If you remain, your presence at this **taping** will constitute your approval of the foregoing.

PLACE IN AN "AREA" DURING THE TAPING OR FILMING OF A SHOW:

Please be advised that **filming** is taking place in connection with the production of a **motion picture** tentatively entitled **The Watcher**. People entering this area may appear in the picture. By entering this area, you grant to **XYZ Productions** the right to film and photograph you and record your voice and to use your voice and likeness in connection with the picture and the distribution and exploitation thereof, and you release **XYZ Productions** and its licensees from all liability in connection therein. You agree and understand that **XYZ Productions** will proceed in reliance upon such grant and release. **XYZ Productions** does not assume responsibility for any injury to your person or damage or loss to your property.

The use of cameras and recording equipment is prohibited due to union and copyright regulations.

Smoking is prohibited in this area... Thank you!

SUPPLYING A FILM/TAPE CLIP FOR PROMOTIONAL PURPOSES

JUNE 25, 1993

TALK SHOW PRODUCTIONS
"THE EVENING SHOW"
8336 West Fairfax Avenue
Los Angeles, CA 90036

Gentlemen:

The undersigned hereby authorizes you to use a FILM CLIP from the **motion picture** tentatively entitled **"THE WATCHER"** for promotional purposes only in the program entitled, **"THE EVENING SHOW"** currently scheduled for broadcast on **JUNE 30, 1993**.

The undersigned hereby affirms that neither he nor anyone acting on his behalf or any company which he may represent, gave or agreed to give anything of value (except for the FILM CLIP) which was furnished for promotional purposes solely on or in connection with **"THE EVENING SHOW"** to any member of the production staff, anyone associated in any manner with the program or any representative of **TALK SHOW PRODUCTIONS** for mentioning or displaying the name of any company which he may represent or any of its products, trademarks, trade-names or the like.

The undersigned understands that any broadcast identification of the FILM CLIP (or the name of any company, product, etc. which he may represent) which **XYZ PRODUCTIONS, INC.** may furnish, shall, in no event, be beyond that which is reasonable related to the program content.

The undersigned is aware, as is the company which he may represent, that it is a federal offense unless disclosed to **TALK SHOW PRODUCTIONS** prior to broadcast if the undersigned gives or agrees to give anything of value to promote any product, service or venture on the air.

The undersigned represents that he is fully empowered to execute this letter on behalf of any company which he may represent.

The undersigned warrants that he or the company which he may represent has the right to grant the license herein granted, and agrees to indemnify you for all loss, damage and liability, excluding the payment of any guild related talent fees or performing rights fees in the music included in said clip, if any (which you agree to pay or cause to be paid), arising out of the use of the above material.

Very truly yours,

ACCEPTED & AGREED:

(Please Print Name)

By_____

(Title)

PRODUCT PLACEMENT RELEASE

JUNE 25, 1993

XYZ PRODUCTIONS, INC.
1234 Flick Drive
Hollywood, CA   90028

Gentlemen:

The undersigned ("Company") agrees to provide the following product(s) and/or service(s) to **XYZ PRODUCTIONS, INC.**, for use in the **motion picture** now entitled **"THE WATCHER"** (the "Picture"):

2	dozen pair, assorted sunglasses
1	basketball
1	bat
2	softballs
2	beachballs
3	pairs roller skates

The Company grants to you, your successors, licensees and assigns, the non-exclusive right, but not the obligation to use and include all or part of the trademark(s), logo(s) and/or identifiable characters (the "Mark(s)") associated with the above listed product(s) and/or service(s) in the Picture, without limitation as to time or number of runs, for reproduction, exhibition and exploitation, throughout the world, in any and all manner, methods and media, whether now known or hereafter known or devised, and in the advertising, publicizing, promotion, trailers and exploitation thereof.

The Company warrants and represents that it is the owner of the product(s) or direct provider of the service(s) as listed above or a representative of such and has the right to enter this agreement and grant the rights granted to **XYZ PRODUCTIONS, INC.**, hereunder.

In full consideration of the Company providing the product(s) and/or service(s) to **XYZ PRODUCTIONS, INC.**, **XYZ PRODUCTIONS, INC.** agrees to accord the Company screen credit in the end titles of the positive prints of the Picture in the following form: "**SPORTING GOODS AND SUNGLASSES** furnished by **HOLLYWOOD PROMOTIONS, INC.**"

The Company understands that any broadcast identification of its products, trademarks, trade names or the like which **XYZ PRODUCTIONS, INC.** may furnish, shall in no event, be beyond that which is reasonably related to the program content.

As it applies to any and all television broadcasts of the Picture, the Company is aware that it is a federal offense to give or agree to give anything of value to promote any product, service or venture on the air. The Company affirms that it did not give or agree to give anything of value, except for the product(s) and/or service(s) to any member of the production staff, anyone associated in any manner with the Picture or any representative of **XYZ PRODUCTIONS, INC.** for mentioning or displaying the name of the Company or any of its products, trademarks, trade names, or the like.

(continued on the following page)

PRODUCT PLACEMENT RELEASE—CONT'D

I represent that I am an officer of the Company and am empowered to execute this form on behalf of the Company.

I further represent that neither I nor the Company which I represent will directly or indirectly publicize or otherwise exploit the use, exhibition or demonstration of the above product(s) and/or service(s) in the Picture for advertising, merchandising or promotional purposes without the express written consent of **XYZ PRODUCTIONS, INC.**

Sincerely yours,

AGREED & ACCEPTED BY

_____
(Authorized Signatory)

_____
(Please Print Name)

By_____

_____
(Title)

_____
(Name of Company)

_____

_____
(Address)

_____
(Phone Number)

FILM/TAPE FOOTAGE RELEASE

JULY 22, 1993

LICENSOR: **XYZ PRODUCTIONS, INC.**

LICENSEE: **STOCK SHOTS, INC.**

DESCRIPTION OF THE FILM/TAPE FOOTAGE:
                             ESTABLISHING SHOTS OF WASHINGTON, D.C.

LENGTH OF FOOTAGE: **40'**

PRODUCTION: **"THE WATCHER"** (The "Picture")

LICENSE FEE, if any: **$1,000.00**

Licensor hereby grants to Licensee, Licensor's permission to edit and include all or portion of the above-mentioned Footage in the Picture as follows:

1. Licensor grants to Licensee a non-exclusive license to edit and incorporate the Footage in the Picture. Licensee may broadcast and otherwise exploit the Footage in the Picture, and in customary advertising and publicity thereof, through-out the world in perpetuity in any media now known or hereafter devised.

2. Licensee shall not make any reproductions whatsoever of or from the Footage except as described hereunder.

3. Licensee agrees to obtain, at Licensee's expense, all required consents of any person whose appearances are contained in the Footage pursuant to this agreement, and to make any payments to such persons, guilds or unions to the extent required under applicable collective bargaining agreements for such use.

4. Licensor represents and warrants that: (1) Licensor has the right and power to grant the rights herein granted, and (2) neither Licensee's use of the Footage pursuant to this license nor anything contained therein infringes upon the rights of any third parties.

5. Licensor and Licensee each agree to indemnify and hold the other harmless from and against any and all claims, losses liabilities, damages and expenses, including reasonable attorneys' fees, which may result from any breach of their respective representations and warranties hereunder.

6. As between Licensor and Licensee, the Picture shall be Licensee's sole and exclusive property. Licensee shall not be obligated to use the Footage or the rights herein granted or to produce or broadcast the Picture.

7. Licensor acknowledges that, under the Federal Communications Act, it is a Federal offense to give or agree to give anything of value to promote any product, service or venture in the Picture, and Licensor warrants and represents that Licensor has not and will not do so.

8. This agreement constitutes the entire understanding between the parties, supersedes any prior understanding relating thereto and shall not be

(continued on the following page)

modified except by a writing signed by the parties. This agreement shall be irrevocable and shall be binding upon and inure to the benefit of Licensor's and Licensee's respective successors, assigns and licensees.

Kindly sign below to indicate your acceptance of the foregoing.

Licensor:

_____
(Signature)

_____
(Please Print Name)

_____
(Title)

CONFIRMED:

_____
(Company)

By_____

_____

_____
(Address)

_____
(Phone Number)

REQUEST FOR VIDEOCASSETTE

NOVEMBER 15, 1993

Mr. F. Stopp
8365 Iris Blvd.
Beverly Hills, CA 90212

Dear Fred:

You accept delivery of the (1/2") (3/4") videocassette ("Recording") of "THE WATCHER" (the "Picture"), and in consideration of our delivery of it, agree as follows:

1. You warrant, represent and agree that the Recording shall be used solely for your private, personal library purpose or for screenings in connection with an in-house demo reel; and the Recording will never be publicly exhibited in any manner or medium whatsoever. You will not charge or authorize the charge of a fee for exhibiting the Recording. You will not duplicate or permit the duplication of the Recording. You will retain possession of the Recording at all times.

2. All other rights in and to the Picture, under copyright or otherwise, including but not limited to title to, are retained by **XYZ Productions**.

3. The permission which we have granted to you for the use of the Recording itself will be non-assignable and non-transferable.

4. You agree to indemnify us against and hold us harmless from claims, liabilities and actions arising out of your breach of this agreement.

5. You agree to reimburse us for the cost of making the Recording available to you.

This will become a contract between you and us upon your acceptance of delivery of the Recording.

Sincerely yours,

ACCEPTED & AGREED:

_____
(Signature)

_____
(Please Print Name)

By_____

_____
(Address)

_____

_____
(Phone Number)

CHAPTER 10

MUSIC CLEARANCE

If you are planning to use anything other than originally scored music throughout your entire film, you should contact a music clearance service during the early stages of pre-production. You will want to know if the rights to the copyrighted musical material are available, how much each would cost to license and if your music budget will cover the cost of the music you wish to use. Early music planning could save you a lot of time and money by knowing exactly which pieces of music you can and cannot incorporate into your film.

The following guide, prepared by **Clearing House, Ltd.**, answers the most frequently asked questions about the field of music clearance. Any additional questions you may have about music rights clearances should be directed to your attorney or music clearance service.

A GUIDE TO MUSIC CLEARANCE
Provided By Clearing House, Ltd.

The music we hear every day on radio and television, or see performed in nightclubs and concerts, is subject to federal copyright protection. The U.S. Copyright Act, and other copyright laws around the world, give the owners of copyrighted music certain rights and controls over the use of their music and the fees that will be paid for that use. This system of law, which makes it possible for artist to earn a living from their creations, also requires that producers desiring to use protected musical material secure proper permission to do so.

What are my responsibilities for clearing the used used in my television motion picture of video project?

Both as a matter of copyright law and the producer's own distribution or exhibition agree-

ments, it is the producer's responsibility to secure the clearance of musical material used in his television, motion picture or video production. This is required to avoid liability for copyright infringement, to meet broadcaster or distributor delivery requirements and to comply with errors and omissions insurance procedures. The term "musical material" includes songs and particular recordings of songs as well, since recordings may be protected by copyright law, state anti-piracy statues and other legal theories.

Failure to properly clear copyrighted musical material may result in substantial copyright infringement liability, an injunction against distribution, legal fees, and the very real possibility of massive re-editing of the finished program or the destruction of release prints or dubs. Once the musical material is properly cleared, it may be used to the full extent of the license terms.

What is music clearance?

It is the process of determining who owns the copyright to any given musical material, then negotiating permission for use of that material for the territories and media in which exhibition or distribution is planned, in exchange for the payment of a license fee to the copyright owner. These steps should be taken before recording in order to eliminate songs which are too expensive or which the copyright owners do not want used. After editing is completed, a music cue sheet (listing all the music in order of use) must be prepared and distributed, the license fees paid and the formal contracts granting the rights must be executed.

There are no set clearance patterns because each composition brings with it a unique set of legal and business affairs problems which should be addressed and resolved before production begins. For example, some musical compositions, while popular and in general use in areas such as radio broadcast or nightclub performance, are not available (at any price) in certain other media applications. The unauthorized use of such material could result in an injunction blocking the exhibition of the entire production, as well as other financial penalties, until the uncleared material is removed.

Who owns the music I wish to use?

This is a very complex question since several people can collaborate to create a single composition. Further, a copyright can be divided into separate parts with each part owned either individually or by several parties.

Generally, a writer sells or assigns the copyright in his song to a music publisher who pays the writer a share of the royalties derived from its exploitation. If the writer is an employee of the publisher, the publisher usually owns the work for the life of the copyright and it is the publisher, not the writer, who has the authority to grant permission for its use. In other cases, the publisher who owns the copyright may be contractually required to ask for the writer's approval before allowing its use.

It is possible for ownership of a copyright to be divided by percentages, or even by territories, so that several publishers could own rights in the United States while several others could own rights for the rest of the world. The people who own music copyrights frequently transfer the right to grant permission and the right to collect royalties for specific types of rights to outside agencies who do the collecting and paperwork (administration) for them. All of this may result in situations where several parties must agree to the license, thereby increasing the difficulty in obtaining clearance.

Recordings are usually owned by the record company that pay for the recording session, or that had the recording artist under contract. However, the terms of recording contracts can require certain artist approvals before the record company can grant a license.

What rights do I need to obtain in order to make sure the musical compositions in my production are properly cleared?

In general, the rights commonly required in television and film production may be divided into the following categories:

PUBLIC PERFORMANCE RIGHTS

These refer to the rights to do such things as recite, play, sing, dance, act out or broadcast a composition in public. However, there is a vast difference between the rights required to merely sing a song on a bare stage and the rights required to dramatize or tell the story of a song using sets, costumes, props, etc. While a detailed explanation

of dramatic and non-dramatic rights is beyond the scope of this guide, remember that the rights required and the complexity of their clearance will depend upon the way the song is used.

REPRODUCTION RIGHTS

These are referred to in television and film production as **synchronization rights** because the protected material is recorded as part of a soundtrack in synchronization with visual images. **Sync rights**, as they are called, should not be confused with so-called **mechanical rights** which have historically referred to the reproduction of music on audio records or tapes for distribution to the general public. Recently, mechanical rights has also been used to refer to the right to reproduce and distribute music in the form of videocassettes and discs. The definitions can become confusing.

ADAPTATION RIGHTS

These rights involve the alteration or adaptation of musical compositions by way of arrangement, parody, comedic use, lyric change, translation, etc. and may result in many clearance problems. If a composition is to be used in an adapted form, specific permission directly from the copyright owner may be required before broadcast or release. Some copyright owners, while open to the use of their material as it was originally written, will not grant permission for any adaptations.

The way in which a song is performed or used will determine the applicability of these various rights. The media in which distribution is planned (broadcast television, home video, feature film, etc.) will significantly affect how these rights are negotiated and how much will have to be paid for the rights.

From whom may I obtain these music rights?

The previously mentioned rights are generally not handled at one source, but instead, are licensed individually by separate parties. For certain rights, you may have to deal directly with the author of the material, the author's estate, lawyer, publisher or agent.

Synchronization rights might be obtained by approaching the owner directly or one of the organizations that represent publishers and license those rights on their behalf (i.e., The Harry Fox Agency, Inc. or Finell-Brunow Associates, Inc.)

Public performing rights are customarily obtained by broadcasters for the music performing rights organizations which represent composers and publishers. They are the American Society of Composers, Authors and Publishers (ASCAP), Broadcast Music, Inc. (BMI) or the Society of

European Stage Authors and Composers (SESAC). Pursuant to the ASCAP and BMI consent decrees with the U.S. government, broadcasters have the choice of securing either a **blanket** or **per program license**. With a blanket license, a broadcaster can use any or all of the songs in the ASCAP/BMI catalogues. Under the per program license, the broadcasters pay only for the programs which contain music licensed by the performing rights societies. Performing rights licensing for media other than broadcast television, such as feature films, non-theatrical and non-broadcast uses may be handled in a completely different manner.

In some cases with popular musical material, the writer may hold the actual copyright while the licensing for television or film use may be handled by the writer's representative. If several parties own a composition, each may have to be contacted. If a writer is deceased and his rights have passed on to his heirs, the process can become even more difficult.

What is a music cue sheet and why is it so important?

A music cue sheet is a document which lists all of the music contained in a production including the title, composer(s), publishers, performing rights affiliation, use and timing of each musical cue. It basically tells the performing rights societies which composers and publishers are to receive royalty distributions and helps to determine how much will be paid. The cue sheet should list the publishing company of the producer if musical cues composed specifically for the production are owned by the producer.

The timely delivery of an accurate music cue sheet has always been a requirement in most production/distribution/station license agreements.

Who is entitled to receive music cue sheets?

Producers should send cue sheets to the performing rights societies that control the music in the programs they create. Additionally, program buyers, syndicators and broadcasters are entitled to receive cue sheets by virtue of the contractual delivery requirements in most production and station program license agreements.

Can the copyright owner keep me from using a composition even if I am willing to pay for it?

Yes. The owner of the composition can, except in very rare cases, restrict or deny permission for its reproduction or adaptation. In certain circumstances, the performing rights organizations also allow the owner to restrict the public performance of music that is normally subject to blanket performance clearance. Some popular music, freely broadcast on radio or used in nightclub performances, may be blocked from use on commercial television or in motion pictures. The Copyright Law leaves the final decision up to the owner or owners of the work.

What happens if I use a song without clearing it?

If no one ever catches you — nothing. However, if the matter is discovered by the copyright owner, you, as the producer of the project and any broadcaster or distributor, may be held liable for copyright infringement as well as other actionable claims. Under the Copyright Act, an infringer may be liable for both the damages sustained by the copyright owner, and the profits resulting from the unauthorized use of the protected material. Even if the copyright owner cannot show what the damages or profits are, he can still be awarded substantial statutory damages as provided in the Copyright Act.

You may find yourself facing an injunction, paying an out-of-court settlement to the copyright owner or going back to your finished program and making extensive changes to remove the uncleared material. A producer with a completed project from which release prints or dubs have already been made, may find himself incurring costs many times what the original clearance and license fees might have been.

Quite recently, several "watchdog" operations have been formed to monitor the use of music in all media on behalf of composers, publishers, record companies and artists. Additionally, both ASCAP and BMI have increased their viewing of television programs and monitoring of music cue sheets in order to determine their accuracy and resolve questions involving performing rights payments to composers and publishers. This, of course, only increases the chance that someone may indeed "catch you" — particularly if your project is successful.

What about old songs? Aren't these songs in the public domain and free to be used without restriction?

There is a certain amount of music for which all copyright protection on a worldwide basis has lapsed. Some musical material which may be in the public domain in the United States may still be protected in other countries. Failure to obtain proper international copyright clearance may severely limit exploitation of the project.

With the changes in the U.S. Copyright Law that became effective January 1, 1978, some older material has had its protection extended, and worldwide rights issues have become even more complicated.

If you plan to use public domain material, you must be sure that *any* arrangement created for your use is based on the original public domain version and not a subsequent copyrighted or protected version which would require clearance.

Actual clearance of material should still be carefully undertaken to insure its public domain status and to comply with errors and omissions insurance procedures. It can take as much time and expense to determine whether a composition is in the public domain as to clear one that is not.

How long can music be protected by copyright?

Generally, music created after January 1, 1978, will be protected by copyright for 50 years after the death of the last surviving writer. "Works made for hire" are protected 75 years from publication or 100 years from creation, whichever is less. For songs written before January 1, 1978, if timely renewal of the copyright is made, the term of protection will last for a total of 75 years from the end of the year the copyright was originally secured. Remember that foreign laws may provide for different copyright terms and may have to be verified on a country-by-country basis.

Also, the fact that a musical composition does not contain a copyright notice does not mean that it is in the public domain. When the United States became a member of the Berne International Copyright Convention (in order to increase foreign protection for domestic works), our copyright law had to be amended to eliminate the requirement of a copyright notice as a prerequisite for copyright protection. While copyright notice is still required in order for a copyright owner to be entitled to certain remedies for infringement, it is not required in order for a work to be protected.

May I use eight bars of a song without paying for it?

No! This is one of the most common misconceptions regarding music and its protection under U.S. Copyright Law. Any unauthorized use of material that is recognizable as having come from a copyrighted source is a potential infringement of copyright.

What is "fair use"?

There is an exception to the exclusive rights of copyright owners called "fair use" which permits the limited use of copyrighted material in special circumstances without requiring an owner's consent. In theory, the public interest in the dissemination of ideas and information is served when uses for such purposes as criticism, comment,

news reporting, scholarship, teaching, etc., are freely permitted. Parodies of material for humorous effect or social commentary are usually treated under the same principles. HOWEVER, caution in the area of parody is strongly recommended.

The U.S. copyright law lists the factors which must be considered in each case of a claimed "fair use." These factors include: 1) the purpose and character of the use; 2) the nature of the work; 3) the amount and substantiality of the portion used; and, 4) the effect of the use on the potential market for or value of the work. Since there are no clear and definite guidelines, it is difficult to determine in advance what may or may not be a permissible "fair use." If you are faced with a question of this nature, it would be prudent to contact your attorney or music clearance service.

May I use the title of a song as my program title?

While titles are not protected under copyright law, they may be protected under other legal doctrines. Use of the title and story line of a song may involve the clearance of dramatic rights or require negotiations similar to those required for the acquisition of rights in a literary property. For protection, your attorney should advise you as to whether the title may be freely used, or if specific permission should be obtained from the owner of the song.

Must a license be secured if song lyrics are spoken in dialogue?

The copyright in a song protects the lyrics as well as the music. Therefore, if an identifiable part of a song lyric is used in dialogue, a license may have to be secured in order to avoid potential liability.

May I change the lyrics to an existing song?

Changes made to the copyrighted lyrics of the song, including what may appear to be only minor changes, usually have to be cleared by obtaining specific permission from the copyright owner. This may even apply to the translation of the original lyrics into a foreign language.

If I clear a song for the first episode of a television series, may it be used in subsequent episodes without additional permission?

No. Licenses are normally granted on a show-by-show basis, and unless the song was cleared for the run of the series, it can only be used in that single episode without violating the rights of the owner.

In addition, a new episode containing clips from previous episodes will require additional licenses for the music contained in the clips.

Do I have to clear musi that is to be used in commercials?

Yes. In order for copyrighted music to be used in the advertisement of products and services, the entire procedure for clearing music must be followed. Popular songs are frequently changed or adapted to fit the product or service being promoted. Accordingly, specific permission for use must be obtained from the copyright owner based upon the markets and media to be exploited.

May I use records on my television show?

Be careful. This is a complex and gray area of both law and practice. Some use of records on television teen dance shows, for instance, has been permitted because this use is considered promotional. Other uses of records in television, home video and motion picture productions may require permission in advance from any number of involved parties including the music publisher, record company, artist, performer's unions, etc.

Commercial phonograph recordings made and released after February 15, 1972 are eligible for federal copyright protection. Recordings made prior to that date, though not copyrightable, may still be protectable under state anti-piracy statutes and other legal theories.

Remember that the use of a recording may require the clearance of two separate and distinct items of intellectual property, the recording itself and the song that was recorded.

If I obtain a license to use a film clip from a television program or feature film in my project, will that license include the right to use the music contained on the soundtrack?

Generally no. Film clip licenses are usually granted with the producer acknowledging that he will be responsible for obtaining all third party rights and clearances. The film clip owner may not own the music, or may have acquired rights for its use in his production only. Therefore, if the music on the soundtrack is not specifically covered in the film clip license agreement, it will be your responsibility to obtain additional clearances for its use in your project. The music publishing division of a motion picture company and the production or publicity division of the same company can have completely different outlooks on what you may or may not use.

If a record company gives me a music video clip for use in my project, will I need further music clearances?

The use of so-called "promotional" music videos of musical performing artists has raised a number of music licensing issues which may not be settled for some time to come.

As with other programs, the proper licensing of the music contained in a music video requires public performance rights, synchronization rights and also may require "dramatic" performing rights if the video is telling the story of a song.

A producer wishing to use a music video clip in his program must first determine which of the above music rights, if any, have been granted to him by the licensor of the music video (usually a record company). Music videos are typically licensed with the user being responsible for all third party licensing obligations including the payments required to be made pursuant to the collective bargaining agreements of any performer's unions.

If the performing artist has written the song and owns or controls the publishing rights, the record company, by virtue of its agreement with the artist, may be able to grant you a license for promotional use of the music in your program. However, if the performing artist has no royalty or ownership interest in the song, the record company may not be willing to assume the responsibility of securing or granting synchronization licenses for your purposes.

Since most record sales occur in the first 90 days of distribution, there is a serious legal and business question as to whether use of a music video in a program intended to be distributed for a period substantially longer than 90 days should be considered promotional or commercial. The more your use is considered to be commercial, the greater the likelihood that you will have to make all publisher payments at normal commercial rates along with possible payment to the record company for continued use of the music video itself.

Is it true that a synchronization license is not necessary for the first US Network run of an original live or taped television program?

That is correct. In current practice, this is an exception to traditional licensing procedure. However, network broadcasts occurring more than six months after the first network run and taped or filmed syndicated broadcasts of the material will require full music rights clearances. Therefore, if you are producing a program that will run for less than a six month period on network television, and which has no value in syndication, you may not need synchronization licenses for the music. As very little programming of this nature exists, you will need clearance for almost all other methods of distribution. Even if no synchronization license is required, all other rights, such as performance and adaptation rights, must be cleared for the first network run. Foreign runs may require synchronization licenses from first broadcast.

Will the networks' music clearance department assist me?

The television networks maintain music clearance personnel to carry out the reporting and clearance requirements of their licenses with the performing rights organizations. Each network may have a different policy. However, they generally do not negotiate synchronization or adaptation rights on behalf of independent producers, but primarily maintain the licenses which provide for blanket clearance of performing rights.

In most production contracts, it is the producer's responsibility to inform the broadcaster of the music to be used, to deliver the program with rights secured, and to indemnify the broadcaster or distributor for any resulting liability, no matter who clears the music.

What rights are required to release a program for sale in the home video marketplace?

Home video distribution, as that term is generally defined in the entertainment industry, requires that the producer obtain the right to reproduce the musical work on the sound track of the program (much like synchronization rights) and the right to manufacture and distribute copies of the program containing the musical work throughout the territories in which distribution is planned. There are currently no public performance rights involved in home video distribution, as long as the program is not displayed at a place open to the public, or any place where a substantial number of people outside of a normal family and its social acquaintances is gathered.

What do publishers charge for home video rights?

Publishers can charge whatever they think the market will bear. Generally, publishers require: 1) a flat fee or royalty per unit sold; 2) a pro-rata percentage of the wholesale or retail sales price; or, 3) a combination of both. These royalty arrangements usually require that the producer account to the publishers on a quarterly or semi-annual basis.

In addition, some publishers may seek fixing fees (one-time flat fee payments similar to synchronization fees), advances or sometimes both. The distinction between the two is that advances are recoupable out of royalties earned while fixing fees are not.

It is now common (particularly with feature films, non-theatrical/educational programs and programs using very little music), to work out arrangements similar to flat fee licenses, or buy-outs, thereby avoiding costly accounting procedures. However, some publishers may not agree to such license terms.

Will the home video royalties apply throughout the world?

This must be answered on a song-by-song basis and will depend on the arrangements between the domestic publisher and its representative (sub-publisher) in each foreign territory. In some cases, the right to grant licenses and collect royalties may have been contractually transferred to the sub-publisher in each territory. If this is the case, the producer may have to deal with the respective sub-publisher in each territory in which distribution is planned.

Although foreign licensing procedures are constantly evolving, a copyright collection society or agent representing the sub-publisher will usually set the rates to be charged. Theses rates are usually based on a percentage of the wholesale or retail sales price in relation to the amount of music used. The foreign rates currently tend to be higher than domestic rates and administratively more difficult to handle.

What about home video rentals?

The U.S. copyright law equally grants the owner of a song and the producer or owner of a home video program the right to control the methods of distribution including sale or rental. However, the right to control rentals is modified by another provision of the U.S. copyright law known as the "first-sale" doctrine. Once a legitimate copy of a program is sold by its owner, the buyer may sell, rent or otherwise dispose of the copy without the consent of or additional payment to the original owner. The buyer may not, however, make a copy of the program.

This means that the producer has little or no control over the rental of the home video program once it has been sold and therefore receives little or no accountable rental income. Pending legislation may alter this in the future. There is no current standard music royalty for accountable rental transactions.

How are feature films licensed?

In feature films, music rights, whether for a song or a recording, are usually licensed worldwide for duration of copyright. This is partly because of the tremendous investment required to make a feature film and the complicated contractual arrangements involved in feature film distribution.

Unlike other types of production for which rights may be licensed on a medium by medium basis, the producer of a feature film will usually secure a very broad grant of rights so that the film can be exploited in all possible media existing now or in the future.

For anti-trust reasons, the performing rights

societies are not allowed to collect performing fees from motion picture theaters in the U.S. Therefore, a producer must secure a United States theatrical performance license directly from the publisher or its agent when securing a synchronization license. Outside the United States, local performing rights societies collect a percentage of the net box office receipts from theaters exhibiting feature films.

Feature film producers must pay particular attention to the way home video rights are acquired, as the major studios and distributors strongly resist paying any kind of continuing home video music royalty. There are well known cases where studios have required producers of feature films in current theatrical release to delete material which carried a royalty obligation prior to home video distribution.

What happens when a program is produced for distribution on public broadcasting stations?

The U.S. copyright law provides that a copyright owner must grant a license (a "compulsory" license) for the public (non-commercial) broadcasting of non-dramatic musical works and popular recordings. Compulsory license rates are established by the copyright royalty tribunal and are published in the Federal Register.

The law also allows public broadcasters and copyright owners or their representatives to enter into voluntary agreements which prevail over compulsory license rates. Such agreements with The Harry Fox Agency, SESAC and others for the licensing of synchronization rights, and with ASCAP and BMI for the licensing of performance rights, allow covered music to be incorporated in a production at the negotiated rates without the necessity of pre-clearing the music with the publisher.

Popular music not covered by voluntary agreements may be used pursuant to the compulsory license; however, this only applies to "non-profit" producers. "For-Profit" producers must negotiate synchronization licenses directly with any publisher who is not signatory to a negotiated agreement.

Regardless of the above, dramatic uses and other adaptations will still require permission in advance from the copyright owners. Remember that the license covers only public broadcasting use. Any non-PBS exhibition of the program will require licenses from all of the parties involved.

How much will it cost to clear a song for use in my television or film project?

This depends on a number of factors, including the nature of the clearance you are attempting to obtain. Many television producers can get by with a one, three or five year synchronization license for just the United States; others need worldwide rights and/or possibly longer terms. Feature film producers must make sure they obtain perpetual worldwide motion picture rights as well as television rights for eventual domestic and foreign syndication.

The new technologies have complicated the matter even further, and the rights for these areas are frequently obtained on a medium by medium basis. There is no established pattern for these fees, as they vary from composition to composition and must be computed separately for each project's specific rights and releasing requirements.

What if I hire a composer to write original music for my television or film project?

Depending on your agreement with the composer, the musical material created for your project on an "employee for hire" basis may belong to you as the employer. If the composer has incorporated existing compositions into the score, care must be taken to make sure those existing compositions have been cleared. Also, the actual status of any public domain material which may have been used should be thoroughly reviewed.

What is a needle drop?

This refers to the use of a single portion, or "cue", of an existing recording (placing the needle down on the recording and then lifting it) in synchronization with filmed or taped images.

If you use a needle drop or "cue" from a commercially produced popular recording, you may have to deal with all of the normal clearance requirements discussed earlier with respect to the song, the recording of the song, the recording artist and the performer's unions.

There are organizations known as "production music" libraries that provide commercially produced recordings specifically for background broadcast and film use at a variety of reasonable license rates. Most production music libraries have reporting requirements which can be satisfied by filing a music cue sheet with the performing rights societies or informing the library of the use. The libraries will usually issue one license which includes the rights for the music and the recording of the music. Some production music companies include so-called "sound alike" recordings of popular artists in their libraries. Remember that if such recordings are used, the producer must still secure a license from the publisher of the song.

If you are a union signatory, or are producing for a union signatory company, be sure to use caution as some production music may not comply with union requirements.

What happens when licenses expire?

If the right to use music contained in your program has been granted for a limited period of time, those licenses will have to be renewed at the end of that period if continued exploitation of the program is contemplated. After that initial period, all rights to use the compositions and/or recordings may expire and any further exhibition of the program may constitute an infringement of the music copyrights. This is seldom an issue in feature films where music is traditionally licensed in perpetuity.

Because of recent legislation, court decisions and business practices, it may not be a simple matter to renew all old licenses. It is possible that the publisher who originally granted the license may no longer control the composition. Also, there are well-known cases where composers and publishers of popular songs have refused to renew expired licenses or have charged exorbitant fees for license renewals.

It may be possible to negotiate for perpetual licenses at the time of initial licensing. However, the price charged by the publisher may increase significantly over the normal price of a limited term license.

May I, or someone on my production staff, obtain the required music rights clearances for my project?

Not unless you or one of the people on your staff has a day-to-day working knowledge of music clearance procedures and the research and computer information at hand necessary to resolve questions of ownership, licensing practice and availability. This is a rapidly evolving and specialized area. Most producers have neither the available full-time staff nor the business affairs support required to carry out the task. While an attorney's direct input is not necessarily required in the process, there are continuing questions which must be addressed in order to comply with both the legal and contractual requirements of production. In common practice, many producers use a music clearance service.

[NOTE: The Clearing House, Ltd., (based in Hollywood) maintains a staff of lawyers and other professionals who specialize in the clearance of music and ancillary rights. They are a single-point producer service that acts to effectively negotiate and obtain required rights and licenses for the use of protected musical material in all media. Utilizing constantly updated industry source data, they deal with producers, artists, publishers, record companies and business affairs staffs worldwide.

The Clearing House, Ltd., has also developed a user-friendly, IBM-compatible computer program which standardizes both the format and methodology of preparing music cue sheets. The program, **Cue Sheets**, is available, upon request, as a service to the industry.]

Chapter 11

Miscellaneous Production Forms

An actor claims he did not receive the script revisions you know you sent by runner yesterday. A vendor claims not to have received the check you think you mailed with a stack of others last Wednesday. The assistant cameraman wants you to order more raw stock, but you think there should be enough on hand for at least another week.

Production means a lot of details to: take care of, keep track of and remember; and these forms should help make doing that a lot easier.

You may not need all of them, but take advantage of the ones that will help you the most. They are not necessarily considered *standard* and do take time to fill out and keep up, but they will keep you better **organized** and being better organized will save you time.

FORMS INCLUDED IN THIS SECTION

Abbreviated Production Report 127
Daily Cost Overview.....................................128
Cast Information Sheet 129
Box/Equipment Rental Inventory 130
Inventory Log 131
Purchase Order Log.....................................132
Crew Start-up and Data Sheet 133
Time Car/Invoices Weekly Checklist 134
Individual Petty Cash Account 135
Invoice 136
Cash or Sales Receipt 137
The Check's in the Mail 138
Mileage Log 139
Raw Stock Inventory 140
Daily Raw Stock 141
Request for Pick-up 142
Request for Delivery 143
Drive-to 144
Walkie-Talkie Sign-out Sheet 145
Beeper Sign-out Sheet 146
Vehicle Rental Sheet 147
Residual Cut-off 148

ABBREVIATED PRODUCTION REPORT

SHOW **THE WATCHER**   PROD# **0100**

DAY **MONDAY** DATE **6-7-93**   DAY# **6** OUT OF **30**

LOCATION **CITY HALL - DOWNTOWN**

CREW CALL **7AM**

FIRST SHOT **9:30A**   MEAL PENALTY **1**

LUNCH **1:30** TO **2P**   OVERTIME **½HR**

SECOND MEAL _____ TO _____

WRAP **8PM**

SCENES **3, 4, 5, 26, 27, 30**

SCENES SCHEDULED BUT NOT SHOT _____

	SCENES	PAGES	MINUTES	SETUPS
PREVIOUS	76	35 2/8	31:37	83
TODAY	6	5 3/8	2:15	23
TOTAL	82	40 5/8	33:52	106

FILM FOOTAGE

GROSS **4590**   GROSS TO DATE **28,830**

PRINT **2720**   PRINT TO DATE **19,630**

N.G. **1510**

WASTE **360**

NOTES **- SCARLET STARLET 30 MIN. LATE TO SET**
- KATIE KANDU (SCRIPT SUPV'R) TOOK ILL ON
SET & REQUESTED TO BE REPLACED. REPLACEMENT
ARRIVED @ NOON.

DAILY COST OVERVIEW

SHOW _THE WATCHER_ PROD# _0100_

DATE _6-7-93_ DAY# _6_

START DATE _5-29-93_

SCHEDULED FINISH DATE _7-8-93_

REVISED FINISH DATE _7-9-93_

	PER CALL SHEET	SHOT	AHEAD/BEHIND
# OF SCENES	6	4	2 BEHIND
# OF PAGES	5 3/8	4 5/8	6/8 BEHIND

	AS BUDGETED AND/OR SCHEDULED	ACTUAL	COST (OVER)/UNDER
CAST OVERTIME	$500 -	$650 -	$150 -
COMPANY SHOOTING HOURS	12	13 -	$10,000 -
MEAL PENALTY (5 SAG ACTORS)	$500 -	$300 -	($200 -)
EXTRAS & STAND-INS	$632 -	$577 -	($55)
CATERING	$840 -	$960 -	$120
RAW STOCK (5,000')	$2,250 -	$1,687 -	($563)

UNANTICIPATED EXPENSES:

ADD'L. PROP ASST.	10 HRS. @ $22/HR.		$242 -
FRINGE			$ 44 -

TOTAL FOR TODAY _$9,738 -_

PREVIOUS TOTAL _$4,000 -_

GRAND TOTAL _$13,738 - (OVER)_

PREPARED BY _ADAM ACCOUNTANT_ APPROVED BY _Fred Filmer_

© ELH Form #19

CAST INFORMATION

SHOW: THE WATCHER
EPISODE: Boys' Night Out
PROD# D100

(Please fill squares in with dates)

ACTOR	ROLE	START DATE	# OF DAYS WORKING	DEAL MEMO	STATION 12	TRAVEL/HOTEL ACCOMODATIONS	MEDICAL EXAM	SENT SCRIPT	NOTIFIED WARDROBE	SCRIPT REVISIONS (BLUE)	SCRIPT REVISIONS (PINK)	SCRIPT REVISIONS (GREEN)	CONTRACT RECEIVED	CONTRACT TO AGENT/ACTOR	CONTRACT RETURNED	CONTRACT SIGNED BY PRODUCER	COPIES DISTRIBUTED	NOTES
CLARK GRABLE	HERBY	9/18	14	5/27 5/28	5/27 5/28	✓	5/11	5/3 5/3	5/3	9/10	9/6		9/11	9/7	9/9	9/11	9/11	
ROCKY RIZZO	JAKE	9/18	14	5/27 5/28	5/27 5/28	✓	5/11	5/5 5/5	5/5				9/11	9/7	9/9	9/11	9/14	
SCARLET STARLET	LAURA	9/21	9	5/29 5/29	5/29 5/29	✓	5/20 5/20	5/11 5/11	5/11				9/8	9/7	9/9	9/11	9/14	
NANCY NICELY	MOM	9/20	11	9/10 9/04	9/10 9/04	✓	5/28 5/28	5/18 5/18	5/8				9/8	9/9	9/15	9/16	9/18	
HOLLYWOOD MANN	GEORGE	9/22	5	9/10 9/10	9/10 9/10	✓	9/3	5/8 5/8	9/8				9/4 9/15	9/15	9/22	9/22	9/24	
KENNY SMILES	MARC	9/20	8	9/24 9/24	9/24 9/24	✓	—	5/25 5/25	9/25 9/25				9/7	9/18	9/15	9/24	9/30	
WILL PERFORMER	JED	9/20	8	9/9 9/9	9/9 9/9	✓	—	5/25 5/25	9/25 9/25				9/7	8/10	9/25	9/24	9/20	
LLOYD LOCAL	POLICE SGT.	9/24	1	9/15 9/15	9/15 9/15	✓	—	8/9 8/9	8/10	✓	✓		9/18	8/19	9/22	6/23/94	9/24	

BOX/EQUIPMENT RENTAL INVENTORY

PRODUCTION COMPANY __XYZ PRODUCTIONS, INC.__

SHOW __THE WATCHER__   PROD# __0100__

EMPLOYEE __SAM SHUTTER__   POSITION __STILL PHOTOGRAPHER__

Address __8436 LENS AVE.__   SOC.SEC.# __331-42-9759__

__CANOGA PARK, CA__   PHONE# __818/ 555-3222__

LOAN OUT COMPANY _____   FED.I.D.# _____

RENTAL RATE $ __200__   PER   [] DAY   [✓] WEEK

                             [] SUBMIT WEEKLY INVOICE

                             [✓] RECORD ON WEEKLY TIME CARD

RENTAL COMMENCES ON __6-18-93__

INVENTORIED ITEMS: 2 NIKON BODIES   SER# 123456XXX
                                        SER# 247654XXX
                3 LENSES   70-210 ZOOM
                            35-105 /MACRO
                            28 mm
                MISC. FILTERS
                MOTOR DRIVE
                TRII-POD
                BLIMP

Please note: 1.   *Box and equipment rentals are subject to 1099 reporting.*

               2.   *The Production Company is not responsible for any claims of loss or damage to box/equipment rental items that are not listed on the above inventory.*

EMPLOYEE SIGNATURE   DATE   6 / 2 / 93

APPROVED BY   DATE   6 / 2 / 93

INVENTORY LOG

SHOW: THE WATCHER PROD# 0100 DEPARTMENT: SET DRESSING

| ITEM(S) | PURCHASED FROM (Name/Address) | PURCHASE DATE | PURCHASE PRICE | P.O.# | AT COMPLETION OF PRINCIPAL PHOTOGRAPHY | | | |
					IF PORTION USED, HOW MUCH REMAINS	IF SOLD, FOR HOW MUCH	IF RET'D. TO COMPANY, IN WHAT CONDITION	LOCATION OF ITEM
2 OIL PAINTINGS	OTTO'S GALLERY	6/2/93	$1200	1235		$600		
FIREPLACE SET	DELL'S DEPT STORE	6/10/93	$150	1576			GOOD	COMPANY'S STORAGE
HALL MIRROR	COUNTRY ANTIQUES	6/11/93	$300	1592			SCRATCHED	''

PURCHASE ORDER LOG

SHOW: THE WATCHER   PROD# 0100

P.O.#	DATE	TO	FOR	PRICE	PURCHASE	RENTAL	SERVICE	RENTAL RET'D	TO INVENTORY	P.O. ASSIGNED TO
1001	6/21	LARRY'S LUMBER	MISC CONST	$2500	✓					CONST. COORDINATOR
1002	6/21	PAUL'S PROP HOUSE	HAND PROPS	$250		✓		7/3/93		PROPERTY MASTER
1003	6/22	JONES SANITATION	TRASH REMOVAL	$500			✓			CONST. COORD.

(CHECK ONE: PURCHASE / RENTAL / SERVICE)

CREW START-UP AND DATA SHEET

NAME	POSITION	SOC. SEC. #	NAME OF CORP. FED. I.D. #	DEAL MEMO	START SLIP	W-4 I-9	START DATE	WRAP DATE	PAYCHECK TO EMPLOYEE	PAYCHECK TO MAIL
A. DEES	1ST ASST. DIR	555-21-1234		7/3/93	✓	✓	7/5/93	9/10	✓	
KATIE KANDU	SCRIPT SUPV'R	543-37-3217		7/10/93	✓	✓	7/26	9/14	✓	
MIKE BOOM	SOUND MIXER	435-62-9652	BOOM AUDIO #95-1234567	7/15/93	✓	✓	7/30	9/13	✓	
F. STOPP	DIR. OF PHOTOG.	375-76-2175		7/2/93	✓	✓	7/19	9/10		✓

TIME CARDS/INVOICES
WEEKLY CHECKLIST

NAME	POSITION	SOC. SEC. # / FED. I.D. #	W/E 7/31	W/E 8/7	W/E 8/14	W/E 8/21	W/E 8/28	W/E 9/4	W/E 9/11	W/E 9/18
A. Dees	1st Asst. Director	555-21-1234	✓	✓	✓	✓	✓	✓	✓	
Katie Kajdu	Script Suprv'r.	543-37-3217		✓	✓	✓	✓	✓	✓	
Mike Boom	Sound Mixer	#95-1234567		✓	✓	✓	✓	✓		
Paula Props	Property Master	321-77-6513	✓	✓	✓	✓	✓	✓	✓	✓
F. Stopp	Dir. of Photog.	375-76-3115	✓	✓	✓	✓	✓	✓	✓	✓

TIME CARDS AND/OR INVOICES TURNED IN EACH WEEK

INDIVIDUAL PETTY CASH ACCOUNT

NAME __PAULA PROPS__   DEPARTMENT __PROPERTY__

SHOW __THE WATCHER__   PROD# __0100__

FLOAT $ __500__

DATE	CHECK#/CASH RECV'D FROM	AMOUNT RECV'D	ACCOUNTED FOR	BALANCE
7/2	CHECK # 1243	$500		500
7/10			$432	68
7/11	CHECK # 1536	$432		500
7/15	CASH FROM F. FILMER	$250		750
7/23			$830	(80)
7/28	CHECK # 1732	$580		500

INVOICE

TO: XYZ PRODUCTIONS
1234 FLICK DR.
HOLLYWOOD, CA 90038

FROM: ASHLEY WILKES   DATE 3/17/93
(Address) 123 TWELVE OAKS AVE.
ATLANTA, GEORGIA
(Phone #) 555-7676

PAYEE SS# OR FED. ID# 521-63-7234   1099 ✓

FOR SERVICES RENDERED ON _____ OR WEEK/ENDING 3/15/93

DESCRIPTION OF SERVICE/RENTAL/CAR ALLOWANCE

DIALOGUE COACH TO HELP CAST WITH SOUTHERN ACCENT	
22.5 HRS. @ $100 PER HR.	

TOTAL AMOUNT DUE $ 2,250 —

EMPLOYEE SIGNATURE _Ashley Wilkes_

APPROVED BY _Fred Filmer_

PD. BY CHECK # 2376   DATE 3/20/93

© ELH Form #27

CASH OR SALES RECEIPT DATE _8/24_   No._93_

RECIPIENT/
SOLD TO: _IRMA'S SWAP MEET_

ADDRESS: _4226 ORANGE BOWL AVE._
PASADENA, CA

PHONE#: _818/555-4344_

FOR PURCHASE OF: _OLD BOOKS & RECORDS_
(SET DRESSING)

WRITTEN
AMOUNT _FIFTY-TWO DOLLARS_ ————— $ _52_

☑ CASH   ☐ 1099   Soc.Sec.# _555-73-2643_

☐ CHECK   Fed.I.D.#

ACCOUNT CODING _823-51_

APPROVED BY _Fred Filmer_   RECV'D BY _Irma Dull_

© ELH Form #28

THE CHECK'S IN THE MAIL

CHECK MADE OUT TO	CHECK NUMBER	CHECK DATED	ADDRESS SENT TO	DATE MAILED	PAY-ROLL	INV.
CAL'S COMPUTERS	1032	2/14	9876 FLORES ST. STUDIO VILLAGE, CA	2/15		✓
XXX AUDIO SERVICES	1053	2/15	123 MAIN ST. HOLLYWOOD, CA	2/16		✓
A. PAINE, M.D.	1059	2/15	3327 INJECTION BLVD. LOS ANGELES, CA	2/16		✓
ASHLEY WILKES	1075	2/20	327 TWELVE OAKS AVE. ATLANTA, GA	2/22		✓
F. STOPP (D.P.)	1082	2/20	1248 MADONNA LANE. BEV. HILLS, CA	2/22	✓	

MILEAGE LOG

NAME: __CARY GOFER__   WEEK ENDING __3/25/93__
SHOW: __THE WATCHER__   PROD# __0100__

DATE	LOCATION FROM	LOCATION TO	PURPOSE	MILEAGE
3/20	OFFICE	SCREEN ACTORS GUILD	PICK UP RATE BOOK	10
	S.A.G. OFFICE	ORIN'S OFFICE SUPPLY	OFFICE SUPPLIES	5
	ORIN'S	OFFICE		15
3/21	OFFICE	SCARLET STARLET'S HOME	DELIVER SCRIPT	8
	SCARLET STARLET'S	KENNY SMILE'S HOME	DELIVER SCRIPT	5
	KENNY SMILE'S	NANCY NICELY'S APT.	DELIVER SCRIPT	3
	NANCY NICELY'S	OFFICE		7

TOTAL MILES: __53__

__53__ MILES @ __27__ ¢ Per Mile = $ __14.31__

Approved By: __Fred Fulmer__   Date: __3/30/93__

Pd. By Check # __2976__   Date __3/31/93__

RAW STOCK INVENTORY

SHOW __THE WATCHER__   PROD# __0100__

WEEK ENDING _____

	52 _47_	52 _93_	52 _96_	52 _____
EPISODE/WEEKLY TOTALS				
Print	7,865	6,050	7,086	_____
No Good	2,390	1,769	1,807	_____
Waste	980	823	1,230	_____
Total **	11,235	8,642	10,123	_____
PURCHASED				
Previously Purchased	50,000	50,000	50,000	_____
Purchased This Episode/Week	+ 15,000	15,000	20,000	_____
Total Stock Purchased	65,000	65,000	70,000	_____
USED				
Stock Used To Date	33,705	25,926	30,369	_____
Used This Episode/Week **	+ 11,235	8,642	10,123	_____
Total Stock Used	44,940	34,568	40,492	_____
Total Purchased	65,000	65,000	70,000	_____
Total Used	- 44,940	34,568	40,492	_____
Estimated Remaining Stock	20,060	30,432	29,508	_____
(Remaining Stock As Per Assistant Cameraman)	20,060	(28,400)	(29,600)	_____

RAW STOCK PURCHASES MADE DURING
THIS EPISODE/WEEK:

P.O.# _2076_	15,000	15,000	—	_____
P.O.# _2093_	—	—	20,00	_____
P.O.# _____	_____	_____	_____	_____
P.O.# _____	_____	_____	_____	_____
TOTAL	_____	_____	_____	_____

NOTES:

DAILY RAW STOCK LOG

SHOW ___THE WATCHER___ PROD# ___0100___

DATE ___OCT 21, 1993___ DAY # ___32___

CAMERA	ROLL #	GOOD	N.G.	WASTE	TOTAL
A	1	550	350	100	1000
B	1	210	140	60	410
C	1	100	100	200	400
A	2	330	210	20	560
B	2	190	130	140	460
B	3	310	80	70	460
B	4	160	140	20	320

	DRAWN	GOOD	N.G.	WASTE	TOTAL
PREVIOUS	15,463	6,186	3788	2,010	27,447
TODAY	4,730	1,850	1150	610	3,610
TOTAL	20,193	8,036	5,038	2,620	31,057

UNEXPOSED ON HAND 18,820'	TOTAL EXPOSED 31,057

REQUEST FOR PICK UP

DATE ___7-5-93___

SHOW ___THE WATCHER___   PROD# ___0100___

PICK UP REQUESTED BY ___FRED FILMER___

ITEM(S) TO BE PICKED UP_____

___SAG THEATRICAL CONTRACT BOOKS___

_____

_____

_____

PICK UP FROM ___FRONT RECEPTION DESK___

(COMPANY) ___SCREEN ACTORS GUILD___   PHONE# ___465-4600___

ADDRESS ___7065 HOLLYWOOD BLVD.___
___HOLLYWOOD___

DIRECTIONS (if needed)_____

_____

_____

_____

☐ MUST BE PICKED UP AT _____ (A.M.) (P.M.)

☑ PICK UP AS SOON AS POSSIBLE

☐ PICK UP TODAY. NO SPECIFIC TIME

☐ NO RUSH -- WHENEVER YOU CAN

COMMENTS/SPECIAL INSTRUCTIONS ___BOOKS ARE "ON HOLD" AT___
___RECEPTION DESK. ASK FOR PICK UP FOR___
___XYZ PRODUCTIONS.___

_____

DATE & TIME OF PICK UP ___11:30 AM 7/5/93___

ITEM(S) DELIVERED TO ___FRED FILMER___

(ALL PICK UP SLIPS ARE TO BE KEPT ON FILE IN THE PRODUCTION OFFICE)

THE COMPLETE FILM PRODUCTION HANDBOOK   © ELH Form #33

REQUEST FOR DELIVERY

DATE _7/23/93_

SHOW _THE WATCHER_   PROD# _0100_

DELIVERY REQUESTED BY _CASTING DEPT._

ITEM(S) TO BE DELIVERED _____

SCRIPT

DELIVER TO _ROBERT BLUFORD_

(COMPANY)_____   PHONE# _555-7321_

ADDRESS _7364 SUNDANCE DR._
HOLLYWOOD HILLS, CA

DIRECTIONS (if needed)_____

[✓] MUST BE DELIVERED BY _10_   ((A.M.)) (P.M.)

[ ] DELIVER AS SOON AS POSSIBLE

[ ] DELIVER TODAY, NO SPECIFIC TIME

[ ] NO RUSH -- WHENEVER YOU CAN

COMMENTS/SPECIAL INSTRUCTIONS: _IF NO ONE ANSWERS_
DOOR, LEAVE ON FRONT PORCH

DATE & TIME OF DELIVERY _9:55 AM_

RECEIVED BY _R Buford_

(ALL DELIVERY SLIPS ARE TO BE KEPT ON FILE IN THE PRODUCTION OFFICE)

DRIVE-TO

SHOW __THE WATCHER__   DATE __8-10-93__

EPISODE __" BOYS NIGHT OUT "__   PROD# __0100__

LOCATION __TARA LAKE__

MILEAGE: __18__   MILES @ __30__   ¢ PER MILE = $ __5.40__

NAME	SOC. SEC.#	POSITION	SIGNATURE
1. F. STOPP	111-76-3251	DIR OF PHOTOG	F. Stopp
2. A. DEES	723-42-7476	1ST ASST DIR	A. Dees
3. K. KANDU	536-22-9759	SCRIPT SUPVR	K. Kandu
4. A. WILKES	331-62-5960	DIALOGUE COACH	A Wilkes
5.			
6.			
7.			
8.			
9.			
10.			
11.			
12.			
13.			
14.			
15.			
16.			
17.			
18.			
19.			
20.			
21.			
22.			
23.			
24.			
25.			
26.			
27.			
28.			

TOTAL ALLOCATION: __75__ People X $ __5.40__ = $ __405__

Fred Filmer   DATE __8/10/93__

WALKIE-TALKIE SIGN-OUT SHEET

SHOW ___THE WATCHER___   PROD# ___0100___

SERIAL #	PRINT NAME	DATE OUT	DATE IN	SIGNATURE
AB376227	A. DEES	7/5	7/5	A. Dees
AB376228	B. JONES	7/5	7/5	B. Jones
AB376229	F. FILMER	7/8	7/8	F. Filmer
AB376230	S. SCOUT	7/8	7/8	S. Scout

WALKIE-TALKIES RENTED FROM: ___XXX AUDIO SERVICES___

ADDRESS ___123 MAIN ST.___   PHONE# ___555-5311___

___HOLLYWOOD, CA___   FAX# ___555-5312___

CONTACT ___GEORGE___   HOURS ___8A-6P___

BEEPER SIGN-OUT SHEET

SHOW ___THE WATCHER_____ PROD# ___0100___

SERIAL #	PRINT NAME	DATE OUT	DATE IN	SIGNATURE
XXX 123	FRED FILMER	4/13	5/20	A. Filmer
XXX 124	A. DEES	4/15	5/18	A. Dees
XXX 125	SWIFTY DEALS	3/25	6/30	Swifty Deals

BEEPERS RENTED FROM: ___XXX CELLULAR, INC._____

ADDRESS ___1717 HIGHLIGHT DR._____ PHONE# ___555-4321___

___LOS ANGELES, CA_____ FAX# ___555-4322___

CONTACT ___JOE_____ HOURS ___9A-7P___

© ELH Form #37

VEHICLE RENTAL SHEET

PRODUCTION COMPANY ___XYZ PRODUCTIONS, INC.___ DATE ___2-17-93___

ADDRESS ___1234 FLICK DR.___

___HOLLYWOOD, CA___

PHONE# ___555-3331___

The vehicle as described below is to be rented for use on the film tentatively entitled: ___"THE WATCHER"___

YEAR, MAKE, MODEL ___1992 MERCEDES BENZ-SL___

LICENSE NUMBER ___1 PAL 222___

SERIAL ID# ___X 944 31296___

VALUE ___$45,000___

SPECIAL EQUIPMENT/ATTACHMENTS _____

RENTAL PRICE $ ___250___ Per (Day) Week/Month

OWNER'S NAME ___ROMEO JONES___

ADDRESS ___4321 BEVERLY HILLS LANE___

___BEVERLY HILLS, CA___

PHONE# ___555-6643___

DRIVER OF VEHICLE (if not owner) _____

START DATE ___2-19-93___ COMPLETION DATE ___2-19-93___

INSURANCE TO BE SUPPLIED BY ___XYZ PRODUCTIONS, INC.___

INSURANCE COMPANY ___ABC INSURANCE CO.___

POLICY # ___5362732LT___

INSURANCE AGENCY REP. ___DARRYL DEDUCTIBLE___

PHONE# ___555-7373___

REQUIRED MAINTENANCE _____

FUEL _____

VEHICLE TO BE USED FOR ___PICTURE VEHICLE FOR SC.#25/PROPS___ (DEPARTMENT)

CERTIFICATE OF INSURANCE ☑ TO OWNER ☑ IN VEHICLE ☑ ON FILE

AGREED TO:

BY: ___Romeo Jones___
        OWNER

BY: ___Alex Autos___
        TRANSPORTATION COORDINATOR

CHAPTER 12
LOCATIONS

There are many aspects to consider before deciding to shoot at any one location besides how much the owner of the property will charge you for the right to shoot on the premises.

How much will the permit cost? How much lead time do you need to get a permit? Will you require police and fire safety officers and how many of each? Can you use an off-duty fire officer, or must it be one on active duty? Does this location have restricted hours in which you can shoot? If you are shooting past a certain time at night or before a certain time in the morning, will you need permission from the surrounding neighbors? Will you need neighborhood consent and/or special permits for the use of firearms or special effects at this location? Will you need to close a street? Will you need additional motorcycle police officers for intermittent traffic control?—If so, how many? Will you need to *post for parking*? Will you have sufficient parking for your cast and crew at the location or will you have to find a near-by parking lot and *shuttle* everyone to the location site? Will you need to provide evidence of special or additional insurance coverage for use of this location?

The answers will vary from city, to county, to state, to country—each having its own set of fees and regulations. The sphere of Los Angeles County film permits alone encompasses approximately 35 individual cities in the Los Angeles area plus Los Angeles City and Los Angeles County, each with its own filming guidelines.

Each state has its own film commission office and there are approximately 56 metropolitan U.S. cities and 49 international cities (outside of the U.S.) that have their own film office. These offices are set up to enforce their specific film regulations, offer information, promote filmmaking in their city and to assist the filmmakers who choose to shoot in their area.

A good location manager will be able to help determine not only where each location should be but also ascertain the specific fees, regulations and restrictions that come with. On bigger shows and/or shows with several locations to find, it is usually necessary to have an assistant location manager as well.

There are independent location services that will help you find all your locations. Some that represent specific properties and others that specialize in specific types of locations (*only* warehouses and office buildings, *only* mansions, *only* schools and hospitals, etc.).

There are also film permit services that provide information, permits (they will pick them up and bring them right to you), police and fire safety officers and will arrange to post for parking and/or collect neighborhood signatures when they're necessary.

The number of locations you need to find, the cost of each and consideration of your budget will determine the combination of location staff and/or services utilized on your show. Clearly, a location manager (or service) working in conjunction with a film permit service is ideal.

FORMS INCLUDED IN THIS SECTION

Location Information Sheet 150
Location List 151
Request to Film During Extended Hours 152

LOCATION INFORMATION SHEET

SHOW __THE WATCHER__
LOCATION MANAGER __B. SCOUT__
PERMIT SERVICE __PAT'S PERMIT SERVICE__
CONTACT __PAT__
PHONE # __555 - 1172__

PRODUCTION # __0100__
(SCRIPTED) LOCATION
__HERBY'S DAD'S OFFICE__
DATE(S) __6-15-93__
[✓] INT.   [ ] EXT.   [✓] DAY   [ ] NIGHT

ACTUAL LOCATION
(Address & Phone #)

__1000 ATLANTIC BLVD., SUITE 700__
__LOS ANGELES, CA__
__555 - 7000__

DATE & DAYS

	# of days	dates
Prep:	1	6-14-93
Shoot:	1	6-15-93
Strike:	1	6-16-93

LOCATION OF NEAREST EMERGENCY MEDICAL FACILITY

__BEVERLY HILLS HOSPITAL__
__2000 TINSELTOWN RD.__
__BEVERLY HILLS__

CONTACTS

Owner(s)
OFFICES OF:
DEWEY, CHEATEM & HOWE
Name(s) __CHARLES CHEATEM__
Address __1000 ATLANTIC #700__
__L.A. 90067__
Phone/FAX# __555 - 7000__
Beeper # _____

Representative(s)

Company: __LOCATION FINDERS, INC.__
Contact: __BORIS__
Address: __5153 RAILROAD DR.__
__LA   90003__
Phone/FAX# __555 - 3172__
Beeper # __555 - 3000__

LOCATION SITE RENTAL FEE

Full Amount $ __2,000__
Amount for PREP days $ __500__
Amount for SHOOT days $ __1,000__
Amount for STRIKE days $ __500__
Deposit $ __500__   Due on __6/1/93__
[ ] Refundable   [✓] Apply to total fee
Balance $ __1,500__   Due on __6/13/93__

O.T. after __12__ hrs. per day @ $ __100__ per hr.
__ANY__ Additional days @ $ __1,000__ per day

Additional charges:
Phone $ __50/DAY__
Utilities $ __INCL.__
Parking $ __150__
(Other) _____ $ _____

CHECK OFF LIST

[✓] Location Agreement	[ ] Signed Release from Neighbors	[✓]	Allocated Parking For
[✓] Certificate of Insurance	[✓] Prepared map to Location	[✓]	Equipment
[✓] Permit	[ ] Heaters/Fans/Air Conditioners	[✓]	Honeywagons
[✓] Fire Safety Officer(s)	[✓] Lay-out Board/Drop Clothes	[✓]	Cast Vehicles
[ ] Police	[ ] Utilities/Power Supply	[✓]	Crew Vehicles
[✓] Location Fee	Allocated Areas For	[✓]	Buses
[✓] Security	[✓] Extras	[ ]	Picture Vehicles
[ ] Intermittent Traffic Control	[✓] Dressing Rms.	[ ]	Extra Tables & Chairs/Tent
[✓] Post for Parking	[✓] Eating	[ ]	Locate Parking Lot if
	[✓] Hair/Makeup		Shuttle is Necessary

© ELH Form #39

LOCATION LIST

SHOW _THE WATCHER_ PRODUCTION # _0100_

SET LOCATION	ACTUAL LOCATION (ADDRESS & PHONE)	DATE & DAYS (PREP/SHOOT/STRIKE)	CONTACTS (OWNER & REPRESENTATIVE)			
HERBY'S DAD'S OFFICE	OFFICES OF: DEWEY, CHEATEM & HOWE 1000 ATLANTIC BLVD., SUITE 700 LA 90067 555-7000	PREP: 6-14-93 SHOOT: 6-15-93 STRIKE: 6-16-93	CHARLES CHEATEM 555-7000 LOCATION FINDERS, INC. ATTN: BORIS 555-3172			
HERBY'S HOUSE	DREGER HOME 12436 SHERMAN OAKS BLVD. SHERMAN OAKS 555-3211	PREP: 6-16-93 SHOOT: 6-17 & 18 STRIKE: 6-19-93	S. DREGER H: 555-3211 O: 555-7665			

REQUEST TO FILM DURING EXTENDED HOURS

Dear Resident:

This is to inform you that **XYZ Productions** will be shooting a film entitled **The Watcher** in your neighborhood at _____. Filming activities in residential areas are normally allowed only between the hours of _____ and _____. In order to extend the hours before and/or after these times, the City requires that we obtain a signature of approval from the neighbors. The following information pertains to the dates and times of our scheduled shoot and any specific information you may need to know regarding our filming activities.

We have obtained or applied for all necessary City permits and maintain all legally required liability insurance. A copy of our film permit will be on file at the City Film Office and will also be available at our shooting location.

FILMING DAYS/HOURS REQUESTED: on_____ (date(s)
 from _____ (a.m.) (p.m.) to _____ (a.m.) (p.m.)
 and _____ (date(s)
 from _____ (a.m.) (p.m.) to _____ (a.m.) (p.m.)

THE FOLLOWING ACTIVITIES ARE PLANNED FOR THE EXTENDED HOURS:
_____

We appreciate your hospitality and cooperation. We wish to make filming on your street a pleasant experience for both you and us. If you have any questions or concerns before or during the filming, please feel free to call our Production Office and ask for me or the Production Manager.

Sincerely yours,

_____
Location Manager

_____
Production Company

_____
Phone No.

We would appreciate it if you would complete and sign where indicated below. A representative from our company will be by within the next day or two to pick-up this form.

_____

❏   I DO NOT OBJECT TO THE EXTENDED FILMING HOURS
❏   I DO OBJECT TO THE EXTENDED FILMING HOURS

COMMENTS:

NAME: _____
ADDRESS: _____
PHONE #: (Optional) _____

Chapter 13
Distant Location

Additional Distant Location Checklist

☐ Establish a relationship with local film commission office

☐ Make travel arrangements

☐ Secure hotel accommodations

☐ Prepare a Movement List

☐ Prepare a list of airline schedules to and from the location(s)

☐ Arrange with the airline or travel agency to have someone at the airport to meet cast and crew members and help with arriving equipment

☐ Open an account with the airline for the shipment of dailies

☐ Obtain a supply of packing slips, air bills, labels, heavy tape, etc., for shipping the film each night

☐ Open a local bank account

☐ Have outside phone line(s) installed in the production office if at all possible

☐ Locate a source for hiring local crew, drivers, office help, extras, etc.

☐ Rent typewriters and a copier machine for the production office

☐ Order a portable screen & projector or a VCR and monitor to screen dailies

☐ Open an account at a local gas station

☐ Locate a source for rental cars and motor homes

☐ Prepare a room list

☐ Prepare a local contact list that includes the:
   (1) names, addresses and phone numbers of a doctor, a dentist, paramedics and a hospital **
   (2) local weather reports in the area

☐ Prepare a list of local restaurants, laundry facilities, car rental agencies, etc. for cast/crew members **

☐ Prepare a list of local shooting locations **

☐ Locate a source for flowers, fruit baskets, etc. for cast and VIP arrivals

☐ Locate clothing racks for the Wardrobe Department (if needed)

☐ Arrange to rent a refrigerator, coffee machine, etc. for the production office

☐ Find out if refrigerators are available for cast and crew to rent

** *(Add directions and/or maps whenever possible)*. Keep maps of how to get to each location in the production office at all times.

Tack a call sheet and map to the next day's location on the production office door when you close-up for the night.

WORKING WITH THE HOTEL

Supply the hotel with a listing of arrivals (names, dates and times of arrival), what type of room each person is to have and/or requests based on the hotel's availability (a suite, a king-size bed, two beds, a room on the ground floor, etc.) and indicate when each of the rooms is to be vacated. Keep the reservations clerk alerted as to any last-minute additions and/or changes in arrivals and departures.

Reserve additional hotel rooms for: a production office, an accounting office, a transportation office, camera and sound equipment, an editing room and a wardrobe room. Rooms for equipment, editing and wardrobe should be on the ground floor and should have dead-bolt locks on the doors.

Make sure the hotel is aware of the Company's parking needs and can supply sufficient parking space for production vehicles and trucks.

Make sure the hotel has rooms ready for check-in when cast and crew members arrive—even if they arrive early in the day (before "check-in" time.)

Arrange with the hotel management for cast and crew members to pay for their own incidental charges.

Keep your own list (HOTEL ROOM LOG) of when each person checks in and out to compare against hotel bills. It may be helpful to keep two lists — one in alphabetical order for quick reference and one according to the cast/crew list.

Channel all complaints about hotel rooms and facilities through the production office.

If the hotel is busy, think about reserving a couple of extra rooms—just in case the schedule changes and additional cast/crew members have to be brought to location earlier than anticipated (most hotels will not charge you for holding the extra rooms, as long as you release the ones you won't be needing early each afternoon, so they can be rented that night.)

Find out the status of available rooms should your show run over schedule and the Company have to stay longer than anticipated.

Check-out the availability of rooms at other hotels/motels in the area should they be needed.

Find out if the hotel has a (banquet or conference) room that could be used to screen dailies each evening or for production meetings if needed.

Check the hours of the hotel's coffee shop. If they do not open early enough or stay open late enough, they may be willing to make special arrangements to open early for breakfast (before "call" time) and stay open after wrap.

If the hotel has a beauty shop, check to see if it could be made available to the Company early each morning for cast members to have their hair and make-up done before leaving for location.

If the Company is shooting nights, make arrangements with "Housekeeping" for the maids not to awaken cast/crew in the morning (and let the coffee shop know your hours have changed.)

Get permission to post a call sheet in the hotel lobby each night.

SHIPPING DAILIES

You will be opening an account with the Air Cargo division of the airline you choose for the shipment of dailies, and you will be sending each night's shipment **Over the Counter**

Select an airline that flies non-stop to your destination with the most evening flights. If it's impossible to get a direct flight, choose a route that has as few stops as possible. This will lessen the chances of the film being unloaded at the wrong stop.

If you call the airline, a representative will usually come to your office to open an account and to give you blank waybills and flight schedules.

Keep the flight schedules of more than the one airline in case there's a problem with the airline or their flight schedule does not meet your needs in a *rush* situation and you have to ship dailies via another carrier. You should not have to open accounts with other airlines. On the rare occasion you would be using another carrier, your driver can pay *cash* and fill out a new waybill at the counter.

Be sure to keep a copy of each waybill in case your shipment is delayed, mislaid or lost. (They also provide back-up to the shipping bills.) It is a good idea to keep a log of every shipment that leaves the production office indicating: date, way-bill number, flight number, arrival and departure times and the contents of your shipment (the number of reels you're shipping, the number of rolls of sound tape and still film, any equipment you may be returning, etc.)

It is best to have a runner from the office or a courier pick up your daily shipment. This person should go to the airport before you start shipping dailies and introduce herself to the airline personnel who will be handling the film shipment when it comes in each night. (A gratuity or two might also be a good idea in this situation.) Should there be a problem with the flight or the routing of the dailies, it would help to know the airport routine and to be on good terms with the staff.

Once the film starts arriving, your runner/courier will open the box(es) and separate the film for the lab, the 1/4" sound tapes, the still film, the envelope(s) for the office (you should "pouch" copies of all your daily paperwork back to the home office via the daily shipment each night) and whatever else you have sent. The runner will drop the film and sound off that night and deliver the remainder to the office first thing the next morning for distribution.

Labels on the box(es) should be addressed to the production office (always include the office phone number) with the notation: **Hold for Pickup** boxes should also indicate or have labels that read: UNDEVELOPED FILM—DO NOT X-RAY.

It is best to ship film on the same flight each evening. The last flight out is the one usually selected to allow a full day's worth of shooting (or most of one) to be sent out. If shooting for the day is not completed by the time the driver has to leave, the camera crew will have to "break" at a designated time and send what they have.

The driver making the airport run should have the packed boxes, a completed waybill, a memo indicating the flight information and a description of what is in each of the boxes you are sending. He should call the production coordinator from the airport to confirm that the boxes got on board and that the flight was on schedule. Or if there is a problem that the boxes had to be sent on another airline or that the flight is going to be delayed. The production coordinator will in turn call the runner or courier on the other end to confirm an estimated arrival time and to give him the waybill number. When the driver returns, he will give the production coordinator a completed copy of the waybill.

As most labs are closed from Friday night to Sunday night, you will ship Friday and Saturday's footage on Sunday afternoon so it arrives before midnight on Sunday.

FORMS INCLUDED IN THIS SECTION

Travel Movement 156
Hotel Room Log 157
Hotel Room List 158
Meal Allowance... 159
Sample Travel Memo
    to Cast and Crew 160-161

TRAVEL MOVEMENT

PROD# 0100

SHOW __The Watcher__
TRAVEL FROM __Los Angeles__ TO __Milwaukee, Wisconsin__
DAY/DATE __Monday, Sept. 20, 1993__ AIRLINE __Wisconsin Air__
TYPE OF AIRCRAFT __747__ MEAL(S) __Lunch__ MOVIE __Yes__
FLIGHT# __220__ DEPARTURE TIME __11 Am__ ARRIVAL __5:15 Pm__ FLIGHT STOPS IN _____
CHANGE TO FLIGHT # _____ DEPARTURE _____ ARRIVAL _____

NAME	POSITION	GROUND TRANSPORTATION TO AIRPORT	TO BE PICKED UP @	GROUND TRANSPORTATION FROM AIRPORT
Swifty Deals	Producer	Driver to Pickup	10 A	Milwaukee Prod. Asst. to Pick up Crew
Sid Celluloid	Director	Driver to Pickup	9:45A	Outside of Baggage
Fred Filmer	UPM	Airport Shuttle Van	9:30A	Area
F. Stopp	Dir. of Photog.	Airport Shuttle Van	9:45A	

HOTEL __Milwaukee Grand__ DIRECT # TO PRODUCTION OFFICE (414) 555-2276
Address __1234 Wisconsin Blvd.__ FAX# (414) 555-2352
__Milwaukee Wisconsin__ ADDITIONAL INFO. _____
Phone # __(414) 555-7000__

© ELH Form #41

HOTEL ROOM LOG

SHOW __THE WATCHER__
HOTEL __MILWAUKEE GRAND__
LOCATION __MILWAUKEE, WISCONSIN__

PROD# __0100__
CONTACT __JEAN__
PHONE# __(414) 555-2000__

NAME	POSITION	ROOM#	TYPE OF ROOM	RATE	DATE IN	DATE OUT	TOTAL DAYS
SWIFTY DEALS	PRODUCER	215	SUITE	150	9/20/93	10/23/93	33
SID CELLULOID	DIRECTOR	220	SUITE	150	9/20/93	10/24/93	34
FRED FILMER	UPM	112	KING	85	9/20/93	10/30/93	40
F. STOPP	DP	103	KING	85	9/20/93	10/23/93	33
A. DEES	1ST ASST. DIR	330	QUEEN	80	9/20/93	10/23/93	33

HOTEL ROOM LIST

SHOW ___THE WATCHER___

HOTEL ___MILWAUKEE GRAND___

ADDRESS ___12345 WISCONSIN BLVD.___
___MILWAUKEE, WISCONSIN___

PHONE# ___(414) 555-2000___ FAX# ___(414) 555-2001___

PROD# ___0100___

LOCATION ___MILWAUKEE, WIS.___

LOCATION DATES ___9-20-93___

Through
___10-30-93___

NAME	POSITION	ROOM #	DIRECT #
Production Office	--------	101	555-2376
Accounting Office	--------	103	555-2372
Transportation Office	--------	105	555-2373
Editing Room	--------	107	555-3275
SWIFTY DEALS	PRODUCER	215	
SID CELLULOID	DIRECTOR	220	
A. DEES	1ST ASST. DIR.	330	
KATIE KANDU	SCRIPT SUPV'R.	307	
PAULA PROPS	PROPERTY MSTR.	217	
MIKE BOOM	SOUND MIXER	302	

© ELH Form #43

MEAL ALLOWANCE

SHOW __THE WATCHER__ PROD# __0100__

LOCATION __MILWAUKEE, WISCONSIN__ WEEK OF __9/20 - 26/93__

MEAL RATES
BREAKFAST $ 8—
LUNCH $ 12—
DINNER $ 20—

NAME	MON 9-20 B	L	D	TUE 9-21 B	L	D	WED 9-22 B	L	D	THUR 9-23 B	L	D	FRI 9-24 B	L	D	SAT 9-25 B	L	D	SUN 9-26 B	L	D	TOTAL	SIGNATURE
A. DEES	-	-	20	8	-	20	8	-	20	8	-	20	8	-	20	8	-	20	8	12	20	200—	*(signature)*
K. KANDU		20		8	-	20	8	-	20	8	-	20	8	-	20	8	-	20	8	12	20	200—	*(signature)*
M. BOOM	20	8		8	-	20	8	-	20	8	-	20	8	-	20	8	-	20	8	12	20	200—	*(signature)*
P. PROPS	20	8		8	-	20	8	-	20	8	-	20	8	-	20	8	-	20	8	12	20	200—	*(signature)*
C. COORDINATOR	8	12	20	8	12	20	8	12	20	8	12	20	8	12	20	8	12	20	8	12	20	280—	C. Coordinator
A. ACCOUNTANT	8	12	20	8	12	20	8	12	20	8	12	20	8	12	20	8	12	20	8	12	20	280	Accountant

TOTAL: **$1360—**

APPROVED __Fred Filmer__

TRAVEL MEMO TO CAST AND CREW

TO: **F. STOPP**

FROM: **FRED FILMER**

RE: TRAVEL & HOTEL ACCOMMODATIONS/LOCATION INFORMATION FOR
            CAST & CREW TRAVELING TO **MILWAUKEE, WISCONSIN**

As per your [✓] contract [ ] deal memo, you will be provided with **one (1), business-class**, round-trip airfare(s) to **MILWAUKEE, WISCONSIN** (destination). At the present time, you are scheduled to travel on **MONDAY, SEPTEMBER 20, 1993** with plane reservations as follows:

        AIRLINE: **WISCONSIN AIR** FLIGHT **#237**
        DEPARTS FROM: **LAX** AT: 11:00 ((a.m.))(p.m.)
        ARRIVAL TIME: 5:15 (a.m.)((p.m.))

The following meals will be served during your flight:
        [ ] Breakfast [✓] Lunch [ ] Dinner [✓] Snack

There [✓] will [ ] will not be a movie shown during your flight.

The following ground transportation will be provided for you:
        TO AIRPORT: **AIRPORT SHUTTLE VAN**
        You will be picked-up at: **9:45** ((a.m.))(p.m.)
        FROM AIRPORT: **UPON ARRIVAL**

You will be staying at:
        MILWAUKEE GRAND HOTEL
        12345 WISCONSIN BLVD.
        MILWAUKEE
        414/555-2000

The following accommodations have been reserved for you:
        [ ] Condo/Apartment [ ] Hotel Suite [ ] Rm. w/a kitchenette
        [✓] Rm. w/a king-sz. bed [ ] Rm. w/a queen sz. bed
        [ ] Rm. w/two beds [ ] Rm. on the ground floor
        [ ] Other_____

On location,   [✓] you will be provided with a vehicle
                [ ] we're not able to provide you with a vehicle
                [ ] you will be sharing the use of a vehicle

Your per diem will be **$40** per day.

Please be aware that upgrading your air fare, bringing guests, reserving a larger room, etc. is to be done at your expense. You can make additional plane reservations through **STAR STUDDED TRAVEL AGENCY** at **555-4032**, and you will be informed as to the additional costs. All hotel incidental charges (room service, long distance phone calls, etc.) will be charged directly to you by the hotel.

All department heads are requested to supply **CONNIE** with a list of any equipment/wardrobe/props, etc., that will need to be shipped to location. We will need to know

(continued on the following page)

how many pieces each department will be shipping and if any of the pieces are oversized. Shipping tags and labels can be picked-up at the production office.

Let **CONNIE** know as soon as possible as to any special requests you might have such as renting a car (if one is not provided for you) or a small refrigerator for your room. Every effort will be made to accommodate your requests.

Reports indicate that current weather conditions in **MILWAUKEE** are **RAINY & APPROXIMATELY 70 degrees** and will become [ ] warmer [ ] much warmer [ ] cooler [✓] much colder [ ] wetter as our schedule progresses. We will be shooting **FIVE (5)** nights and the weather at night for this time of year is anticipated to be **25 DEGREES**. Please pack accordingly.

At the present, your return flight is scheduled for **SATURDAY, OCTOBER 23RD** on **WISCONSIN AIR**, Flight #236, leaving MILWAUKEE at **9:15** (a.m.) (p.m.) and arriving in **LAX** at **11:30** (a.m.) (p.m.)

If there are changes in our shooting schedule or unforeseen delays that would extend our location shooting, you will be informed and your return reservations updated.

Your room will be reserved until the completion of [ ] your role [✓] production, and your return flight will be booked accordingly. If you wish to remain in **MILWAUKEE**, or to travel elsewhere at the completion of [✓] principal photography [ ] your role, please check with us first as your services may be needed for looping and/or pick-up shots. We may not know immediately if and/or when, but would let you know ASAP. If you choose to remain in **MILWAUKEE**, however, it will be your responsibility to make further arrangements with the hotel and to re-book your own airline tickets. Please just let us know of your plans and that you will not be returning with the rest of the company.

If you have any additional questions regarding your travel or location accommodations, please contact **CONNIE COORDINATOR** at **555-3331**.

CHAPTER 14

IMMIGRATION, CUSTOMS AND VISA INFORMATION

Our business continues to become increasingly *international* as more U.S. based films are being shot in other countries and cast and crew members from other countries are being recruited to work on U.S. films. There is a definite controversy over this continuing trend; but whether you agree or not, you should have a basic knowledge of what it entails. The following is a brief description of immigration, customs and visa information. As this is an area that requires a considerable amount of legal expertise in addition to the precise preparation of petitions and applications, consultations with labor and management organizations, documentation of work searches, etc.,—it is an area primarily handled by attorneys who specialize in immigration-related matters. Consult with your attorney before any definitive plans are made to shoot out of the country or bring foreign performers or crew members into the U.S.

FILMING IN A FOREIGN COUNTRY

Producers, name directors and top-name performers are generally welcome in most foreign countries; but justification for bringing in lesser-known talent is considerably more difficult in an effort to protect local work forces.

As each country has its own set of regulations, the first step is to call the embassy or consulate of the country where you wish to film to find out their specific immigration policies and requirements. Be aware that in addition to requirements to enter certain foreign countries, several also impose a **Departure Tax**: a fee to leave their country. Some will require this tax paid in its exact amount in their country's currency. Others will accept the fee in U.S. Dollars. Your travel agent or the embassy you are dealing with will inform you if the country you wish to travel to has a Departure Tax, how much it is and how it is to be paid.

Some countries have their own film office and/or film industry representatives to handle inquiries and to work with you. Less-developed countries tend to have less stringent policies; but regardless of which country it is, assume you will have to apply for a permit; and allow plenty of time to do so.

Arrangements for cast and crew members to work in a foreign country are made through **Immigration**. Arrangements for the shipment of equipment, wardrobe, props, etc., to that same foreign country are made through **Customs**. It is important to select and retain a local **Customs Broker** specializing in the entertainment industry who will assist with all your import needs and interact with an affiliate broker at your point of entry if necessary.

Depending on your destination, one of three different procedures will be required in the importation of any necessary items: 1) carnets, 2) duplicate lists, and 3) duplicate lists with bond or cash deposit requirements.

A **carnet**, which is not accepted in all countries, is a document which lists all the equipment by serial number and description. The goods are inspected by Customs prior to departure and at each point of entry and departure to ensure that all goods stay with the carriers. A **bond** based on 40 percent of the value of the goods is required to protect against claims on the carnet (although in a couple of countries, the figure is slightly higher.) The bond will cost one percent of the 40 percent figure, or a financial statement of the company applying may be sufficient to underwrite the bond. Information on carnets, carnet applications and bond forms can be obtained from one of the eight **U.S. Council for International Business** offices throughout the country which are located in:

New York/Midtown	(212) 354-4480
New York/Downtown	(212) 747-1800
Massachusetts	(617) 737-3266
Florida	(305) 592-6929

Illinois	(708) 490-9696
California/Los Angeles	(213) 386-0767
California/San Francisco	(415) 956-3356
Texas	(713) 869-5693

Some countries require less-complicated **duplicate lists**. At importation, the equipment is checked against a list, again with serial numbers required, and then re-checked at exportation to ensure that nothing has remained in the country. On the list, a **CIF value (Cost Including Freight)** will be required, which is the value of the goods at the point of entry, plus the insurance and freight paid to get the shipment there added to the total cost of the goods.

Some countries require **cash deposits**, others will accept banker's guarantees or you may be able to obtain a **T.I.B. (Temporary Importation Bond)** from the customs broker in that country.

Again, each country has different regulations. Canada, for example, has what they call an **Equivalency Requirement**: if equivalent equipment is available in Canada, you may have difficulty bringing similar U.S. goods across the border. So allow yourself enough lead time to ascertain requirements and restrictions, apply for permits, fill out applications, gather serial numbers and the value of your equipment and post bonds and/or deposits.

Customs and Immigration are government entities and no matter how urgent our needs may be, they will work within their own time-frame and will not make exceptions for anyone... even filmmakers.

TEMPORARAILY EMPLOYING TALENT AND TECHNICAL PERSONNEL FROM OTHER COUNTRIES

The following summarizes the requirements for bringing cast and crew members from other countries into the U.S.

The **Immigration Act of 1990** introduced the newly-created **O and P Visa Classifications** for the entry of importation of artists, entertainers, athletes, performers and related support personnel. Prior to the 1990 Act, these individuals would have entered under the H-1B classification of distinguished merit and ability. With the introduction of the O and P visas, the **H-1B Classification** is now limited to individuals in *specialty occupations*. The **H-2B Classification**, although more complicated to qualify for, remains an option for those who do not qualify in the **O Non-Immigrant Visa** and **P Non-Immigrant Visa** categories.

O VISAS

The O-1 Visa: This visa is granted to those who possess *extraordinary ability* in the arts, sciences, education, business or athletics, or have a demonstrated record of extraordinary achievement in the motion picture and television industry.

The O-2 Visa: Granted to those entering the U.S. temporarily and solely for the purpose of accompanying and assisting an O-1 alien of extraordinary ability. These individuals must be highly skilled, possess all appropriate qualifications and significant prior experience and perform support services that cannot be readily performed by U.S. workers. Documentation is not only required to establish the qualifications of the O-2 petitioner, but also the past working relationship with the O-1 alien.

The O-3 Visa: Granted to accompanying family members of O-1 or O-2 aliens.

Before a petition may be approved for the O category, a **Consultation Requirement** must be met. In the field of motion picture and television, consultation with a labor union or guild and management organization in the area of the alien's ability is required. The mandatory consultation requirement allows unions to have input on all O-1 and O-2 petitions requiring services in the motion picture and television industry, which affects the adjudication of these petitions. However, it is important to note that consultation with a management organization is also required, which may not be consistent with the union. Further, these consultations are advisory in nature only and are not binding on the ultimate decision of the Immigration Service.

The O-1 and O-2 visa petition may only be approved for the time required to complete a specific event or performance and may not exceed three years. Extensions are granted one year at a time to continue or complete the same event or activity.

P VISAS

The P-1 Visa: This classification pertains to athletes who perform at an internationally recognized level of performance and seek to enter the U.S. temporarily for the purpose of competing at a specific competition or tournament, or for a limited athletic season. It also pertains to those who are members of internationally recognized entertainment groups. (The Attorney General may waive the international recognition requirement under special circumstances for a group that is nationally recognized.)

A **P-1 entertainment group** must have been established for at least one year, and 75 percent of the performers and entertainers in the group must have been performing in the group for at least one year. This classification additionally covers aliens who function as support personnel to individual athletes, an athletic team or an entertainment group.

The P-2 Visa: This category is reserved for an alien who performs as an artist or entertainer, either individually or as part of a group, and is to perform under a **Reciprocal Exchange Program** which is between an organization(s) in the U.S. and an organization in one or more foreign states. The P-2 entertainer petition must be accompanied by evidence that the group has been established and performing regularly for a period of at least one year and contain a statement from the petitioner listing each member of the group and the exact dates which that member has been employed on a regular basis by the group. Evidence must also be submitted to substantiate the international recognition of the group. These petitions must also include: 1) a copy of the formal reciprocal exchange agreement; 2) a statement from the sponsoring organization describing the reciprocal exchange as it relates to the specific petition for which P-2 classification is sought; 3) evidence that the appropriate labor organization in the U.S. was involved in negotiation, or has concurred with, the reciprocal exchange; and 4) evidence that the aliens and U.S. artists or entertainers subject to the reciprocal exchange possess comparable skills and experience.

The P-3 Visa: An alien who performs as an artist or entertainer, individually or as part of a group, and seeks to enter the U.S. to perform, teach or coach as such an artist or entertainer or with such a group under a commercial or noncommercial program that is culturally unique may qualify for this classification. A P-3 petition must be accompanied by substantiation from recognized experts attesting to the authenticity and excellence of the alien's or group's skills in performing or presenting the unique or traditional art form. Evidence must also be submitted indicating that most of the performances or presentations will be culturally unique events sponsored by educational, cultural or governmental agencies.

The P-4 Visa: The family of a P-1, P-2 or P-3 alien who is accompanying or following to join such alien may enter on this visa.

As with the O non-immigrant category, a **consultation requirement** is also required with the P non-immigrant category. Written evidence of consultation with an appropriate labor organization regarding the nature of the work to be done and the alien's qualifications is mandatory. The permitted length of stay for all P classifications is generally the time necessary to complete the event or events for which non-immigrant status is sought with a maximum period of one year. Extensions of stay may be granted for periods of one year to complete the event.

Performers' agents, who routinely negotiate employment for their clients, are allowed to file O and P classification petitions on their behalf. Such petitions must provide a complete itinerary of the event(s) as well as the contract(s) between the third-party employer(s) and the alien. The contract between the agent and the alien specifying the wage offered and the conditions of employment must also be submitted.

Once the Immigration Service approves a petition on Form I-797, the applicant must apply for a visa at a U.S. Consulate abroad by presenting the original Approval Notice and completing a visa application form. When the visa is issued, the applicant may enter the US and work on the project authorized by the approved petition.

H-2B Visas

Entertainment personnel who do not qualify as aliens of extraordinary or exceptional ability to be classified in the O and P categories, or as support personnel of an O-1 or P alien, will have to consider using the H-2B classification. For a lesser known entertainer or technician or support personnel involved with a project begun abroad that needs to be completed in the U.S. where the principal entertainer is a U.S. citizen, this category is the best option available.

Requirements for the H-2B classification are: 1) the position to be filled by the alien is one for which the employer has a temporary need, and 2) certification is sought from the U.S. Department of Labor that unemployed persons capable of performing the labor are not available in the U.S. and the employment of the alien will not adversely affect the wages and working conditions of workers similarly employed in the U.S.

The **Department of Labor** (DOL) has published detailed guidelines for the criteria and procedures to be followed for all H-2 requests in the entertainment industry. Applications for temporary **Labor Certification** should be filed at least forty-five days prior to the proposed commencement of services to ensure completion and processing by the DOL. In addition to submitting **Form ETA-750, Part A**, the application must include an itinerary of locations where the alien will work, together with duration of work in each location, as well as documentation of any recruitment efforts taken by the employer. Proof is required to establish that there are not sufficient U.S. workers able, willing, qualified and available for the employment.

Two principal sources of recruitment are always required—an advertisement placed in a national (trade) publication six weeks prior to filing the paperwork, advertising for this particular position/role and a request to the appropriate labor union regarding membership availability.

When it comes to **Talent**, casting session information and a letter from the Casting Director stating the particulars of the casting search in the

U.S. and reasons for the use of an actor from another country should be included. It must be stressed in the letter that this particular actor is the only one who can properly portray the part as it is written.

The Department of Labor grants labor certifications for periods not exceeding 12 months. If the intended duration of employment is more than one year, a new application must be submitted for any additional year or part thereof; but *temporary employment* must not exceed three (3) years.

All applications, itineraries, labor certifications, letters and documentations are to be submitted to the **Employment Development Department—Alien Certification Office.** After reviewing said materials, they will then forward everything to the **United States Department of Labor**. The Department of Labor will then certify or turn down all requests for U.S. work permits.

With regard to talent, a copy of all applications and documentations should also be sent to the **Screen Actors Guild** where they are reviewed and a recommendation of acceptance or denial is then issued and forwarded to the **Immigration and Naturalization Service** (INS). Check with your local SAG office to find out who your contact is pertaining to the employment of aliens.

After certification approval has been obtained from the Department of Labor, the **temporary labor certification** together with completed **I-129H Forms** are sent to the Regional Service Center of the **Immigration and Naturalization Service** having jurisdiction over the intended place of employement. Covering three pages, this form requires information on the petitioner, the beneficiary and a third page requiring the signature of the petitioner.

As the DOL determination is only advisory, INS can still approve H-2B classification even in the absence of the certification. Petitions submitted to the INS should include a statement from the employer explaining the reasons it is infeasible to hire U.S. workers to fill the position offered and the factors that make the position offered temporary in nature.

Once the I-129-H form is processed and labor certification is cleared, the applicant can go to the **American Consulate** in their country and apply for their visa. They cannot apply until it has been approved and cleared in this country. The Immigration Service will notify the petitioning employer as well as the appropriate consulate that said individual has been approved for a visa.

With respect to talent, when the Immigration Service has finalized everything, the actors must be cleared with SAG—either checked through **Station 12** or **Taft-Hartleyed** before they can work.

For further information, first, contact your attorney—then: **Employment Development Department—Alien Certification Office, United States Department of Labor** and **Immigration and Naturalization Service** office closest to your base of operations.

[Note: The information on visas was provided by Peter Loewy, Esq., Managing Partner of the law firm, Fragomen, Del Rey and Bernsen, P.C., a national law firm practicing solely in the area of immigration and nationality law. Mr. Loewy is based in the West Los Angeles, California, office.]

Chapter 15
A Little Post-Production

Most production people, even very experienced ones, find they know very little about post-production. They are hired in pre-production, work through the end of production and then usually turn everything over to a post-production supervisor and move on to the next picture.

Post-production is such a huge and complicated subject—made even more complicated by all the new technology—that it could warrant an entire book in itself. However, even with a good post-production supervisor handling everything for you, production personnel often find themselves involved with certain facets of post-production prior to the end of principal photography. A basic understanding of post-production (and post-production related costs) is needed to prepare a more accurate budget. It is also important to be aware of just how significant post-production is to your finished picture.

Basics that are always good to know are: how to plan a post-production schedule, guidelines for preparing screen credits and some essential terminology.

It is also helpful to be familiar with standard delivery requirements—those elements (e.g., film, sound track, script, contracts, cast list, stills) that must be turned over to the distributor of your film when post-production has been completed. Much of the necessary paperwork can be accumulated ahead of time (during principal photography) to save on time during post.

Sample Post-Production Schedule

Post-production schedules can vary from four to six weeks on a quick television movie to eight to ten months on some theatrical features. The following is a reasonable schedule based on a modestly-budgeted film—not overly extravagant, yet allowing enough time to make sure everything is done properly.

This schedule reflects a picture that is being cut on film as opposed to videotape. (Editing on videotape will decrease the amount of time it takes to cut the picture, although your costs will remain relatively the same, if not more, due to the high expense of the videotape editing equipment.) There are several videotape editing systems available (i.e., Ediflex, CMX 6000, Laser Edit, etc.); and although many producers prefer the speed they offer, the majority of films are still being edited on Moviolas and flatbeds.

The process of editing begins during principal photography—as soon as filming has been completed on an entire sequence. The following reflects the weeks following the completion of principal photography.

WEEK NUMBER ONE
The Editor receives the last batch of dailies and the Script Supervisor's final notes. She continues her "assembly".

WEEK NUMBER TWO
The Producer should start assembling a list of tentative screen credits. By the end of this week, the Editor should have a completed assembly of the picture (sometimes referred to as the **Editor's cut**).

WEEKS NUMBER THREE THROUGH SIX

Once the Editor has completed her cut, the Director then takes the next several weeks to add his changes. It is reasonable to assume that he will complete a "first" cut by the end of Week Number Four, and a final "Director's cut" by the end of Week Nunber Six

DGA regulations specify that the Director of a feature film budgeted over $1,500,000 is to receive up to ten weeks, or one day of editing time for each two days of originally scheduled photography, whichever is greater, (following the editor's assembly of the picture) to complete the Director's cut. The Director has up to 20 days to complete his cut on a television motion picture running 120 minutes or less; and on a television motion picture running more than two (2) hours, he has 20 days plus five days for each additional hour in excess of two hours. Although the Director is entitled to the above-specified number of days in which to have his cut, those who work well with their editor(s) and are also cognizant of delivery date requirements and the financial concerns of the company, will not usually take the full allotted time and will complete their cut within a reasonable time frame.

WEEK NUMBER SEVEN

The Producer will screen the Director's cut and start adding her own changes to the picture.

Although not final, a cassette of the picture (without time code) should be given to the composer so he can start thinking about and working on the music

WEEK NUMBER EIGHT

If inserts are needed, they should be shot and cut in no later than this week

The Producer should be completed with his/her picture changes by the end of this week (the "final cut")

WEEK NUMBER NINE

Screen credits should be finalized.

The Assistant Editor will start ordering opticals.

Transfer the final cut to video (with time code) for sound effects, dialogue and music editors, and the composer.

Spot the picture with sound effects and dialogue editors.

Spot the picture with the composer for the second time.

If the picture is a feature, the Editor should start cutting the "television" version.

WEEK NUMBER ELEVEN

Begin looping (A.D.R.) actors.

WEEKS NUMBER TEN THROUGH THIRTEEN

These weeks (while the sound effects and Foley editors, dialogue editor and the composer are preparing their work), the opticals are finalized, opticals and credits cut into the picture and the negative cutter begins cutting the negative.

WEEKS NUMBER FOURTEEN AND FIFTEEN

Assuming that the sound track of this picture will be recorded in stereo, it will take approximately four weeks to dub the show. It would be cost effective to spend the first two weeks pre-dubbing the dialogue.

If pre-dubbing is done during these two weeks, this is also the time in which the picture is scored (prior to the final dub.)

WEEK NUMBER SIXTEEN AND SEVENTEEN

Final dub (or mix).

WEEK NUMBER EIGHTEEN

Add any sound "Fixes" to (or Sweeten) the picture. If there are any major sound fixes, they should be made to the master tracks. Minor fixes can be done at the same time as print mastering.

Make a Print Master.

Make a Mono Master.

Make M & E (music and effects) tracks for foreign distribution

If required, make a television/stereo version and in some cases, a television/mono version of the picture.

Time the picture for color.

WEEK NUMBER NINETEEN

Strike a First Trial Print.

Make additional color adjustments as necessary.

WEEK NUMBER TWENTY

Strike an Answer Print.

Prepare your delivery requirements.

BASIC POST-PRODUCTION TERMINOLOGY

The terms are listed in order of how a film progresses through the post-production process.

WORK PRINT (OR DAILIES)

A positive print made from the Director's selected takes. This is what the editor works with in assembling the picture.

NEGATIVE CUTTER

Your negative cutter is responsible for accepting the exposed negative from the lab. She breaks the negative down into individual scenes and maintains a log of each scene by key numbers (numbers on the edge of the film used to match the work print to the negative.) The negative cutter pulls sections of negative for reprints and opticals and most importantly, cuts the negative to match the final cut work print. This person is hired prior to the start of principal photography.

SYNCING DAILIES

The matching or synchronization of the sound track to the picture. This is accomplished by matching the sound of the clapping slate from the sound track with the exact spot in the picture where the slate comes together.

CODING DAILIES

Printing matching numbers on the edge of the work print and the sound track for the purpose of maintaining synchronization while cutting the picture.

OPTICALS

Visual effects such as dissolves, fades and enlargements. This may also include titles when they appear over action.

INSERTS

Inserts are brief shots which are used to accentuate a story point. They are usually close-ups or extreme close-ups and can include anything from the time on a wrist watch to a hand writing a note. If time restrictions did not allow for inserts to be shot during production or if it is decided after the completion of principal photography that an insert is needed, they can easily be shot on a small insert stage anywhere and at any time. Depending on the shot, the actual actors are generally not needed. It's important, however, that the props and the wardrobe match exactly.

SPOTTING

Running the picture with the Composer to determine where music will begin and end for each scene. And separately running the picture for the Sound Effects Editors to determine where and what sound effects are to be added and/or enhanced and for the Dialogue Editor to determine where dialogue needs to be replaced and/or added.

SOUND EFFECTS

The adding, replacing or enhancing of sounds of any kind which are not recorded during production or were recorded but deemed unusable. Sound effects can include anything from the sound of a kiss to that of a major explosion.

FOLEY

A method of recording sound effects that involve physical movement—such as footsteps—which can be duplicated on a sound stage. These effects are recorded by a Foley Artist who reproduces the exact movement on the stage while watching the action being projected on a screen.

LOOPING OR A.D.R. (AUTOMATIC DIALOGUE REPLACEMENT)

Re-recording production dialogue that has been deemed unusable for any number of reasons (airplane flying overhead during the take, unintelligible word, etc.). The actors record the dialogue while watching themselves projected on a screen and listening to the dialogue as it had been recorded on the set. The new dialogue that is being recorded must match the lip movement of the actor on the screen.

Looping also encompasses the adding of off-stage dialogue that had not been previously recorded or miscellaneous crowd or background voices ("walla"). These are also done while the actors view the projected scene.

SCORING

The recording of the music that is to be used in the film.

DUBBING

As a film term, this can also be referred to as **mixing**, i.e., the blending of dialogue, music and sound effects.

PRE-DUBBING

When there are so many sound tracks being used that it makes it difficult to maintain control, it is advantageous to mix several sound tracks together prior to the final mix. This is usually done with dialogue when mixing in stereo. However, if you have a large number of sound effects tracks, you may also want to pre-mix some of them. Once the dialogue tracks are mixed, the effects and the music are balanced accordingly.

FIXES OR SWEETENING

This involves going back after the dubbing

has been completed to make minor adjustments to the sound track.

PRINT MASTER

Combining all mastered stereo tracks into a single piece of sound track. This is the final track used to make the optical sound track for release prints.

OPTICAL SOUND TRACK

This is the transferring of the print master from magnetic tape stock to optical stock which is then combined with the negative to make a release print.

TIMING

This is a process in which the color and density of the picture is balanced from one scene to another throughout the picture. It is done at the lab with the lab's color timer, the Editor and occasionally the Director of Photography.

FIRST TRIAL PRINT

This is a first complete print of the film with sound track, opticals and titles struck from the cut negative. This print will indicate where additional minor color and density adjustments have to be made. Several trial prints may be necessary before an Answer Print is struck.

ANSWER PRINT

The first acceptable release print struck from the negative.

SCREEN CREDITS

One of the things a Production Manager or Production Coordinator is often asked to do before wrapping a show is to supply the company or Producer with a list of tentative screen credits. Screen credits vary a lot from show to show, but there are some basic guidelines that all shows follow.

Guild and/or union requirements govern the placement of certain screen credits. Some credits are given based on an unwritten industry-accepted pecking order, some are negotiated before the beginning of principal photography and others are given at the sole discretion of the producer after the completion of principal photography.

The following are some basic guild/union guidelines pertaining to screen credits and a couple of examples of what a *reasonable* set of credits might look like for a motion picture and a movie for television. Note that you are not bound by any of the union/guild requirements if you are not a signatory to that particular union/guild; however, many of the union rules pertaining to screen credit placements are also routinely utilized on non-union shows. And again, be aware that much of the positioning is negotiated and/or determined by the Producer.

DIRECTORS GUILD OF AMERICA (DGA)

DIRECTOR—THEATRICAL MOTION PICTURE

The director of the film shall be accorded credit on a separate card on all positive prints and all videodiscs/videocassettes of the film in size of type not less than 50 percent of the size in which the title of the motion picture is displayed or of the largest size in which credit is accorded to any other person, whichever is greater. Such credit shall be on the last title card appearing prior to principal photography, or the first card following the last scene of the picture.

DIRECTOR—TELEVISION

The director shall be given credit in the form *Directed by* on a separate card which shall be the last title card before the first scene of the picture or the first title card following the last scene of the picture. However, in the case of split credits where credit is given to any person before the first scene of the picture, the director shall be given the last solo credit card before the first scene of the picture. The director's name on the screen shall be no less than 40 percent of the episode or series title, whichever is larger.

UNIT PRODUCTION MANAGER/FIRST ASSISTANT DIRECTOR/SECOND ASSISTANT DIRECTOR—THEATRICAL MOTION PICTURE AND TELEVISION

Employer shall accord credit in a *prominent place* (no less than a separate card, or its equivalent in a crawl, shared by no more than three names) on all positive prints of each feature or television motion picture. The only *technical* credits which may receive a more prominent place shall be those of the Director of Photography, the Art Director and the Film Editor. The order of names on the card shall be the Unit Production Manager, First Assistant Director and Second Assistant Director; and each of such names on the card or crawl shall be of the same size and style of type. If you wish to give your Unit Production Manager the screen credit of *Production Manager*, it must be with the prior approval of the DGA.

Note: The DGA requires that you submit your tentative screen credits to them for approval of "compliance with credit provisions." The above is a brief synopsis of their credit provisions. Check the DGA basic agreement for a complete list of their credit guidelines.

SCREEN ACTORS GUILD (SAG)

PERFORMERS—THEATRICAL MOTION PICTURE

Producer agrees that a cast of characters on at least one card will be placed at the end of each theatrical feature motion picture, naming the performer and the role portrayed. All credits on this card shall be in the same size and style of type, with the arrangement, number and selection of performers listed to be at the sole discretion of the Producer. In all feature motion pictures with a cast of 50 or less, all performers shall receive credit. In all other feature motion pictures, not less than 50 shall be listed in the cast of characters required at the end of each feature motion picture in connection with theatrical exhibition, excluding performers identified elsewhere in the picture. Stunt performers need not be identified by role.

PERFORMERS—TELEVISION MOTION PICTURE

As above, at least one card at the end of each television motion picture naming the performer and role portrayed. Any performer identified by name and role elsewhere in the picture, or any performer playing a major continuing role and identified by name elsewhere in the picture, need not be listed in the cast of characters at the end of the picture.

WRITERS GUILD OF AMERICA (WGA)

WRITERS—THEATRICAL MOTION PICTURE

Credit shall be accorded as follows:

Screenplay by (single card): Indicates authorship of the screenplay, but not necessarily of the story upon which it was based. This credit must always have a "story by" credit accompanying it.

Story by: Indicates authorship of a story upon which a resulting screenplay is based.

From a Story by or **Based on a Story by: Screenplay** is based on source material other than an original story for the screenplay.

Written by: Indicates that the story and the screenplay were authored by the same person or team of writers. (Written by = Story and Screenplay by)

Writing credits as finally determined shall appear on a card immediately preceding the cards for the producer and director, provided the producer's card immediately precedes the director's card, otherwise the Writer's card shall immediately precede the director's card. No other credit except source material credit may appear on the writer's card. Credit for screenplay writer shall be in the same style and size of type as that used for the individual producer or director, whichever is larger.

WRITERS—TELEVISION

Credit shall be accorded as follows:

Teleplay by or **Story by:** based on a story with no source material, but that the writer(s) of the teleplay and the writer(s) of the story are not necessarily the same.

Written by (for story and teleplay). Indicates that the teleplay and the story were authored by the same person or team of writers. (Written by = Teleplay and Story by)

Writing credit, including source material credit, may appear on a separate card or cards immediately following the title card of a particular episode; or immediately prior to or following immediately after the director's credit.

Note: Check your Writers Guild Basic Agreement for requirements relating to the of submission of Tentative Screen Credits.

MISCELLANEOUS LOCAL CRAFT UNIONS

DIRECTOR OF PHOTOGRAPHY

Credit shall be given on a separate card adjacent to the group of cards for the Writer, Producer and Director in whichever order such cards appear in such grouping.

FILM EDITOR

Credit shall read: *Edited by* or *Editor*, and such credit shall be on a separate card in a prominent place (it is generally placed adjacent to the Art Director credit.) This credit is given only to the editor who edits the material for content, continuity and narration concept.

ART DIRECTOR

Credit shall be on a separate card adjacent to the Director of Photography credit and read **Art Director** or **Art Directors**. If the latter is used and joint credit is given, the names shall be joined by the word *"and."* If you wish to give **Production Designer** or **Production Design(ed) by** credit, prior permission must be obtained from the Local Union.

COSTUME DESIGNER

While credit is not mandatory, it may only be given to a member of the Costume Designers Guild. If given, it should read: **Costumes Designed by, Costumes by** or **Costume Designer**.

SET DECORATOR

There is no regulation calling for the specific placement of this credit other than in a *prominent place*. It usually appears directly after or shortly after the DGA (UPM, 1st Assistant Director and 2nd Assistant. Director) card in the end credits.

MAKE-UP ARTIST/HAIR STYLIST

The requirement of this Local is just that both the Make-up Artist and the Hair Stylist receive screen credit. Placement is at the discretion of the Producer.

MAIN TITLES AND END TITLES

Main Titles refer to the screen credits that appear before the picture begins and **End Credits** appear following the picture.

If your film is for television, check the network's delivery requirements as to their format which indicates the amount of time you have to run screen credits. The number of screen credits a producer is able to give (other than those which are contractual or required by the guilds/unions) is greatly influenced by the limited amount of time allowed to run them. Producers of theatrical features, on the other hand, do not share the same time restrictions and have the freedom to give credit to whomever they wish.

Before your screen credits are finalized, check them over carefully and have them approved by your legal and/or business affairs office and/or your production executive.

Sample Main Titles

Movie For Television

Card #1	(SHOW TITLE)	
Card #2	Starring	
	_____	(lead cast)
Card #3	_____	(cast)
Card #4	_____	(cast)
Card #5	_____	(cast)
Card #6	And	
	_____	(last cast member as listed as and the "And/as"
makes	_____	this a "special" credit)
Card #7	Editor (or "Edited by")	_____
Card #8	Art Director	
	(or "Production Designer")	_____
Card #9	Director of Photography	_____
Card #10	Executive Producer	_____
Card #11	Produced by	_____
Card #12	Written by	_____
Card #13	Directed by	_____

Sample Main Titles

Theatrical Motion Picture

Card #1	_____	Presents	(name of producing entity)
Card #2 A	_____	Production	(name of producer or producer's company)
Card #3 A	_____	Film (name of director)	
Card #4	_____	(lead cast)	
Card #5	_____	(2nd lead)	
Card #6	(PICTURE TITLE)		
Card #7	Starring		
	_____	(cast)	
Card #8	_____	(cast)	
Card #9	_____	(all cast members may	
	_____	not receive single card	
	_____	credit)	
Card #10	And		(the last cast credit is
	_____		almost as special as the
			first and is accentuated by
			the "And...")
Card #11	Casting by	_____	
Card #12	Music by	_____	
Card #13	Costume Designer	_____	(this credit is sometimes listed in the end credits)
Card #14	Associate Producer	_____	
Card #15	Edited by	_____	
Card #16	Production Designed by	_____	
Card #17	Director of Photography	_____	
Card #18	Executive Producer	_____	
Card #19	Screenplay by	_____	
Card #20	Produced by	_____	
Card #21	Directed by	_____	

SAMPLE END CREDITS
THEATRICAL MOTION PICTURE

Note: Depending upon your contractual obligations, the amount of time you have to run the end credits, and the producer's "discretion" as to the exact placement of names, your credits will look different. This is merely a simplified example of what your end credits might look like.

Card #1   Associate Producer   _____

Card #2   Co-Starring

            _____   as   _____

            _____   as   _____

            _____   as   _____

Card #3   Featuring

            _____   as   _____

            _____   as   _____

            _____   as   _____

            _____   as   _____

Card #4   Casting by   _____   (If #4 & #5 are not in the main titles, this is a good place for them)

Card #5   Music Composed by

Card #6   _____   Unit Production Manager

            _____   First Assistant Director

               Second Assistant Director

Card #7   _____   Set Decorator

            _____   Gaffer

            _____   Property Master

            _____   Script Supervisor

               Sound Mixer

Card #8   _____   Camera Operator

            _____   Costume Supervisor

            _____   Key Grip

            _____   Location Manager

               Production Coordinator

Card #9   _____   Post-production Supervisor

            _____   Assistant Film Editor

            _____   Music Editor

            _____   Sound Editor

            _____   Negative Cutter

               Rerecording Mixer

Card #10   _____   Make-up Artist

            _____   Hair Stylist

            _____   Production Accountant

            _____   Transportation Coordinator

               Extra Casting

Card #11   Catering by   _____

           Color by   _____

           Titles and Opticals by   _____

           Lenses and Camera

           Equipment by   _____

           Re-recorded at   _____

Card #12   Copyright © 1993 by   _____

           All Rights Reserved

           Music Copyright © 1993 by

           All Rights Reserved

                                I.A.T.S.E. bug (if applicable)

Card #13   Executive In Charage of Production   _____

Card #14   (Production Company Logo)

SAMPLE END CREDITS

MOVIE FOR TELEVISION

Note: These credits will probably run on a "crawl"; and again... remember, this is just an example.

CAST OF CHARACTERS

_____	as	_____
_____	as	_____
_____	as	_____

_____ Unit Production Manager
_____ First Assistant Director
_____ Second Assistant Director

_____ Second Unit Director

_____ Choreographer

_____ Art Director
_____ Set Decorator

_____ Costume Supervisor
_____ Men's Costumer
_____ Women's Costumer

_____ Camera Operator
_____ Steadicam Operator
_____ First Assistant Cameraman
_____ Second Assistant Cameraman
_____ Script Supervisor

_____ Sound Mixer
_____ Boom Operator
_____ Utility Sound Technician

_____ Additional Film Editor
_____ Assistant Film Editor
_____ Apprentice Editor

_____ Supervising Sound Editor
_____ ADR Editor
_____ Sound Editor
_____ Music Editor

_____ Chief Lighting Technician (or "Gaffer")
_____ Asst Chief Lighting Tech ("Best Boy")
_____ Electricians
_____ Key Grip
_____ Second Company Grip ("Best Boy/Grip")
_____ Dolly Grip
_____ Grips

_____ Set Designer
_____ Property Master
_____ Assistant Property Master
_____ Lead Man
_____ Swing Gang

SAMPLE END CREDITS—CONT'D.

MOVIE FOR TELEVISION

_____	Supervising Make-up Artist
_____	Make-up Artist
_____	Supervising Hair Stylist
_____	Hair Stylist
_____	Construction Coordinator
_____	Stand-by Painter
_____	Production Illustrator
_____	Art Department Coordinator
_____	Special Effects Coordinator
_____	Stunt Coordinator
_____	Location Manager
_____	Production Coordinator
_____	Production Secretary
_____	Production Accountant
_____	Assistant Production Accountant
_____	Unit Publicist
_____	Still Photographer
_____	First Aid
_____	Extras Casting
_____	Craft Service
_____	Transportation Coordinator
_____	Transportation Captain
_____	Drivers
_____	Head Wrangler
_____	Wranglers
_____	Assistant to (Producer)
_____	Assistant to (Director)
_____	Production Assistants
_____	Musical Supervision
_____	Music Coordinator
_____	Re-recording Mixers
_____	Music Engineer
_____	Music Scoring Mixer
_____	Orchestrations
_____	Orchestra Conductor
_____	Negative Cutter
_____	Color Timer
_____	Titles & Opticals

(SECOND UNIT CREW)

_____	First Assistant Director
_____	Second Assistant Director
_____	Camera Operator
_____	Script Supervisor

Movie for Television

(STUNTS BY)

_____	_____
_____	_____
_____	_____
_____	_____

(MUSIC CREDITS)

"Song Title"
Written by   _____
Performed by   _____
Courtesy of   _____ Record

THIS FILM WAS SHOT ON LOCATION IN   _____

_____

THE PRODUCERS WISH TO THANK

_____
_____
_____

Color by   _____
Lenses & Cameras by _____
Re-recorded at   _____

Dolby Stereo (R) (logo)

MPAA (logo)   I.A.T.S.E. (bug)

Copyright © 1991 by _____
All Rights Reserved

The events, characters, and firms depicted in this photoplay are fictitious, any similarity to actual events or firms, is purely coincidental. Ownership of this motion picture is protected by copyright and other applicable laws, and any unauthorized duplication, distribution or exhibition of this motion picture could result in criminal prosecution as well as civil liability.

A (Name of Producing Entity) Production

Distributed by_____

(Company Logo)

STANDARD DELIVERY REQUIREMENTS

DELIVERY REQUIREMENTS

Those elements that have to be turned over to the Distributor of your film at the completion of post-production.

The sooner you get a list of delivery requirements from your distributor, the sooner you can start assembling the necessary elements.

The following is a list of some standard delivery requirements. Your distributor may not ask for everything in this listing or may ask for something that is not here, but his specifications will be similar as these are fairly standard requirements.

Your distributor will let you know the quantity needed of each element requested.

COMPOSITE ANSWER PRINT OR 35MM RELEASE PRINT

A complete first class composite 35mm positive print of the Picture, fully color corrected with complete main and end titles and composite sound track.

NEGATIVE

The complete 35mm picture negative and the optical sound negative in perfect synchronization with the picture negative cut and assembled to conform in all respects to the answer print.

INTERPOSITIVE (IP)

A fine grain positive print of the Picture made from the cut negative and used to make a duplicate (dupe) negative.

DUPLICATE NEGATIVE

A second-generation negative made from the INTER-POSITIVE for the purpose of striking additional release prints.

LOW-CONTRAST (LOW-CON) PRINT

A positive print of the Picture made from the dupe negative on special low-contrast film stock for the purpose of transferring the Picture to videotape.

ONE-INCH VIDEOTAPE

A master videotape format of the Picture transferred from the low-con print. The one-inch videotape is used to make (dub) additional (3/4" and 1/2") videotapes of the Picture. One-inch videotapes are often supplied to television and cable networks.

ORIGINAL SOUND RECORDING

Complete original 1/4" master magnetic recording of the soundtrack of the Picture (original production sound.)

MAGNETIC MASTER COMPOSITE MIX

A magnetic 1/4" or 35mm master composite recording of the complete soundtrack of the Picture conforming in all respects to the Answer Print.

MAGNETIC MUSIC MASTER

A magnetic 1/4" track of the original music score for the Picture.

TEXTLESS BACKGROUND

A clear background interpositve and dupe negative of all scenes, including main and end titles, which would normally have lettering superimposed over them. (Used to make foreign-language prints.)

WORK PRINT

The edited work picture and all corresponding dialogue, music and sound effects work tracks.

THREE-STRIPE MAGNETIC MASTER

A complete dubbed and rerecorded 35mm magnetic master of the soundtrack of the Picture composed of separate dialogue, music and sound effects tracks (3-stripe.)

MUSIC & EFFECTS (M & E) TRACK

A 35mm sound track of the dubbed music and sound effects (each on separate channels) for purposes of looping dialogue into foreign language versions of the Picture.

TELEVISION VERSION

The negative, positive print(s) and sound tracks for all alternate scenes and/or takes, cover shots, looped dialogue lines and other material which can be used in place of all scenes containing nudity, violence and objectionable language in the Picture for the purpose of conforming to rating or television requirements.

FOREIGN VERSION

The negative, positive print(s) and sound tracks for any alternate scenes and/or takes, cover shots, etc. which may contain nudity, violence or language which were shot for the purpose of foreign distribution.

CUTS & TRIMS

The negative and positive prints of all outtakes, trims, second takes, tests, sound effects tracks, dialogue tracks and music tracks made in connection with the Picture which may be used to manufacture trailers and for the purposes of exhibiting and exploiting the Picture.

ACCESS LETTERS

Letters sent by the Producer to the lab(s) and/or any storage facility where elements of the Picture (not already delivered to the Distributor) are being stored which give the Distributor access to these elements. The Distributor will require copies of all access letters in addition to the name(s) and location(s) of the facilities where all undelivered elements are being stored and a detailed inventory of the elements being kept at each location.

STILLS

Original black and white and color negatives, black and white contact proof sheets, still photographs and color transparencies taken in connection with the Picture.

PUBLICITY MATERIAL

All publicity material which may have been prepared in connection with the Picture, including press books and posters.

CONTINUITY SCRIPT

A script containing the dialogue and action continuity of the completed Picture.

SCREENPLAY

The final screenplay or shooting script, the script supervisor's lined script and notes and the film editor's notes and code books.

SYNOPSIS

A brief synopsis of the story of the Picture.

MUSIC CUE SHEETS

Copies of the music cue sheets of the Picture and any other materials which contain music. The music cue sheets are to include: 1) the title of the musical compositions and sound recordings if applicable; 2) names of the composers and their performing rights society affiliation; 3) names of the recording artists; 4) the nature, extent and exact timing of the uses made of each musical composition in the Picture; 5) name and address of the owner of the copyright of each musical composition and sound recording, and 6) the name and address of the publisher and company which controls the sound recording.

COMPOSER'S SCORE

The entire musical score used by the composer and/or conductor together with all original music, manuscripts, instrumental and vocal parts and other music prepared in connection with the Picture.

CONTRACTS

Copies of all licenses, contracts, releases, assignments and/or other written permissions from the proper parties for the use of any musical, literary, dramatic and other materials of whatever nature used in the production of the Picture (including but not limited to all employment contracts with actors, directors, producers, writers and composers.)

M.P.A.A. RATING

A paid rating certificate from the *Code and Rating Administration of America, Inc.* and production code number.

SCREEN CREDITS

A complete list of screen credits and the names of all persons to whom the Producer is contractually obligated to accord credit in any paid advertising, publicity or exploitation of the Picture.

FINAL CAST & CREW LISTS

FINAL COST REPORT

PROOF OF ERRORS AND OMISSIONS INSURANCE

A certificate of insurance evidencing Producer's Errors and Omissions policy covering the Picture and adding the Distributor as an additional named insured.

TELEVISION RESIDUALS

A statement containing the following information for purposes of determining television residual payments: 1) Date principal photography commenced; 2) name and address (and loan-out information if applicable) of each writer, director, actor, unit production manager, first and key second assistant directors and any other personnel entitled to residuals together with the following information concerning each: a) Social Security number, b) W-4 classification (marital status and number of dependents claimed), c) length of employment of SAG personnel, d) a copy of Notice of Tentative Writing Credits, and e) a list of all DGA personnel employed on the Picture.

OWNERSHIP

A certified statement containing the name and address of each participant in net profits to whom the Distributor must account and make payment.

INDEX

A

Abbreviations viii
Access letters 178
Accounting 8
Accounts
    Setting up with labs 1
Actors
    Advice regarding employment of 28
    Checklist 3
    Letter to agent re: contract 23
Actors Production Time Report 25
AD viii. *See* Assistant Directors
Adaptation Rights 118
Additional Insured 11
    Loss Payee/Equipment 11
    Managers or Lessors of Premise 11
Additional Taxable Income 8
ADR 168. *See also Automatic Dialogue Replace-
    ment*
Affirmative action 28
Agency
    Extras casting 3
Agent
    Actors 24
Agreements 1, 4
    Certificates of insurance 4
    Distribution 3
    Financing 3
    Location 4
Air conditioners 4
Aircraft 4, 11, 14
Airline 154
Airplanes
    Employees flying on 13
Alien Certification Office 166
All States' Endorsement 12
Alliance of Motion Picture and Television
    Producer. *See* AMPTP
American Consulate 166
American Humane Association 5, 28
AMPTP 9
Animal handlers 5
Animals 1, 5, 14
    Rules governing 28
    When it's okay to kill them 28
Answer Print 170
Anti-piracy statues 117
Art Director 172

Artistic vii
ASCAP 119, 123
Aspirin 5
Assembly 167
Assistant Directors 23, 25
Assistant location manager 149
Atmosphere 95
Attorney vii, 3, 95, 117
Attorney General 164
Auto insurance 7
Auto liability
    Hired, loaned or donated 12
Automatic Dialogue Replacement 169
Automobile accident report forms
    Blank 5

B

Background 95
Bank
    Account 3
    Information 5
    Reconciliation 5
Beauty shop 154
Beepers 7
    Order 3
Benefits 12
    Pension and Health 27
Bids
    Insurance company 4
Billing 28
Bills
    Approving of 3
    Coding 3
Black bags 4
Blank forms viii
Blue (script changes) 69
BMI 119, 123
Boats 4
Bond 163
Bonds 1
Book
    Final production 5
Booking Slip 23
Bottled water 3
Box rental 8
Breakdown 12
    Script 3
    Sheet vii
Breakdowns 4

Atmosphere 4
Locations 4
Production vehicles 4
Special effects 4
Stunt 4
Travel 4
Budget 69
Finalize 4
Modest 1
Buff (script changes) 69
Bullhorns 4, 7
Business affairs 95
Business licenses 3

C

CAL-OSHA 9
California Senate Bill 198 9
Call sheets 5, 25
Blank 5
Camera car 4
Camera reports 4
Canada 164
Carnet 163
Cars
Picture 4
Cash deposits 164
Cash flow 69
Chart 4
Cast Insurance 13
Cast List 5
Extra copies of 5
Final SAG 5
Cast Lists 15, 23
Cast physicals 4
Casting
Finalize 3
Casting Director 165
Casting Office 23, 25
Casting sessions 4
Catering 1, 4
Cellular phone 4
Certificate holder 11
Certificates of Insurance 4, 11
Chairs 4
Chargers
For walkie talkies 7
Chart-of-accounts 3, 5
Check requests 8
Blank forms 5
Needed immediately 8
Check-in time 154
Checklist
Additional distant location 153
Chemicals 9
Cherry (script changes) 69
Child labor laws 26

CIF (Cost Including Freight) 164
Claims
Insurance 11
Processing 15
Claims reporting
Procedures 15
Clearance
Copyrighted music
Failure to clear 117
Music
Responsibilities for 117
Using a song without obtaining the rights 119
Clearances 95
Clearing House, Ltd. 117, 124
Clothing racks 153
CMX 6000 167
Coding Dailies 169
Coffee maker 3
Company Nurse 4
Company policies 7
Completion bond 3
Completion bond company
Sending script to 4
Composer 123, 169
Composer's Score 179
Composite Answer Print 178
Comprehensive general liability 11
Computer 3, 7
Computer software
Bugeting and scheduling 69
For preparing music cue sheets 124
Condition of employment 7
Condor 4
Consecutive employment 25, 28
Rules concerning performers 25, 26
Consultation Requirement 164, 165
Contact list 3, 5
Extra copies of 5
Continuity Script 70, 179
Contracts 1, 3, 5, 179
Costume designer 3
Day-player 24
Director 3
Director of photography 3
Fully-executed 25
Literary material 3
Minors 3
Producer 3
Production designer 3
SAG three day-player 23
SAG Weekly 23
Stunt
Daily performer 24
Weekly performer 24
Stunt performer 24
Union and guild 3

Copy machine 3, 5
Copyright 118, 120
  Infringement 117
Copyright Act 119
Copyrighted music 1
Cores 4
Corporate (signatory papers) information 5
Corporate seal 3
Correspondence
  Key 5
Cost report 69
  Final. *See* Final: cost report
Costume Designer 172
Courier 154
Cover letter 23
Cover sets 1
Coverage
  Guild/union accident 13
  Special insurance 4
Crane 4
Crawl 175
Credits
  Notice of tentative writing
    Television 31
    Theatrical 31
  WGA 171
  Writers 171
    Television 171
Crew vii
  Hiring of 1
  Post production 1
  Treatment of vii
Crew cabs 4
Crew deal memos 3, 7
  Blank forms 5
Crew list 3, 69, 179
Crew members
  How to get in touch with 1
Cue 123
Cue Sheets 124
Customs 163
  Broker 163
Cuts 178
Cycs 5

D

Dailies 1, 169
  Routing of 1, 4
  Screening of 4
Daily production report 12
Dancers 28
Dates
  Series production 3
Dates of delivery 5
Day performer 26
  Converting to weekly performer 26

Upgrade from extra 27
Day-out-of-days vii, 4, 15
  Extra copies of 5
  Final 5
Day-player contracts 24
Dead-bolt locks 153
Deal memos viii, 15, 23, 31, 87
  Crew 3
  DGA 3
Delivery requirements 5, 11, 70, 117, 168
Department of Labor 165
Departure Tax 163
  How to pay 163
Depiction of Identification of Actual Products 96
Depiction of Public Authorities 96
Deposits
  Cash, for customs bonds 164
DGA 170. *See also* Directors Guild of America
  Basic Agreement
    Addendum to for 1993 87
  Deal memo 87
Dialogue 168
Dialogue Coach 3
Dialogue Editor 169
Director 70
  Television 170
  Theatrical Motion Picture 170
Director of Photogaphy (DP) viii
Director of Photography 171
Directors 163
  Working in a foreign country 163
Director's cut 87, 168
Directors Guild of America viii, 31, 87, 170
  Regulations 168
Distant Location 153
Distribution 9
Distribution list 23
Distributor 178
Doctor 4
DOL. *See* Department of Labor
Dolly 4
Doubles
  Photo 3
  Stunt 3
Dressing rooms 4
Drop cloths 4
Dubbing 169
Dubbing facilities 1
Duplicate lists 163, 164
Duplicate Negative 178
Duties
  Production assistant 7

E

Ediflex 167

Editing
  Equipment 7
  Room 1, 153
  Rooms
    Set-up 1
  Videotape 167
Editing time
  DGA rules regarding 168
Editor's cut 167
Eight bars 120
Electric equipment 4
Electric truck 4
Embassy 163
Employee for hire 123
Employer 13
Employer of record 12
Employer's Report of Injury 10
Employment
  Consecutive
    SAG members 25
  First day of
    SAG 25
  SAG
    On hold 25
Employment contract 28
Employment Development Department 166
  Alien Certification 166
Employment of minors 26
Empty cans 4
End credits 172
  Movie for television 175
  Theatrical motion picture 174
Episode Files 21
Episodes
  List of 3
Equipment 1, 4, 7, 13
  Grip and electric 4
  Securing additional 1
  Sound 4
Equipment rental agreements 15
Equivalency Requirement 164
Errors and omissions 117
Exams
  Doctor's 3
Executive Staff List 85
Expendables 7
  Grip, electric and camera 4
Extra expense 14
Extras 3, 28
  Types of 27
  Vouchers 3

F

Fair use 120
Fans 4
Favors

Backfiring 10
Fax machine 3
Feature film 121
Federal ID number 3, 8
Federal Register 123
Fees 149
  Permits 149
Fictional character 95
Files
  Episode 21
  General production 21
  Series 21
  Setting up production 3
Film
  Polaroid 4
  Still 4
Film and Video Clips 96
Film clip 121
  Licenses 121
Film commission 149
Film Editor 171
Film office
  Foreign 163
Films
  Low budget 1
Final
  Budget 5
  Cost report 5
  Day-out-of-days 5
  Production Book 5
  SAG cast list 5
  Shooting schedule 5
Final call
  Actors 25
Final Cast 179
Final Cost Report 179
Final draft
  Script 69
Fire and Police officers 4
Fire safety officers 149
First Aid kit 5
First Assistant Director 171. *See also* AD
First cut 168
First trial print 170
First work calls 25
Fitting calls 28
Fixes 169
Flammable liquids 9
Flashlights 5
Flat fee 122
Flatbeds 167
Foley 168, 169
Foreign countries
  Rules regarding working there 163
Foreign distribution 168
Foreign version 178
Form ETA-750 165

Forms viii
    Product Placement Release 96
    Production 125
    Release 3
    Supply of 3
Furniture 3

G

Gas receipts 8
General extras 27
General production files 21
General Safety Guidelines 9
Generator 4
Get started 1
Goldenrod (script changes) 69
Gratuity 154
Gray (script changes) 69
Green (script changes) 69
Grievances 9
Grip equipment 4
Grip truck 4
Group Release 95
Guidelines
    General safety 9
Guild contracts 31
Guilds 1

H

H-1B Classification 164
H-2B Classification 164
H-2B Visas 165
Hair
    Schedule 3
Hair pieces 5
Hair Stylist 172
Hair trailer 4
Hairdressing 28
Harry Fox Agency 123
Headsets 4
Heaters 4
Hiring crew members 1
Hold for Pickup 154
Home video
    Distribution 122
    Marketplace 122
    Rentals 122
    Rights 123
        Charge for 122
    Royalties 122
Honeywagon 4
Hotel 153
    Room log 154
Hotel accommodations 1
Hotel/motel
    Availability of others in area 154
Housekeeping 154

I

I-9s
    Extra copies of 5
Immigration 163
    Labor certifications
        Duration 166
    Policies and requirements of foreign countries 163
Immigration Act of 1990 164
Immigration and Naturalization Service (INS) 166
Independent contractors 12
Information Sheets
    SAG Final Cast List 23
Injury
    Employee 12
        What to do re: insurance 12
INS. *See* Immigration and Naturalization Service
Inserts 169
Insurance 4
    Agency 12
    Auditor 15
    Auto accident claims 12
    Cast 3
    Cast and director 13
    Claim Worksheets 15
    Claims 5, 9
    Costumes and wardrove 13
    Coverage 4
    Delivery requirements 11
    E&O 3
    Errors and omissions 11
    Faulty stock, camera, processing 13
    Miscellaneous rented equipment 13
    Negative film and video direct physical loss 13
    Office contents 13
    Props, sets and scenery 13
    Setting up 11
    Special coverages 11
    Standard motion picture and television 11
    Travel/accident coverage 13
    Workers' Compensation 12
Interpositive (IP) 178
Interviews 28
Inventories 7, 9
Inventory
    Equipment and tools 7
    Log Forms 7
    Logs 5
    Missing 13
    On-going 7
    Props 7
    Raw stock 3
    Set dressing 7

Invoicing 8
IRS 3
Ivory (script changes) 69

K

Keys 7
  Office 3

L

Labor Certification 165
Labs 1
Laser Edit 167
Laundry facilities 153
Law suits 9
Laws
  Copyright 117
Lay-out board 4
Legal 3
Liability 11
Libraries 123
License 95, 121
  Blanket 119
  Compulsory 123
  Expired
    Music 124
  Per program 119
License plates 96
Licensing
  Feature films 122
Likeness 95
Line producers vii
Lists
  Cast 3
  Contact 69
  Crew 5, 69
  Final staff 5
  Vendor 5
Livestock 14
Local Craft Unions 171
Location 28
  Agreements 15, 95, 96
    Blank 5
    Signed copies of 5
  Distant
    Work week 25
  Expenses 28
  List 5
  Maps 4
  Questions before you shoot 149
Location manager 149
  Assistant 149
Location of inventory 5
Location scouts 4
Location services
  Independent 149
Locations 1, 4, 95, 149

Alternate 1
  Managers or Lessors of Premises 11
Log
  Inventory 3
  Purchase order 3
Looping 28, 169
  Facilities 1
Loss Payee 11
Low-contraxt (lo-con) print 178
Lyrics
  Changing 120

M

M.P.A.A. Rating 179
Magnetic master composite mix 178
Magnetic music master 178
Main Titles 172
  Movies for television 173
  Theatrical motion picture 173
Major deals
  Copies of 5
Makeup 28
  Trailer 4
Makeup Artist 172
Maps to the locations
  Extra copies of 5
Materials
  Purchased, rented, built 7
Meal penalty violations 28
Mechanical rights 118
Medical bills 12
Medical exams 3
Medical facilities, emergency
  Location of 4
Memos
  Crew deal 5
  DGA 3
Mileage logs 8
Mileage Reimbursement 8
Miniatures 1
Minors 28
  Employment of
    Outside California 26
  Employment rules
    California 26
  Payment of 26
  Regulations concerning
    SAG 26
Minutes book 3
Missing equipment 14
Mock-ups 1, 5
Models 5
Monitor 4
Mono Master 168
Monopolistic 12
Motor home 4

Motorcycle police officers 149
Moviolas 167
Music 1
    Copyrighted
        Failure to obtain clearance 117
    Originally scored 117
    Ownership 118
Music and effects 168
Music and effects (M & E) track 178
Music Clearance 1
    Costs 123
    Department 122
    In subsequent television episodes 120
    Service 95, 117
Music cue sheet 119, 179
    Who receives 119
Music video clip 121
Music videos
    Promotional 121
Musical material 117
Mysterious disappearance 14

N

Names
    Clearance of 95
Names of Actual Businesses or Organizations
    96
ND Stunt 24
Needle drop 123
Negative 178
Negative cutter 169
Night work 28
Non-owned auto liability policy 7
Non-union crews 31
Notice of Tentative Writing Credits 179
Nude scenes
    Children or infants in 28
    Rules regarding 28

O

O Non-Immigrant Visa 164, 165
O Visas 164
    O-1 Visa 164
    O-2 Visa 164
    O-3 Visa 164
Office
    Accounting 153
    Camera and sound 153
    Production 153
    Transportation 153
Office supplies 3, 5, 7
Old songs 119
Omitted (scene) 69
Omnies 27
One-inch videotape 178
One-Line Schedule vii, 3, 69

Optical sound track 170
Opticals 168, 169
Order film 1
Original music 123
Original sound recording 178
Over the Counter 154
Overtime 28
    Records 28
Ownership 179

P

P Non-Immigrant Visa 164, 165
P Visas 164
    P-1 entertainment group 164
    P-1 Visa 164
    P-2 Visa 165
    P-3 Visa 165
    P-4 Visa 165
Pager 7
Paperwork 3
    Preparation of 1
Paramedics 153
Parking 4
Parking lot
    Where to locate 4
Pay
    Premium for working on sixth and/or seventh
        days 25
Pay scales 28
Payment 28
    Late 28
Payroll company 12
Payroll forms 23
Performer categories 26
Performers 163, 171
    Television motion pictures 171
    Theatrical motion pictures 171
    Working in a foreign country 163
Permit 149
Permits 3, 4, 5
    To Employ Minors 26
    Work
        For minors 3
Personal Release 95
Petitions
    Immigration re: P-2 visas 165
Petty Cash 8
Petty cash envelopes
    Blank 5
Phone system 3
Photo
    Polaroid of performer 27
Photo double 27
Photograph 27
Photograph or Likeness of Actual Person 96
Physicals

Director and cast 4
Picture cars 4
Picture vehicles 1
Pink (script changes) 69
POC viii, 8. *See also* Production coordinators
Polaroid
  Film 4
  Photo 27
Police 149
  Report 14
Policies
  Standard industry 7
Policy guidelines 7
Portable File Box 5
Post-production 167
Pouch 154
Power 4
Pre-dubbing 169
Pre-Production 1, 69
  Checklist 3
  Schedule 2, 4
Pre-rigging 4
Prefix 555 96
Premium pay 25
Prep time 1
Primary policy 11
Principal photography 7, 12, 167
Print Master 168
Print master 170
Procedures
  Music clearance 3
Process photography 5
Process trailer 4
Producer 15, 23, 27, 70, 163, 168
Producers
  Independent 1
  Working in a foreign country 163
Product Placement 9
  Release Form 96
Production vii
  Accountant 8, 15, 23
  Assistants 7
  Board 3
  Coordinator vii, 7, 13, 23, 170
  Designer 172
  Manager vii, 8, 13, 15, 23, 70, 170
  Manuals vii
  Meetings 4
  Music 123
  Office 7, 153, 154
  Reports 5
    Blank 5
  Trailer 4
  Working in vii
Production Companies
  Independent vii
Production Design(ed) by 172

Production Package 13
Production Schedule vii
Production time reports 28
Program title 120
Proof of errors and omissions insurance 179
Props 13
Public broadcasting stations 123
Public domain 119
Public figures 96
Public Performance Rights 118
Publicity material 179
Publisher 118
Publishing rights 121
Purchase orders 8
  Blank 5

R

Railroad 4, 11
Railroads or Railroad Facilities 14
Rates
  Negotiating weekly 4
Raw stock 4, 7
Rear screen 5
Reason for hire 27
Received of petty cash slip 8
Reciprocal Exchange Program 165
Record company 118
Recycling 9
Refrigerator 3
Regulations, locations 149
Rehearsals 4
  Schedule 3
Release form viii, 95
  Blank 5
Releases
  Preparation of 1
Releases From Neighbors
  Signed 4
Repairs 14
Replacement costs 14
Report to work 25
Reports
  Copyright 3
  Title 3
Reproduction Rights 118
Request
  For Delivery 7
  For Pick-up 7
Request to film during extended hours 152
Requirements
  Budget 1
  Delivery 11
  Script 1
Responsibility vii
Rest periods 28
Restaurants 153

Restrictions 149
Resume 27
Reuse of film 28
Riders
  SAG contract 3
Right-to-work state 27
Rights
  Music 118
  Screenplay 3
Room
  Editing 153
  Wardrobe 153
Rules 7
Runner 7, 125, 154
Running inventories 13

S

Safe clothing 9
Safety 28
  General guidelines 9
Safety guidelines 9
SAG viii, 24, 26, 171. *See also Screen Actors Guild*
  Bond 3
  Compensation 26
  Contracts 3, 23, 25, 28
    Blank 5
  Day player Contract
    Signing of 24
  Extras 27
  Final Cast List Information Sheets 23
  Guidelines 27
  Performer Categories
    Schedule A 26
    Schedules A-J 26
  Performer categories 26
  Regulations 26
  Taft/Hartley report
    Blank forms 5
Salmon (script changes) 69
Sample Main Titles 173
Schedule
  Eight-week 1
  Ideal pre-production 1
  Reasonable 1
  Sample post-production 167
  Tentative post-production 4
Schedules 3
Scoring 1, 169
Scratched negative 15
Screen Actors Guild 13, 31, 166. *See also SAG*
  Offices 29
Screen Credit 28
Screen Credits 168, 170, 179
Screenplay 179
  Final draft 69

Script 3, 5
  Changes
    Extra copies of 5. *See also Script Revisions*
  Distributed to cast and crew 3
  Duplicated 3
  Extra copies of 5
  Finalize 3
  Research 3
  Timing 4
  Typed 3
Script Revisions 25, 69
Script revisions 125
Script Supervisor 69
Second Assistant Director 4, 171
Security 4
Serial numbers 7
Series files 21
SESAC 123
Set Decorator 172
Set dressing 13
Sets 1
Sex scenes
  Rules regarding 28
Sheet
  Crew start-up 3
  Data 3
Shipments
  Delayed 154
Shipping Dailies 154
Shoot
  Six-week 1
Shooting schedule 4, 69
  Extra copies of 5
  Final 5
Shuttle 149
Signatory 1
Social Security 179
Software programs vii
  Automatic preparation vii
Songs 117
Sound alike 123
Sound effects 168, 169
Sound Effects Editors 169
Sound equipment 4
Soundtrack 121
Special effects 1
Special makeup 5
Special requirements 1
Spotting 168, 169
Staff and crew lists
  Extra copies of 5
Stand-ins 3, 27
Standard
  Delivery Requirements 178
  Industry policies 7
  Production forms viii, 69
Star wagon 4

Start slips
  Extra copies of 5
Starting from scratch 3
Station 12 3, 24, 27
Station l2 166
Steadicam 4
Still film 4
Stills 179
Stock
  1/4" Mag 4
Stock footage 5
Story by 171
Street Address 96
Strike and Cleaning service 4
Studios, major vii
Stunt double 24
Stunt Performer
  Contracts 24
Stunt performer
  Categories 24
    ND stunt 24
    Stunt double 24
    Utility stunt 24
Stunt performers 28
Stunt work 1, 28
Supplies 7
Sweeten 168
Sweetening 169
Sync rights 118. *See Synchronization: Rights*
Synchronization
  License 121
  Rights 118
Syncing dailies 169
Synopsis 179

T

T.I.B. *See* Temporary Importation Bond
Tables 4
Taft-Hartley 166
Taft/Hartley 27
  Form 27
  When to do 27
Talent 165
Tan (script changes) 69
Tax
  Departure 163
Taxable income 8
Teacher 3
Technical advisor 5
Telephone Numbers 96
Teleplay by 171
Television
  Program 121
  Residuals 179
  Series 3
  Show

Use of records on 121
  Version 178
Temporary Importation Bond 164
Temporary Labor Certification 166
1099 8
Tent 4
Tests
  Makeup 3
Textless background 178
Third Party
  Property Damage 14
  Rights 121
35mm release print 178
Three-stripe magnetic master 178
Time cards 15
Time code 168
Time Report 25
Timing 170
Title
  Song as program title 120
Tracks
  M&E 168
  Music and effects (M&E) 168
Traffic Control 4, 149
Trainers
  Animal 5
Transportation 4, 28
Travel 1
  Accident policy 13
  Movement lists 15
Travel Day 25
Travel time 28
Trial balance 5
Trial Print 168
Trims 178
Truck
  Electric 4
  Fuel 4
  Grip 4
  Prop 4
  Set dressing 4
Typewriter 3, 5, 7

U

U.S. Copyright Act 117
U.S. Council for International Business 163
U.S. Department of Labor 165, 166
U.S. Network run 121
Umbrella (Excess Liability) 14
Undeveloped Film
  X-Ray, Do Not 154
Union
  Requirements for visas 165
Union grievances 9
Union signatory 123
Union/guild

Being signatory to 31
Unions 1
Unit Production Manager 171. *See also Production Managers*
United States Department of Labor 166
UPM viii, 8. *See also* Production managers
Use of
    Literary Material 96
    Name 96
    Trademark or Logo 96
        Release Form 96
Utilities 4
Utility stunt 24

V

Valuables 14
Vans 4
VCR 4, 7
Vehicles 1, 4, 11
    Employees driving own car for business
        purposes 7
Vendor 125
Vendors 8
    Setting up accounts with 3
Video Assist 4
Videocassettes 7
Violations
    Meal penalty 28
VIP 153
Visa
    Consulation requirements 165
Visas 164
    H-1B 164
    H-2B 164, 165
    Non-Immigrant 164
    O Classification 164
    O Visa 164
    P Classification 164
    P Visa 164, 165
    Petition 164
        By agents for clients 165

W

W-4 179
    Extra copies of 5
Walkie-talkies 4, 7
Wardrobe 1, 3, 7, 13, 28
    Trailer 4
Wardrobe Department 153
Wardrobe room 153
Water truck 4
Watercraft 11, 14
Waybill 154
Weather reports 153
Welfare Worker 3
WGA viii

Work Calls 25
    Subject to Change 25
Work days
    Consecutive 25
Work permits
    Minors 3
Work print 169, 178
Work week 25
Work weeks 28
Workers Compensation 3, 4, 10, 12, 26
    Accident report forms
        Blank 5
Working in a foreign country
    Producers, directors, performers 163
Working with Animals 28
Wranglers 5
Writers 171
    Theatrical motion picture 171
Writers Guild 31
    Credits Department 31
Written by 171

Y

Yellow (script changes) 69

INDEX OF FORMS

Note: **Bold face** entries indicate blank form.
Italicized entries indicate a grouping of
forms.

A

Abbreviated Production Report 127, **276**
Actors Production Time Report 53, **224**

B

Beeper Sign-out Sheet 146, **295**
Box/Equipment Rental Inventory 130, **279**
Breakdown Sheet 71, **238**

C

Call Sheet 73-74, **241-242**
Cash or Sales Receipt 137, **286**
Cast Deal Memo 88, **249**
Cast Information Sheet 129, **278**
Cast List 84
Check Request 77, **245**
Check's In The Mail, The 138, **287**
Contact List 85
Crew Deal Memo 89, **250**
Crew List 83
Crew Start-up and Data Sheet 133, **282**

D

Daily Cost Overview 128, **277**
Day-out-of-Days 72, **239**
Directors Guild of America Forms
    Director Deal Memo 92, **252**
    UPM and Assistant Director
        Film Deal Memo 93, **254**
    Employment Data Report 65, **235**
    Weekly Work List 64, **234**
Drive-to   144, **293**

E

Executive Staff List 84
Extra Talent Voucher 94, **255**

F

Film/Tape Clip for Promotional Uses 110, **270**
Film/Tape Footage Release 113-114, **273-274**

G

Group Release 101, **261**

H

Hotel Room List 158, **302**
Hotel Room Log 157, **301**

I

Insurance Claim Worksheets
    Automobile Accident 19-20, **201-202**
    Cast-Extra Expense-Faulty Stock 18, **199**
    Damage 17, **198** Theft 16, **197**
Inventory Log 131, **280**
Invoice 136, **285**

L

Location Agreement 97-98, **257-258**
Location Information Sheet 150, **297**
Location List 151, **298**

M

Meal Allowance 159, **303**
Mileage Log 139, **288**

O

One-Line Schedule 82

P

Personal Release 99, **259**
Personal Release—Payment 100, **260**
Petty Cash Accounting 79, **246**
Petty Cash Account, Individual 135, **284**
Product Placement Release 111-112, **271-272**
Production Report 75-76, **243-244**
Purchase Order 78. **245**
Purchase Order Log 132, **281**

R

Raw Stock Inventory 140, **289**
Raw Stock, Daily 141, **290**
Received of Petty Cash Slip 80, **248**
Request for Delivery 143, **292**
Request for Pick-up 142, **291**
Request for Videocassette 115, **275**
Request to Film During Extended Hours 152,
    299

S

Screen Actors Guild Forms
  Extra Voucher 51, **222**
  Actors Production Time Report 53, **224**
  Casting Data Report 55-56, **225-226**
    Stunt Performers 57-58, **227-228**
    Low Budget/Affirmative Action 59-60,
    229-230
  Daily Contract
    Television, Motion Pictures
      or Videotapes 33-34, **203-204**
    Theatrical Motion Pictures 45, **213**
  Daily Stunt Performer Contract
    Motion Pictures 46, **219**
    Television, Motion Pictures
      or Videotape 39-40, **209-210**
  Final Cast List Information Sheet 61-62,
  231-232
  Member Report—ADR Theatrical/
    Television 63, **233**
  Minimum Freelance Contract
    Theatrical Motion
      Pictures 43-44, **215-216**
  Television, Motion Pictures or
    Videotape 37-38, **207-208**
  Minimum Three-Day Contract
    Television, Motion Pictures or
      Videotape 35-36, **205-206**
  Stunt Performer Minimum Freelance
    Weekly Contract
      Motion Pictures 47-48, **211-212**
      Television 41-42, **211-212**
  Taft-Hartley Report 49, **220**
    SAG Extras 50, **221**
  Theatrical and Television Sign-In 52, **223**
Shooting Schedule 81

T

Travel Memo to Cast and Crew 160-161, **305-306**
Travel Movement 156, **300**
Time Card/Invoices Weekly Checklist 134, **283**

U

Use of Literary Material 104, **264**
Use of Name 102, **262**
Use of Still Photographs
  Copyrighted Owner, Not Person
    in Photo 105, **265**
  Person in Photo/Payment 107, **267**
  Copyrighted Owner, Not Person
    in Photo/Free 108, **268**
  Person in Photo/Free 106, **266**
Use of Trademark or Logo 103, **263**

V

Vehicle Rental Sheet 147, **296**

W

Walkie-Talkie Sign-out Sheet 145, **294**

Writers Guild of America Forms
  Notice of Tentative Screen Credits
    Television 68, **237**
    Theatrical 67, **236**
Wording for Multiple Signs 109, **269**
Writer's Deal Memo 90, **251**
Writing Team Deal Memo 91, **252**

BLANK FORMS

From Chapter 3
Insurance Claim Worksheets
Theft   197
Damage   198
Cast/Extra Expense/Faulty Stock   199
Automobile Accident   201-202

From Chapter 6
Screen Actors Guild Forms
Daily Contract for Television
    Motion Pictures or Videotapes   203-204
Minimum Three-Day Contract for
    Television, Motion Pictures or
    Videotape   205-206
Minimum Freelance Weekly Contract
    for Television, Motion Pictures
    or Videotape   207-208
Daily Stunt Performer
    Contract for Television,
    Motion Pictures or Videotape   209-210
Stunt Performer Minimum Freelance
    Weekly Contract for Television,
    Motion Pictures or Videotape   211-212
Daily Contract for
    Theatrical Motion Pictures   213
Minimum Freelance Contract
    for Theatrical Motion Pictures   215-216
Daily Stunt Performer
    Contract for Theatrical Motion
    Pictures   217-218
Stunt Performer Minimum Freelance
    Weekly Contract—Motion Pictures   219
Taft-Hartley Report   220
Taft-Hartley Report—SAG Extras   221
SAG Extra Voucher   222
Theatrical and Television Sign-In   223
Actors Production Time Report   224
Casting Data Report   225-226
Casting Data Report for
    Stunt Performers   227-228
Casting Data Report—
    Low Budget/Affirmative Action   229-230
Final Cast List Information Sheet   231-232
Member Report—
    ADR Theatrical/Television   233
Directors Guild of America Forms
Weekly Work List   234

Employment Data Report   235-236

Writers Guild of America Forms
Notice of Tentative
    Screen Credits—Theatrical   237
Notice of Tentative
    Screen Credits—Television   238

From Chapter 7
Breakdown Sheet   239
Day-out-of-Days   240
Call Sheet   241-242
Production Report   243-244
Check Request   245
Purchase Order   246
Petty Cash Accounting   247
Received of Petty Cash Slip   248

From Chapter 8
Cast Deal Memo   249
Crew Deal Memo   250
Writer's Deal Memo   251
Writing Team Deal Memo   252
DGA Director Deal Memo   253
DGA UPM and Assistant Director
    Film Deal Memo   254
Extra Talent Voucher   255

From Chapter 9
Location Agreement   257-258
Personal Release   259
Personal Release—Payment   260
Group Release   261
Use of Name   262
Use of Trademark or Logo   263
Use of Literary Material   264
Use of Still Photographs (Copyrighted
    Owner, Not Person in Photo)   265
Use of Still Photographs
    (Person in Photo/Free)   266
Use of Still Photographs
    (Person in Photo/Payment)   267
Use of Still Photographs
    (Copyrighted Owner,
    Not Person in Photo/Free)   268
Wording for Multiple Signs   269

Film/Tape Clip for Promotional Uses   270
Product Placement Release   271-272
Film/Tape Footage Release   273-274
Request for Videocassette   275

From Chapter 11

Abbreviated Production Report   276
Daily Cost Overview   277
Cast Information Sheet   278
Box/Equipment Rental Inventory   279
Inventory Log   280
Purchase Order Log   281
Crew Start-up and Data Sheet   282
Time Car/Invoices Weekly Checklist   283
Individual Petty Cash Account   284
Invoice 285
Cash or Sales Receipt   286
The Check's in the Mail   287
Mileage Log   288
Raw Stock Inventory   289
Daily Raw Stock   290
Request for Pick-up   291
Request for Delivery   292
Drive-to   293
Walkie-Talkie Sign-out Sheet   294
Beeper Sign-out Sheet   295
Vehicle Rental Sheet   296

From Chapter 12

Location Information Sheet   297
Location List   298
Request to Film During Extended Hours   299

From Chapter 13

Travel Movement   300
Hotel Room Log   301
Hotel Room List   302
Meal Allowance   303
Sample Travel Memo
    to Cast and Crew   305-306

INSURANCE CLAIM WORKSHEET

DAMAGE TO [ ] EQUIPMENT
[ ] WARDROBE
[ ] PROPS
[ ] SET DRESSING
[ ] LOCATION/PROPERTY

PRODUCTION_____

DATE OF OCCURRENCE_____ TIME_____

WHAT WAS DAMAGED_____
_____
_____

LOCATION OF OCCURRENCE_____
_____

HOW DID DAMAGE OCCUR_____
_____
_____
_____
_____

WITNESS_____ POSITION_____
PHONE#_____

DAMAGED ITEM(S)   [ ] PURCHASED FOR SHOW -- PURCHASE PRICE $_____
[ ] RENTED FROM/OWNER_____
ADDRESS_____
_____
PHONE#_____
CONTACT_____

RENTAL PRICE $_____ PER [ ] DAY
[ ] WEEK
[ ] MONTH

VALUE OF DAMAGED ITEM(S) $_____
ESTIMATE(S) TO REPAIR $_____

[ ] ATTACHMENTS_____
_____

SUBMITTED TO INSURANCE AGENCY ON_____
ATTENTION_____
CLAIM #_____
INSURANCE COMPANY CLAIMS REP._____

INSURANCE CLAIM WORKSHEET COMPLETED BY_____
DATE_____ TITLE_____

AMOUNT CREDITED TO AGGREGATE DEDUCTIBLE $_____ DATE_____
REIMBURSEMENT CHECK PAID TO_____
AMOUNT $_____ DATE_____

INSURANCE CLAIM WORKSHEET
(THEFT)

STOLEN   [ ] EQUIPMENT
[ ] WARDROBE
[ ] PROPS
[ ] SET DRESSING
[ ] VEHICLE

PRODUCTION_____

DATE ITEM(S) WERE DISCOVERED MISSING _____

DESCRIPTION OF ITEM(S) STOLEN (Include I.D.#'s If Available)_____
_____
_____
_____
_____
_____

DEPARTMENT USED BY_____

PERSON USED BY_____

WHERE WERE ITEM(S) LAST SEEN _____

WHO DISCOVERED ITEM(S) MISSING_____

ITEM(S)   [ ] PURCHASED FOR SHOW -- PURCHASE PRICE $_____
[ ] RENTED FOR SHOW
    RENTED FROM_____
    ADDRESS_____
    _____

    PHONE#_____
    CONTACT_____

    VALUE $_____
    RENTAL PRICE $_____ PER [ ] DAY
    [ ] WEEK
    [ ] MONTH

[ ] POLICE REPORT ATTACHED
[ ] OTHER ATTACHMENTS_____
    _____

SUBMITTED TO INSURANCE AGENCY ON_____
ATTENTION_____
CLAIM #_____
INSURANCE COMPANY CLAIMS REP._____

INSUR. CLAIM WORKSHEET COMPLETED BY_____
DATE_____ TITLE_____

AMOUNT CREDITED TO AGGREGATE DEDUCTIBLE $_____ DATE_____
REIMBURSEMENT CHECK PAID TO_____
AMOUNT $_____ DATE_____

       © ELH Form #2

INSURANCE CLAIM WORKSHEET

[ ] CAST
[ ] EXTRA EXPENSE
[ ] FAULTY STOCK

PRODUCTION_____

DATE OF OCCURRENCE_____ TIME_____

DESCRIPTION OF INCIDENT_____
_____
_____
_____
_____
_____
_____
_____

IF CAST CLAIM, WHICH ARTIST_____

WAS A DOCTOR CALLED IN [ ] YES [ ] NO

NAME OF DOCTOR_____
        ADDRESS_____
        PHONE#_____

COULD COMPANY SHOOT AROUND INCIDENT [ ] YES [ ] NO
IF YES, FOR HOW LONG_____

HOW MUCH DOWN TIME WAS INCURRED DUE TO THIS INCIDENT_____
_____
_____

AVERAGE DAILY COST $_____

BACKUP TO CLAIM TO INCLUDE_____
_____
_____
_____
_____

SUBMITTED TO INSURANCE AGENCY ON_____
                    ATTENTION_____
                     CLAIM #_____
    INSURANCE COMPANY CLAIMS REP._____
              INSURANCE AUDITOR_____

INSURANCE CLAIM WORKSHEET COMPLETED BY_____
DATE_____ TITLE_____

AMOUNT CREDITED TO DEDUCTIBLE $_____ DATE_____
REIMBURSEMENT CHECK PAID TO_____
                    AMOUNT $_____ DATE_____

INSURANCE CLAIM WORKSHEET

AUTOMOBILE ACCIDENT

PRODUCTION_____

DATE OF OCCURRENCE_____ TIME_____

LOCATION OF OCCURRENCE_____
_____
_____

HOW DID ACCIDENT OCCUR_____
_____
_____
_____
_____
_____
_____
_____

<u>INSURED VEHICLE</u> (Year, Make, Model)_____
VEHICLE I.D.#_____ LIC. PLATE#_____
OWNER OF VEHICLE_____
ADDRESS_____
PHONE#_____ CONTACT_____

DRIVER_____
POSITION_____
DRIVER'S LIC.#_____USED W/PERMISSION [ ] YES [ ] NO
ADDRESS_____
_____
PHONE#_____

WHERE CAN CAR BE SEEN_____
WHEN_____

DAMAGE TO CAR_____
_____
_____

ESTIMATE(S) TO REPAIR $_____ $_____

<u>DAMAGE TO OTHER VEHICLE</u>(Year, Make, Model)_____
_____ LIC. PLATE#_____
DRIVER OF OTHER VEHICLE_____
ADDRESS_____
_____
PHONE(S)#_____ #_____

WHERE CAN CAR BE SEEN_____
WHEN_____

DAMAGE TO CAR_____
_____
_____

ESTIMATE(S) TO REPAIR $_____ $_____

INSURANCE CLAIM WORKSHEET - AUTOMOBILE ACCIDENT
PAGE #2

INJURED _____   _____
ADDRESS_____   _____

PHONE#_____   _____
EXTENT OF INJURY_____   _____

_____   _____
_____   _____

WITNESS(ES)_____   _____
    ADDRESS_____   _____

    PHONE#_____   _____

[ ] POLICE REPORT ATTACHED
[ ] OTHER ATTACHMENTS_____
_____
_____

SUBMITTED TO INSURANCE AGENCY ON _____
ATTENTION_____
CLAIM #_____
INSURANCE COMPANY CLAIMS REP._____

INSURANCE CLAIM WORKSHEET COMPLETED BY_____
DATE_____ TITLE_____

INSURANCE ADJUSTER TO SEE INSURED VEHICLE ON_____
TO SEE OTHER VEHICLE ON_____

AMOUNT CREDITED TO DEDUCTIBLE $_____ DATE_____
REIMBURSEMENT CHECK PAID TO_____
AMOUNT_____ DATE_____
TO_____
AMOUNT_____ DATE_____

NOTES:_____
_____
_____
_____
_____
_____
_____
_____
_____

SCREEN ACTORS GUILD

DAILY CONTRACT
(DAY PLAYER)
FOR TELEVISION MOTION PICTURES OR VIDEOTAPES

Company_____

Date Employment Starts_____

Role_____

Production Title_____

Production Number_____

Date_____

Actor Name_____

Address:_____

Telephone No. (_____)_____

Social Security No._____

Daily Rate $_____

Weekly Conversion Rate $_____

Wardrobe supplied by Actor _____Yes _____No

If so, number of outfits _____ @ $ _____

(formal) _____ @ $ _____

Date of Actor's next engagement_____

Complete for "Drop-And-Pick-Up" Deals ONLY:

Firm recall date on _____ or

on or after* _____

("On or after" recall only applies to pick-up as Weekly Player.)

As ☐ Day Player ☐ Weekly Player

*Means date specified or within 24 hours thereafter

THIS AGREEMENT covers the employment of the above-named Player by _____ _____ in the production and at the rate of compensation set forth above and is subject to and shall include, for the benefit of the Player and the Producer, all of the applicable provisions and conditions contained or provided for in the 1986 Screen Actors Guild Television Agreement (herein called the "Television Agreement"). Player's employment shall include performance in non-commercial openings, bridges, etc., and no added compensation shall be payable to Player so long as such are used in the role and episode covered hereunder in which Player appears; for other use, Player shall be paid the added minimum compensation, if any, required under the provisions of the Screen Actors Guild agreements with Producer.

Producer shall have all the rights in and to the results and proceeds of the Player's services rendered hereunder, as are provided with respect to "photoplays" in Schedule A of the Producer-Screen Actors Guild Codified Basic Agreement and the right to supplemental market use as defined in the Television Agreement.

Producer shall have the unlimited right throughout the world to telecast the film and exhibit the film theatrically and in supplemental markets in accordance with the terms and conditions of the Television Agreement.

If the motion picture is rerun on television in the United States or Canada and contains any of the results and proceeds of the Player's services, the Player will be paid for each day of employment hereunder the additional compensation prescribed therefor by the Television Agreement, unless there is an agreement to pay an amount in excess thereof as follows:

_____

_____

_____

_____

If there is foreign telecasting of the motion picture as defined in the Television Agreement, and such motion picture contains any of the results and proceeds of the Player's services, the Player will be paid in the amount in the blank space below for each day of employment hereunder, or if such blank space is not filled in, then the Player will be paid the minimum additional compensation prescribed therefor by the Television Agreement.

If the motion picture is exhibited theatrically anywhere in the world and contains any of the results and proceeds of the Player's services, the Player will be paid $_____, or if this blank is not filled in, then the Player will be paid the minimum additional compensation prescribed therefor by the Television Agreement.

If the motion picture is exhibited in supplemental markets anywhere in the world and contains any of the results and proceeds of the Player's services, then Player will be paid the supplemental market fees prescribed by the applicable provisions of the Television Agreement.

If the Player places his or her initials in the box below, he or she thereby authorizes Producer to use portions of said television motion picture as a trailer to promote another episode or the series as a whole, upon payment to the Player of the additional compensation prescribed by the applicable provisions of the Television Agreement.

Initial

By _____

Producer

_____

Player

Production time reports are available on the set at the end of each day, which reports shall be signed or initialed by the Player.

Attached hereto for your use are the following: (1) Declaration Regarding Income Tax Withholding ("Part Year Employment Method of Withholding") and (2) Declaration Regarding Income Tax Withholding. You may utilize the applicable form by delivering same to Producer. Only one of such forms may be used.

NOTICE TO ACTOR: IT IS IMPORTANT THAT YOU RETAIN A COPY OF THIS CONTRACT FOR YOUR PERMANENT RECORDS.

MINIMUM THREE-DAY CONTRACT
FOR TELEVISION MOTION PICTURES OR VIDEOTAPES
THREE-DAY MINIMUM EMPLOYMENT

THIS AGREEMENT is made this _____ day of _____, 19____, between_____, a corporation, hereinafter called "Producer," and _____, hereinafter called "Performer."

WITNESSETH:

1.   Photoplay; Role and Guarantee. Producer hereby engages Performer to render service as such in the role of _____, in a photoplay produced primarily for exhibition over free television, the working title of which is now _____. Performer accepts such engagement upon the terms herein specified. Producer guarantees that it will furnish Performer not less than _____ days' employment. (If this blank is not filled in, the guarantee shall be three (3) days.)

2.   Salary. The Producer will pay to the Performer, and the Performer agrees to accept for three (3) days (and pro rata for each additional day beyond three (3) days) the following salary rate: $ _____.

3.   Producer shall have the unlimited right throughout the world to telecast the film and exhibit the film theatrically and in Supplemental Markets in accordance with the terms and conditions of the applicable Screen Actors Guild Television Agreement (herein referred to as the "Television Agreement").

4.   If the motion picture is rerun on television in the United States or Canada and contains any of the results and proceeds of the Performer's services, the Performer will be paid the additional compensation prescribed therefor by the Television Agreement, unless there is an agreement to pay an amount in excess thereof as follows:

_____

_____

5.   If there is foreign telecasting of the motion picture as defined in the Television Agreement, and such motion picture contains any of the results and proceeds of the Performer's services, the Performer will be paid the amount in the blank space below plus an amount equal to one-third (1/3) thereof for each day of employment in excess of three (3) days, or, if such blank space is not filled in, then the Performer will be paid the minimum additional compensation prescribed therefor by the Television Agreement. $ _____.

6.   If the motion picture is exhibited theatrically anywhere in the world and contains any of the results and proceeds of the Performer's services, the Performer will be paid $_____, plus an amount equal to one-third (1/3) thereof for each day of employment in excess of three (3) days. If this blank is not filled in, the Performer will be paid the applicable minimum additional compensation prescribed therefor by the Television Agreement.

7.   If the motion picture is exhibited in Supplemental Markets anywhere in the world and contains any of the results and proceeds of the Performer's services, the Performer will be paid the supplemental market fees prescribed by the applicable provisions of the Television Agreement.

8.   Term. The term of employment hereunder shall begin on _____ _____, on or about* _____ and shall continue thereafter until the completion of the photography and recordation of said role.

_____

* The "on or about clause" may only be used when the contract is delivered to the Performer at least three (3) days before the starting date.

9. Incorporation of Television Agreement. The applicable provisions of the Television Agreement are incorporated herein by reference. Performer's employment shall include performance in non-commercial openings, closings, bridges, etc., and no added compensation shall be payable to Performer so long as such are used in the role and episode covered hereunder and in which Performer appears; for other use, Performer shall be paid the added minimum compensation, if any, required under the provisions of the Screen Actors Guild agreements with Producer. Performer's employment shall be upon the terms, conditions and exceptions of the provisions applicable to the rate of salary and guarantee specified in Paragraphs 1. and 2. hereof.

10. Arbitration of Disputes. Should any dispute or controversy arise between the parties hereto with reference to this contract, or the employment herein provided for, such dispute or controversy shall be settled and determined by conciliation and arbitration in accordance with and to the extent provided in the conciliation and arbitration provisions of the Television Agreement, and such provisions are hereby referred to and by such reference incorporated herein and made a part of this agreement with the same effect as though the same were set forth herein in detail.

11. Performer's Address. All notices which the Producer is required or may desire to give to the Performer may be given either by mailing the same addressed to the Performer at _____ , or such notice may be given to the Performer personally, either orally or in writing.

12. Performer's Telephone. The Performer must keep the Producer's casting office or the assistant director of said photoplay advised as to where the Performer may be reached by telephone without unreasonable delay. The current telephone number of the Performer is (_____) _____ .

13. If Performer places his initials in the box, he thereby authorizes Producer to use portions of said television motion picture as a trailer to promote another episode or the series as a whole, upon payment to the Performer of the additional compensation prescribed by the Television Agreement.

14. Furnishing of Wardrobe. The Performer agrees to furnish all modern wardrobe and wearing apparel reasonably necessary for the portrayal of said role; it being agreed, however, that should so-called "character" or "period" costumes be required, the Producer shall supply the same. When Performer supplies any wardrobe, Performer shall receive the cleaning allowance and reimbursement specified in the Television Agreement.

15. Next Starting Date. The starting date of Performer's next engagement is _____ .

IN WITNESS WHEREOF, the parties have executed this agreement on the day and year first above written.

By _____

Producer

_____

Performer

_____

Social Security No.

Production time reports are available on the set at the end of each day. Such reports shall be signed or initialed by the performer.

Attached hereto for your use is a Declaration Regarding Income Tax Withholding ("Part Year Employment Method of Withholding"). You may utilize such form by delivering same to Producer.

NOTICE TO PERFORMER: IT IS IMPORTANT THAT YOU RETAIN A COPY OF THIS CONTRACT FOR YOUR PERMANENT RECORDS.

SCREEN ACTORS GUILD

MINIMUM FREE LANCE WEEKLY CONTRACT
FOR TELEVISION MOTION PICTURES OR VIDEOTAPES

Continuous Employment - Weekly Basis - Weekly Salary
One Week Minimum Employment

THIS AGREEMENT is made this _____ day of _____, 19____, between_____, a corporation, hereinafter called "Producer," and _____ hereinafter called "Performer."

WITNESSETH:

1.   **Photoplay; Role and Guarantee.** Producer hereby engages Performer to render services as such, in the role of _____, in a photoplay produced primarily for exhibition over free television, the working title of which is now _____. Performer accepts such engagement upon the terms herein specified. Producer guarantees that it will furnish Performer not less than _____ weeks employment. (If this blank is not filled in, the guarantee shall be one week).

2.   **Salary.** The Producer will pay to the Performer, and the Performer agrees to accept weekly (and pro rata for each additional day beyond guarantee) the following salary rate: $ _____ per "studio week." (Schedule B Performers must receive an additional overtime payment of four (4) hours at straight time rate for each overnight location sixth day).

3.   Producer shall have the unlimited right throughout the world to telecast the film and exhibit the film theatrically and in Supplemental Markets, in accordance with the terms and conditions of the applicable Screen Actors Guild Television Agreement (herein referred to as the "Television Agreement").

4.   If the motion picture is rerun on television in the United States or Canada and contains any of the results and proceeds of the Performer's services, the Performer will be paid the additional compensation prescribed therefor by the Television Agreement, unless there is an agreement to pay an amount in excess thereof as follows:

_____

_____

_____

5.   If there is foreign telecasting of the motion picture, as defined in the Television Agreement, and such motion picture contains any of the results and proceeds of the Performer's services, the Performer will be paid $ _____ plus pro rata thereof for each additional day of employment in excess of one week, or, if this blank is not filled in, the Performer will be paid the minimum additional compensation prescribed therefor by the Television Agreement.

6.   If the motion picture is exhibited theatrically anywhere in the world and contains any of the results and proceeds of the Performer's services, the Performer will be paid $ _____ plus pro rata thereof for each additional day of employment in excess of one week, or, if this blank is not filled in, the Performer will be paid the minimum additional compensation prescribed therefor by the Television Agreement.

7.   If the motion picture is exhibited in Supplemental Markets anywhere in the world and contains any of the results and proceeds of the Performer's services, the Performer will be paid the supplemental market fees prescribed by the applicable provisions of the Television Agreement.

8.   Term. The term of employment hereunder shall begin on _____ _____, on or about* _____ and shall continue thereafter until the completion of the photography and recordation of said role.

9.   Incorporation of Television Agreement. The applicable provisions of the Television Agreement are incorporated herein by reference. Performer's employment shall include performance in non-commercial openings, closings, bridges, etc., and no added compensation shall be payable to Performer so long as such are used in the role and episode covered hereunder and in which Performer appears; for other use, Performer shall be paid the added minimum compensation, if any, required under the provisions of the Screen Actors Guild agreements with Producer. Performer's employment shall be upon the terms, conditions and exceptions of said provisions applicable to the rate of salary and guarantee specified in Paragraphs 1. and 2. hereof.

10.   Arbitration of Disputes. Should any dispute or controversy arise between the parties hereto with reference to this contract, or the employment herein provided for, such dispute or controversy shall be settled and determined by conciliation and arbitration in accordance with and to the extent provided in the conciliation and arbitration provisions of the Television Agreement, and such provisions are hereby referred to and by such reference incorporated herein and made a part of this agreement with the same effect as though the same were set forth herein in detail.

11.   Performer's Address. All notices which the Producer is required or may desire to give to the Performer may be given either by mailing the same addressed to the Performer at _____, or such notice may be given to the Performer personally, either orally or in writing.

12.   Performer's Telephone. The Performer must keep the Producer's casting office or the assistant director of said photoplay advised as to where the Performer may be reached by telephone without unreasonable delay. The current telephone number of the Performer is (_____)_____.

13. If the Performer places his initials in the box, he thereby authorizes Producer to use portions of said television motion picture as a trailer to promote another episode or the series as a whole, upon payment to the Performer of the additional compensation prescribed by the Television Agreement.

14.   Furnishing of Wardrobe. The Performer agrees to furnish all modern wardrobe and wearing apparel reasonably necessary for the portrayal of said role; it being agreed, however, that should so-called "character" or "period" costumes be required, the Producer shall supply the same. When Performer supplies any wardrobe, Performer shall receive the cleaning allowance and reimbursement specified in the Television Agreement.

15.   Next Starting Date. The starting date of Performer's next engagement is _____.

IN WITNESS WHEREOF, the parties have executed this contract on the day and year first above written.

By   _____
                                    Producer

       _____
                                    Performer

       _____
                          Social Security No.

Production time reports are available on the set at the end of each day. Such reports shall be signed or initialed by the performer.

NOTICE TO PERFORMER: IT IS IMPORTANT THAT YOU RETAIN A COPY OF THIS CONTRACT FOR YOUR PERMANENT RECORDS.

_____
* The "on or about clause" may only be used when the contract is delivered to the performer at least three (3) days before the starting date.

SCREEN ACTORS GUILD

STUNT PERFORMER

DAILY STUNT PERFORMER CONTRACT
FOR TELEVISION MOTION PICTURES AND VIDEOTAPES

TELEVISION DAILY

Company _____

Date Employment Starts _____

Role _____ , or

     Stunt Double for* _____ , or

     Other (description) _____

Production Title _____

Date _____

Stunt Performer Name _____

Address _____

Telephone No. _____

Social Security No. _____

Daily Rate $ _____

Weekly Conversion Rate $ _____

Stunt Adjustment(s):

$ _____ for _____ No. of takes _____

$ _____ for _____ No. of takes _____

Wardrobe supplied by Stunt Performer _____ Yes _____ No

If so, number of outfits_____ @ $ _____

     (formal) _____ @ $ _____

Date of Stunt Performer's next engagement: _____

COMPLETE FOR ''DROP & PICK-UP'' DEALS ONLY:

Firm recall date on _____ , or

on or after**   _____

(''On or after'' recall only applies to pick-up as
Weekly Performer.)

As _____ Day Player _____ Weekly Player

**Means date specified or within 24 hours thereafter.

WITNESSETH:

1. THIS AGREEMENT covers the employment of the above-named Performer by _____
    in the production and at the rate of compensation set forth above and conditions contained or provided for in the Screen Actors Guild Television
    Agreement (herein called the ''Television Agreement''). Performer's employment shall include performance in non-commercial openings, bridges,
    etc., and no added compensation shall be payable to Performer so long as such are used in the role and episode covered hereunder in which
    Performer appears.

2. Producer shall have the unlimited right throughout the world to telecast the film and exhibit the film theatrically and in supplemental markets
    in accordance with the terms and conditions of the Television Agreement.

3. If the motion picture is rerun on television in the United States or Canada and contains any of the results and proceeds of the Performer's services,
    the Performer will be paid for each day of employment hereunder the additional compensation prescribed therefor by the Television Agreement,
    unless there is an agreement to pay an amount in excess thereof as follows: _____

4. If there is foreign telecasting of the motion picture as defined in the Television Agreement, and such motion picture contains any of the results
    and proceeds of the Performer's services, the Performer will be paid in the amount in the blank space below for each day of employment hereunder,
    or if such blank space is not filled in, then the Performer will be paid the minimum additional compensation prescribed therefor by the Television
    Agreement. _____

*NOTE: STUNT DAY PERFORMERS MUST RECEIVE A SEPARATE DAY'S PAY AND CONTRACT FOR EACH PERSON DOUBLED.

5. If the motion picture is exhibited theatrically anywhere in the world and contains any of the results and proceeds of the Performer's services, the Performer will be paid $ _____ , or if this blank is not filled in, then the Performer will be paid the minimum additional compensation prescribed therefor by the Television Agreement.

6. If the motion picture is exhibited in supplemental markets anywhere in the world and contains any of the results and proceeds of the Performer's services, then Performer will be paid the supplemental market fees prescribed by the applicable provisions of the Television Agreement.

By _____

Producer

_____

Stunt Performer

Production time reports and/or time cards are available on the set at the end of each day, which reports shall be signed or initialed by the Performer and must indicate any agreed stunt adjustments.

Attached hereto for your use are the following: (1) Declaration Regarding Income Tax Withholding ("Part Year Employment Method of Withholding") and (2) Declaration Regarding Income Tax Withholding. You may utilize the applicable form by delivering same to Producer. Only one of such forms may be used.

NOTICE TO STUNT PERFORMER: IT IS IMPORTANT THAT YOU RETAIN A COPY OF THIS CONTRACT FOR YOUR PERMANENT RECORDS.

TELEVISION WEEKLY

SCREEN ACTORS GUILD

STUNT PERFORMER

MINIMUM FREE LANCE WEEKLY CONTRACT
FOR TELEVISION MOTION PICTURES OR VIDEOTAPES

Weekly Basis — Weekly Salary
One Week Minimum Employment

THIS AGREEMENT, made this_____day of_____ , 19_____, between

_____ , a corporation, hereinafter called "Producer,"

and _____ , hereinafter called "Performer."

WITNESSETH:

1. PHOTOPLAY, ROLE AND GUARANTEE. Producer hereby engages Performer to render services as such,

   Check One:

   ☐ in the Role of _____ , or

   ☐ as Stunt Double for_____ , or

   ☐ as Utility Stunt Performer, or

   ☐ other (describe work)_____

   in a photoplay produced primarily for exhibition over free television, the working title of which is now _____
   _____ . Performer accepts such engagement upon the terms herein specified. Producer guarantees that it will furnish Performer
   not less than _____ weeks employment. (If this blank is not filled in, the guarantee shall be one week).

2. SALARY. The Producer will pay to the Performer, and the Performer agrees to accept weekly (and pro rata for each additional day beyond guarantee)
   the following salary rate: $ _____ per "studio week." (Schedule H-II Performers must receive an additional overtime payment
   for four (4) hours at straight time rate for each overnight location Saturday.)

3. STUNT ADJUSTMENTS. It is understood between the parties that the salary rate specified above may require adjustment depending upon the
   nature of the stunt activities Producer requires. If so, a Stunt Adjustment will be agreed upon between the parties through good faith bargaining
   and said adjustment shall be noted on the Performer's daily time sheet or time card. Such adjustment shall increase the Performer's compensation
   for the week in the manner prescribed in Schedule H of the Screen Actors Guild Codified Basic Agreement.

4. Producer shall have the unlimited right throughout the world to telecast the film and exhibit the film theatrically and in supplemental markets,
   in accordance with the terms and conditions of the Screen Actors Guild Television Agreement (herein referred to as the "Television Agreement").

5. If the motion picture is rerun on television in the United States or Canada and contains any of the results and proceeds of the Performer's services,
   the Performer will be paid the additional compensation prescribed therefor by the Television Agreement unless there is an agreement to pay an
   amount in excess thereof as follows:_____

6. If there is foreign telecasting of the motion picture as defined in the Television Agreement, and such motion picture contains any of the results
   and proceeds of the Performer's services, the Performer will be paid $ _____ plus pro rata thereof for each day of
   employment in excess of one week, or, if this blank is not filled in, then the Performer will be paid the minimum additional compensation
   prescribed therefor by the Television Agreement.

7. If the motion picture is exhibited theatrically anywhere in the world and contains any of the results and proceeds of the Performer's services,
   the Performer will be paid $ _____ plus pro rata thereof for each day of employment in excess of one week, or, if
   this blank is not filled in, the Performer will be paid the minimum additional compensation prescribed therefor by the Television Agreement.

8. If the motion picture is exhibited in supplemental markets anywhere in the world and contains any of the results and proceeds of the Performer's services, then Performer will be paid the supplemental market fees prescribed by the applicable provisions of the Television Agreement.

9. TERM. The term of employment hereunder shall begin

on _____ , OR on or about* _____

10. CONTINUOUS EMPLOYMENT AND RIGHT TO ROLE. If the Stunt Performer portrays a role or has dialogue, such Performer shall be entitled to continuous employment and "right to role" and shall receive payment for the entire period from the Performer's first call to work on the picture until completion of the photography and recordation of said role.

11. INCORPORATION OF TELEVISION AGREEMENT. The applicable provisions of the Television Agreement are incorporated herein by reference. Performer's employment shall include performance in non-commercial openings, closings, bridges, etc., and no added compensation shall be payable to Performer so long as such are used in the role(s) and episode(s) covered hereunder and in which Performer appears. Performer's employment shall be upon the terms, conditions and exceptions of said provisions applicable to the rate of salary and guarantee specified in Paragraphs 1 and 2 hereof.

12. PERFORMER'S ADDRESS. All notices which the Producer is required or may desire to give to the Performer may be given either by mailing the same addressed to the Performer at_____ or such notice may be given to the Performer personally, either orally or in writing.

13. PERFORMER'S TELEPHONE. The Performer must keep the Producer's casting office or the assistant director of said photoplay advised as to where the Performer may be reached by telephone without unreasonable delay. The current telephone number of the Performer is _____ .

14. NEXT STARTING DATE. The starting date of the Performer's next engagement is _____ .

IN WITNESS WHEREOF, the parties have executed this agreement on the day and year first above written.

PRODUCER _____ STUNT PERFORMER _____

BY _____ SOCIAL SECURITY # _____

*The "on or about" clause may only be used when the contract is delivered to the Performer at least three (3) days before the starting date.

The Production time reports are available on the set at the end of each day, which reports shall be signed or initialed by the Performer and must indicate any agreed stunt adjustments.

Attached hereto for your use is a Declaration Regarding Income Tax Withholding.

NOTICE TO STUNT PERFORMER: IT IS IMPORTANT THAT YOU RETAIN A COPY OF THIS CONTRACT FOR YOUR PERMANENT RECORDS.

SCREEN ACTORS GUILD

**DAILY CONTRACT
(DAY PLAYER)
FOR THEATRICAL MOTION PICTURES**

Company_____

Date Employment Starts_____

Production Title_____

Production Number_____

Role_____

Daily Rate $_____

Weekly Conversion Rate $_____

Date_____

Actor Name_____

Address_____

Telephone No. (_____)_____

Social Security No._____

Date of Birth_____

Legal Resident of (State)_____

Citizen of U.S._____Yes _____No

Wardrobe supplied by Actor _____Yes _____No

If so, number of outfits _____ @ $ _____

(formal) _____ @ $ _____

Date of Actor's next engagement_____

Complete for "Drop-And-Pick-Up" Deals ONLY:

Firm recall date on _____ or

on or after* _____

("On or after" recall only applies to pick-up as Weekly Player.)

As ☐ Day Player ☐ Weekly Player

*Means date specified or within 24 hours thereafter

The employment is subject to all of the provisions and conditions applicable to the employment of DAY PLAYERS contained or provided for in the Producer-Screen Actors Guild Codified Basic Agreement of 1986 as the same may be supplemented and/or amended.

The Player (does) (does not) hereby authorize the Producer to deduct from the compensation hereinabove specified an amount equal to _____ per cent of each installment of compensation due the Player hereunder, and to pay the amount of so deducted to the Motion Picture and Televison Relief Fund of America, Inc.

Special Provisions:

PRODUCER_____ PLAYER_____

BY_____

Production time reports are available on the set at the end of each day.
Such reports shall be signed or initialed by the Player.

Attached hereto for your use is Declaration Regarding Income Tax Withholding.

NOTICE TO ACTOR: IT IS IMPORTANT THAT YOU RETAIN A COPY OF THIS CONTRACT FOR YOUR PERMANENT RECORDS.

SCREEN ACTORS GUILD
MINIMUM FREE LANCE CONTRACT
FOR THEATRICAL MOTION PICTURES

Continuous Employment—Weekly Basis—Weekly Salary
One Week Minimum Employment

THIS AGREEEMENT, made this _____ day of _____, 19____, between_____ _____, hereafter called "Producer", and _____, hereafter called "Player".

WITNESSETH:

1. PHOTOPLAY, ROLE, SALARY AND GUARANTEE. Producer hereby engages Player to render services as such in the role of_____, in a photoplay, the working title of which is now _____, at the salary of $_____ per "studio week" (Schedule B Players must receive an additional overtime payment of four (4) hours at straight time rate for each overnight location Saturday). Player accepts such engagement upon the terms herein specified. Producer guarantees that it will furnish Player not less than_____week's employment (if this blank is not filled in, the guarantee shall be one week). Player shall be paid pro rata for each additional day beyond guarantee until dismissal.

2. TERM: The term of employment hereunder shall begin on

   on _____

   on or about* _____
   and shall continue thereafter until the completion of the photography and recordation of said role.

3. BASIC CONTRACT. All provisions of the collective bargaining agreement between Screen Actors Guild, Inc. and Producer, relating to theatrical motion pictures, which are applicable to the employment of the Player hereunder, shall be deemed incorporated herein.

4. PLAYER'S ADDRESS. All notices which the Producer is required or may desire to give to the Player may be given either by mailing the same addressed to the Player at _____ or such notice may be given to the Player personally, either orally or in writing.

5. PLAYER'S TELEPHONE. The Player must keep the Producer's casting office or the assistant director of said photoplay advised as to where the Player may be reached by telephone without unreasonable delay. The current telephone number of the Player is _____

6. MOTION PICTURE AND TELEVISION RELIEF FUND. The Player (does) (does not) hereby authorize the Producer to deduct from the compensation hereinabove specified an amount equal to _____ per cent of each installment of compensation due the Player hereunder, and to pay the amount so deducted to the Motion Picture and Television Relief Fund of America, Inc.

7. FURNISHING OF WARDROBE. The (Producer) (Player) agrees to furnish all modern wardrobe and wearing apparel reasonably necessary for the portrayal of said role; it being agreed, however, that should so-called "character" or "period" costumes be required, the Producer shall supply the same. When Player furnishes any wardrobe, Player shall receive the cleaning allowance and reimbursement, if any, specified in the basic contract.

   Number of outfits furnished by Player _____ @ $_____
   (formal) _____ @ $_____

8. ARBITRATION OF DISPUTES. Should any dispute or controversy arise between the parties hereto with reference to this contract, or the employment herein provided for, such dispute or controversy shall be settled and determined by conciliation and arbitration in accordance with the conciliation and arbitration provisions of the collective bargaining agreement between the Producer and Screen Actors Guild relating to theatrical motion pictures, and such provisions are hereby referred to and by such reference incorporated herein and made a part of this Agreement with the same effect as though the same were set forth herein in detail.

9. NEXT STARTING DATE. The starting date of Player's next engagement is_____.

10. The Player may not waive any provision of this contract without the written consent of Screen Actors Guild, Inc.

11. Producer makes the material representation that either it is presently a signatory to the Screen Actors Guild collective bargaining agreement covering the employment contracted for herein, or that the above-referred-to photoplay is covered by such collective bargaining agreement under the Independent Production provisions of the General Provisions of the Producer-Screen Actors Guild Codified Basic Agreement of 1983 as the same may be supplmented and/or amended.

IN WITNESS WHEREOF, the parties have executed this agreement on the day and year first above written.

PRODUCER _____ PLAYER _____

BY _____ Social Security No. _____

*The "on or about" clause may only be used when the contract is delivered to the Player at least seven days before the starting date. See Codified Basic Agreement of 1983, Schedule B, Schedule C, otherwise a specific starting date must be stated.

Production time reports are available on the set at the end of each day, which reports shall be signed or initialed by the Player.

Attached hereto for your use are the following: (1) Declaration Regarding Income Tax Withholding ("Part Year Employment Method of Withholding") and (2) Declaration Regarding Income Tax Withholding. You may utilize the applicable form by delivering same to Producer. Only one of such forms may be used.

NOTICE TO ACTOR: IT IS IMPORTANT THAT YOU RETAIN A COPY OF THIS CONTRACT FOR YOUR PERMA-NENT RECORDS.

MOTION PICTURE
WEEKLY

SCREEN ACTORS GUILD

STUNT PERFORMER

MINIMUM FREE LANCE WEEKLY CONTRACT
FOR THEATRICAL MOTION PICTURES

Weekly Basis — Weekly Salary
One Week Minimum Employment

THIS AGREEMENT, made this_____day of_____ , 19_____, between

_____ , hereafter called "Producer," and

_____ , hereafter called "Performer."

WITNESSETH:

1. PHOTOPLAY, ROLE, SALARY AND GUARANTEE. Producer hereby engages Performer to render services as such,

   Check One:

   ☐ in the Role of _____ , or

   ☐ as Stunt Double for_____ , or

   ☐ as Utility Stunt Performer, or

   ☐ other (describe work)_____

   in a photoplay, the working title of which is now _____ , at the
   salary of $ _____ per "studio week" (Schedule H-II Performers must receive an additional overtime payment of four (4) hours
   at straight time rate for each overnight location Saturday). Performer accepts such engagement upon the terms herein specified. Producer guarantees
   that it will furnish Performer not less than _____ weeks employment (if this blank is not filled in, the guarantee shall be one week).
   Performer shall be paid pro rata for each additional day beyond the guarantee until dismissal.

2. TERM. The term of employment hereunder shall begin on _____ OR on or about* _____

3. STUNT ADJUSTMENTS. It is understood between the parties that the salary rate specified above may require adjustment depending upon the
   nature of the stunt activities Producer requires. If so, a Stunt Adjustment will be agreed upon between the parties through good faith bargaining
   and said adjustment shall be noted on the Performer's daily time sheet or time card. Such adjustment shall increase the Performer's compensation
   for the week in the manner prescribed in Schedule H of the Screen Actors Guild Codified Basic Agreement.

4. CONTINUOUS EMPLOYMENT AND RIGHT TO ROLE. If the Stunt Performer portrays a role or has dialogue, such Performer shall be
   entitled to continuous employment and "right to role" and shall receive payment for the entire period from the Performer's first call to work
   on the picture until completion of the photography and recordation of said role.

5. BASIC CONTRACT. All provisions of the collective bargaining agreement between Screen Actors Guild, Inc. and Producer, relating to theatrical
   motion pictures, which are applicable to the employment of the Performer hereunder, shall be deemed incorporated herein.

6. PERFORMER'S ADDRESS. All notices which the Producer is required or may desire to give to the Performer may be given either by mailing
   same addressed to the Performer at _____ , or such notice may be given
   to the Performer personally, either orally or in writing.

* The "on or about" clause may only be used when the contract is delivered to the Performer at least seven (7) days before the starting date. See
  Codified Basic Agreement of 1983, Schedule B or Schedule C, otherwise a specific starting date must be stated.

7. PERFORMER'S TELEPHONE. The Performer must keep the Producer's casting office or the assistant director of said photoplay advised as to where the Performer may be reached by telephone without unreasonable delay. The current telephone number of the Performer is _____.

8. MOTION PICTURE AND TELEVISION RELIEF FUND. The Performer (does) (does not) hereby authorize the Producer to deduct from the compensation hereinabove specified an amount equal to _____ per cent of each installment of compensation due the Performer hereunder, and to pay the amount so deducted to the Motion Picture and Television Relief Fund of America, Inc.

9. ARBITRATION OF DISPUTES. Should any dispute or controversy arise between the parties hereto with reference to this contract, or the employment herein provided for, such dispute or controversy shall be settled and determined by conciliation and arbitration in accordance with the conciliation and arbitration provisions of the collective bargaining agreement between the Producer and Screen Actors Guild relating to theatrical motion pictures, and such provisions are hereby referred to and by such reference incorporated herein and made a part of this Agreement with the same effect as though the same were set forth herein in detail.

10. NEXT STARTING DATE. The starting date of the Performer's next engagement is _____.

11. The Performer may not waive any provision of this contract without the written consent of Screen Actors Guild, Inc.

12. Producer makes the material representation that either it is presently a signatory to the Screen Actors Guild collective bargaining agreement covering the employment contracted for herein, or that the photoplay is covered by such collective bargaining agreement under the Independent Production provisions of the General Provisions of the Producer-Screen Actors Guild Codified Basic Agreement as the same may be supplemented and/or amended to date.

IN WITNESS WHEREOF, the parties have executed this agreement on the day and year first above written.

PRODUCER _____ PERFORMER _____

BY _____ SOCIAL SECURITY # _____

Production time reports and/or time cards are available on the set at the beginning and end of each day, which reports shall be signed or initialed by the Performer and must indicate any agreed stunt adjustments.

Attached hereto for your use are the following: (1) Declaration Regarding Income Tax Withholding ("Part Year Employment Method of Withholding") and (2) Declaration Regarding Income Tax Withholding. You may utilize the applicable form by delivering same to Producer. Only one of such forms may be used.

NOTICE TO STUNT PERFORMER: IT IS IMPORTANT THAT YOU RETAIN A COPY OF THIS CONTRACT FOR YOUR PERMANENT RECORDS.

MOTION PICTURE
DAILY

SCREEN ACTORS GUILD
STUNT PERFORMER
DAILY STUNT PERFORMER CONTRACT
FOR THEATRICAL MOTION PICTURES

Company _____

Date Employment Starts _____

Production Title _____

Production No. _____

Role _____ , or

    Stunt Double for* _____ , or

    Other (description) _____

Daily Rate $ _____

Weekly Conversion Rate $ _____

Stunt Adjustment(s):

$ _____ for _____ No. of takes _____

$ _____ for _____ No. of takes _____

Date _____

Stunt Performer Name _____

Address _____

Telephone No. ( ) _____

Social Security No. _____

Date of birth _____

Legal Resident of (State) _____

Citizen of U.S. _____ Yes _____ No

Wardrobe supplied by Stunt Performer _____ Yes _____ No

If so, number of outfits_____ @ $ _____

    (formal) _____ @ $ _____

Date of Stunt Performer's next engagement: _____

COMPLETE FOR "DROP & PICK-UP" DEALS ONLY:

Firm recall date on _____ , or

on or after** _____

("On or after" recall only applies to pick-up as
Weekly Player.)

As _____ Day Player _____ Weekly Player

**Means date specified or within 24 Hours thereafter.

WITNESSETH:

1. The employment is subject to all of the provisions and conditions applicable to the employment of Stunt Performers contained or provided for in the Producers-Screen Actors Guild Codified Basic Agreement as the same may be supplemented and/or amended. Refer to Schedule H.

2. The Stunt Performer (does) (does not) hereby authorize the Producer to deduct from the compensation hereinabove specified an amount equal to _____ per cent of each installment of compensation due the Stunt Performer hereunder, and to pay the amount so deducted to the Motion Picture and Television Relief Fund of America, Inc.

3. Special Provisions: _____
_____
_____
_____

PRODUCER_____ STUNT PERFORMER_____

Production time reports and/or time cards are available on the set at the end of each day. Such reports shall be signed or initialed by the Stunt Performer and must indicate any agreed stunt adjustments.

Attached hereto for your use is Declaration Regarding Income Tax Withholding.

TO STUNT PERFORMER: IT IS IMPORTANT THAT YOU RETAIN A COPY OF THIS CONTRACT FOR YOUR PERMANENT RECORDS.

*NOTE: STUNT DAY PERFORMERS MUST RECEIVE A SEPARATE DAY'S PAY AND CONTRACT FOR EACH PERSON DOUBLED.

SCREEN ACTORS GUILD

#15

TAFT/HARTLEY REPORT

ATTENTION:_____ ATTACHED?:_____ RESUME*_____ PHOTO

_____

EMPLOYEE INFORMATION

NAME_____ SS#_____

ADDRESS_____ AGE (IF MINOR)_____

CITY/STATE_____ ZIP_____ PHONE(   )_____

EMPLOYER INFORMATION

NAME_____ Check_____ AD AGENCY

one:_____STUDIO

ADDRESS_____ _____PRODUCTION

COMPANY

CITY/STATE_____ ZIP_____ PHONE(   )_____

EMPLOYMENT INFORMATION

Check   CONTRACT: _____DAILY   CATEGORY: _____ACTOR
one: _____3-DAY   _____SINGER   _____OTHER_____
                  _____WEEKLY   _____STUNT

WORK DATE(S)_____ SALARY_____

PRODUCTION TITLE_____ PROD'N/COM'L #_____

SHOOTING LOCATION (City & State)_____

REASON FOR HIRE (be specific)_____

_____

_____

_____

_____

_____

Employer is aware of General Provision, Section 14 of the Basic Agreement that applies to Theatrical and Television production, and Schedule B of the Commercials Contract, wherein Preference of Employment shall be given to qualified professional actors (except as otherwise stated). Employer will pay to the Guild as liquidated damages, the sums indicated for each breach by the Employer of any provision of those sections.

SIGNATURE_____ DATE_____
          Producer or Casting Director - Indicate which

PRINT NAME_____ PHONE(   )_____

*PLEASE BE CERTAIN RESUME LISTS ALL TRAINING AND/OR EXPERIENCE IN THE ENTERTAINMENT INDUSTRY.

SAG EXTRA

SCREEN ACTORS GUILD

TAFT/HARTLEY REPORT

ATTENTION:_____ ATTACHED?:_____ RESUME _____PHOTO

_____

EMPLOYEE INFORMATION

NAME_____ SS#_____

ADDRESS_____ AGE (IF MINOR)_____

CITY/STATE_____ZIP_____PHONE(   )_____

EMPLOYER INFORMATION

NAME_____ Check____ CASTING OFFICE
                                        one:____STUDIO
ADDRESS_____   ____PRODUCTION
                                                   COMPANY
CITY/STATE_____ZIP_____PHONE(   )_____

EMPLOYMENT INFORMATION

Check
 one: General Extra ____   Special Ability Extra ____   Dancer ____

WORK DATE(S)_____ SALARY_____

PRODUCTION TITLE_____

SHOOTING LOCATION (City & State)_____

REASON FOR HIRE (be specific)_____

_____

_____

Employer is aware of General Provision, Section 45 of the Producer-Screen Actors
Guild Extra Player Agreement that applies to Theatrical and Television
production, wherein Preference of Employment shall be given to qualified
professional extras (except as otherwise stated). Employer will pay to the
Guild as liquidated damages, a sum which shall be determined by binding
arbitration for each breach by the Employer of any provision of those sections.

SIGNATURE_____ DATE _____
          Producer or Casting Director - Indicate which

PRINT NAME_____ PHONE(   )_____

PRODUCER:

PLEASE PRESS
YOU ARE MAKING FOUR COPIES

DATE	NAME (PRINT)	PRODUCTION NO. OR TITLE		DISMISSAL TIME

SAG NO.

SOCIAL SECURITY NO. MUST BE PROVIDED TO MAKE PAYMENT

TYPE OF CALL

STARTING TIME

☐ SINGLE ☐ MARRIED ☐ MARRIED but withheld at higher single rate

Total number of allowances you are claiming: _____

Additional amount, if any, you want deducted $ _____

If claiming exemption from withholding, write exempt and year in box   19 _____

BASIC WAGE RATE	TRAVEL TIME	PENALTIES		HOURS WORKED
	ARRIVE LOCATION:		INTERVIEW	MEAL PERIODS
	LEAVE LOCATION:			IN
				OUT
	FITTING	MEALS		IN
	☐	B ☐	☐	OUT
		L ☐		ASST. DIR.-APPROVED FOR PAYMENT
		D ☐		

EMPLOYEE: PLEASE PRINT INFORMATION LISTED ABOVE AND SIGN WHERE INDICATED

"I, the undersigned, certify that the number of income tax withholding exemptions claimed on this certificate does not exceed the number of which I am entitled.

"I agree to accept the sum properly computed based upon the times and the basic wage rate shown as payment in full for all services heretofore rendered by me for said employer.

"I further agree that the said sum, less all deduction required by law, may be paid to me by negotiable check issued by said company, said check to be addressed to me at my last reported address and deposited in the United States mail within the time periods provided by law.

"I hereby give and grant to the company named all rights of every kind and character whatsoever in and to all work heretofore done, and all poses, acts, plays and appearances heretofore made by me for you and in to all of the results and proceeds of my services heretofore rendered for you, as well as in and to the right to use my name, likeness and photographs, either still or moving for commercial and advertising purposes. I further give and grant to the said company the right to reproduce in any manner whatsoever any recordations heretofore made by said company of my voice and all instrumental, musical, or other sound effects produced by me. I further agree that in the event of a retake of all or any of the scenes in which I participate, or if additional scenes are required (whether originally contemplated or not) I will return to work and render my services in such scenes at the same basic rate of compensations as that paid me for the original taking.

"By signing this form, I hereby agree that said employer may take deductions from my earnings to adjust previous overpayments if and when said overpayments may occur."

WARDROBE	PROPS	VEHICLE	MILEAGE

DO NOT WRITE IN THIS SPACE

TYPE OF WORK	PAY CODE	HOURS		AMOUNT	BASIC RATE
		WORK	PAY		
DAY		.	.	.	
NIGHT		.	.	.	ADJUSTMENTS
O/T		.	.	.	
WET		.	.	.	OVERTIME
SMOKE					ALLOWANCES
OTHER				.	
OTHER					GROSS
OTHER					
OTHER					

Signature _____ Date _____

Address _____ Apt # _____

City _____ State _____ Zip _____

Phone Number _____

BACK OF WHITE COPY MUST BE COMPLETED

YOUR EMPLOYER OF RECORD IS _____
IF OTHER THAN A PAYROLL COMPANY, EMPLOYER'S FEDERAL I.D. NUMBER IS _____

white—PAYROLL COPY
yellow—PRODUCTION COPY
pink—SAG COPY
golden rod—EXTRAS COPY

Screen Actors Guild
Kenmar Printing   357
Form No. 451

SCREEN ACTORS GUILD
THEATRICAL & TELEVISION SIGN-IN

PLEASE PRINT
ALL INFORMATION

AUDITION DATE_____

Prod'n Co._____ Casting Rep._____ Phone_____
Prod'n Title_____ Director_____ Phone_____
Episode Title/#_____ Producer_____ Phone_____

[ ] FILM
[ ] TV-MOW
[ ] TV-OTHER

PLAYER'S NAME	SOCIAL SECURITY	NAME OF ROLE	AGENT	VIDEO TAPED?	PROVIDED?		PLAYER'S			
					PARKING	SCRIPT	ACTUAL CALL	TIME IN	TIME OUT	INITIALS

_____
SIGNATURE OF AUTHORIZED REPRESENTATIVE

PRODUCER

1. Complete top half of form.
2. Sign your name.
3. Designate person to whom correspondence
   concerning this form shall be sent.

SCREEN ACTORS GUILD
ACTORS PRODUCTION TIME REPORT

PICTURE TITLE: _____

PROD. # _____   DATE _____   IS TODAY A DESIGNATED DAY OFF? • YES ___ NO ___

CAST - WEEKLY & DAY PLAYERS
Worked - W   Rehearsal - R   Finished - F
Started - S   Hold - H   Test - T
Travel - TR

CAST / CHARACTER	W S R T / TR	MAKEUP WDBE.	WORKTIME		B K F S T	MEALS		TRAVEL TIME				STUNT ADJUST.	WARDROBE NO. OF OUTFITS PROVIDED	ACTORS SIGNATURE
			REPORT ON SET	DISMISS ON SET		1ST MEAL	2ND MEAL	LEAVE FOR LOCATION	ARRIVE ON LOCATION	LEAVE LOCATION	ARRIVE AT STUDIO			

• This refers to the 2 days (1 day on overnight location) which producer can designate as day(s) off for the production.

SCREEN ACTORS GUILD

Casting Data Report

See Reverse
For Instructions

THIS FORM MUST BE COMPLETED FOR EACH MOTION PICTURE AND EACH EPISODE OF EACH SERIES PRODUCED FOR THE QUARTER IN WHICH PRINCIPAL PHOTOGRAPHY WAS COMPLETED.

1) PRODUCTION COMPANY _____

2) QUARTER and YEAR _____

3) PROJECT (Title, Prod. No., etc.) _____

4) DESCRIPTION (Feature, M.O.W., TV Series, etc.) _____

5) TOTAL NO. OF DAYS OF PRODUCTION (Principal Photography Only) _____

6) DATA SUBMITTED BY _____ NAME

TELEPHONE NUMBER _____

7) CHECK IF APPROPRIATE ☐ NO STUNTS

PART I

8)

CATEGORY		FORM OF HIRING			9) CAST TOTALS	10) NO. OF DAYS WORKED	11) AGE:					
		DAILY	WEEKLY	SERIES			UNDER 40		40 and OVER		UNKNOWN	
											M	F
MALE	LEAD											
	SUPPORT											
FEMALE	LEAD											
	SUPPORT											

PART II

12)

CATEGORY		FORM OF HIRING						13) NO. OF DAYS WORKED		14) AGE					
		DAILY		WEEKLY		SERIES				UNDER 40		40 and OVER		UNKNOWN	
		M	F	M	F	M	F	M	F	M	F	M	F	M	F
ASIAN / PACIFIC	LEAD														
	SUPPORT														
BLACK	LEAD														
	SUPPORT														
CAUCASIAN	LEAD														
	SUPPORT														
LATINO / HISPANIC	LEAD														
	SUPPORT														
N. AMERICAN INDIAN	LEAD														
	SUPPORT														
UNKNOWN/OTHER	LEAD														
	SUPPORT														

THE COMPLETE FILM PRODUCTION HANDBOOK 225

INSTRUCTIONS

1. Indicate the Production Company (e.g. "THE ABC COMPANY").

2. Indicate the quarter/year (e.g. "1st quarter 1981").

   The quarters consist of:

January — March	(1st)
April — June	(2nd)
July — September	(3rd)
October — December	(4th)

3. Indicate the <u>name</u> of the film for which you are reporting.

4. Indicate the <u>type</u> of project (feature, television movie, television pilot, television series, animation).

5. Use a number to respond to this question.

6. Indicate the name of person completing this form and the telephone number for same.

7. Two separate reports are required, one for <u>Performers</u> only and one for <u>Stunt Performers</u> only. If there were no Stunt Performers employed on the film, check the "No Stunt" box. If Stunt Performers were employed, complete the casting data report form for Stunt Performers.

8. <u>Part I</u>. Indicate the total number of lead and supporting Performers in each of the applicable categories.

9. Use numbers only to indicate the total number of Performers in the category.

10. Use numbers only to indicate the total number of days worked by <u>ALL</u> Performers in the category.

11. Use numbers only to indicate how many Performers were in each age group.

12. <u>Part II</u>. Indicate the total number of males and females in each category.

13. Use number only to indicate the total number of days worked by <u>ALL</u> the Performers in male and female category.

14. Use numbers only to indicate how many performers were in each age group.

**<u>NOTE</u>: PLEASE MAKE EVERY EFFORT TO INSURE THAT YOUR NUMBERS CORRESPOND ACROSS AND AMONG <u>PART I AND PART II</u>.

SCREEN ACTORS GUILD

Casting Data Report for Stunt Performers Only

THIS FORM MUST BE COMPLETED FOR EACH MOTION PICTURE AND EACH EPISODE OF EACH SERIES PRODUCED FOR THE QUARTER IN WHICH PRINCIPAL PHOTOGRAPHY WAS COMPLETED.

See Reverse
For Instructions

1) PRODUCTION COMPANY _____

2) QUARTER and YEAR _____

3) PROJECT (Title, Prod. No., etc.) _____

4) DESCRIPTION (Feature, M.O.W., TV Series, etc.) _____

5) TOTAL NO. OF DAYS OF PRODUCTION (Principal Photography Only) _____

6) DATA SUBMITTED BY _____ NAME

TELEPHONE NUMBER _____

7) NAME OF STUNT COORDINATOR _____

PART I

CATEGORY	8) FORM OF HIRING						9) PERFORMER TOTALS	10) NUMBER DAYS WORKED	11) AGE						12) STUNT SUMMARY			
	DAILY		WEEKLY		SERIES				UNDER 40		40 and OVER		UNKNOWN		DESCRIPT		NON-DESCRIPT	
	M	F	M	F	M	F												
MALE																		
FEMALE																		

PART II

CATEGORY	13) FORM OF HIRING						14) NUMBER DAYS WORKED		15) AGE						16) STUNT SUMMARY			
	DAILY		WEEKLY		SERIES				UNDER 40		40 and OVER		UNKNOWN		DESCRIPT		NON-DESCRIPT	
	M	F	M	F	M	F	M	F	M	F	M	F	M	F	M	F	M	F
ASIAN/PACIFIC																		
BLACK																		
CAUCASIAN																		
HISPANIC																		
N. AMERICAN INDIAN																		
OTHER/UNKNOWN																		

INSTRUCTIONS

**There are two separate report forms required.
Complete one report for Performers and one report for Stunt Performers.

---

1. Indicate the Production Company (e.g. "THE ABC COMPANY").

2. Indicate the quarter/year (e.g. "1st quarter 1981").

   The quarters consist of: January — March   (1st)

   April   — June   (2nd)

   July   — September   (3rd)

   October — December   (4th)

3. Indicate the <u>name</u> of the film for which you are reporting.

4. Indicate the <u>type</u> of project (feature, television movie, television series).

5. Use a number to respond to this question.

6. Provide the name and telephone number of the person who completes this form.

7. Provide the name of the stunt coordinator for the film.

Part I
8. Indicate the total number of males and females in each category.

9. Use numbers only to indicate the total number of stunt performers in the category.

10. Use numbers only to indicate the total amount of days worked by all stunt performers in the category.

11. Use numbers only to indicate how many stunt performers are in a certain age group.

12. Use numbers only to indicate the stunts as descript or non-descript.

Part II
13. Indicate the total number of males and females in each category.

14. Use numbers only to indicate the total number of days worked by <u>all</u> the Performers in each category.

15. Use numbers only to indicate how many performers were in each age group.

16. Indicate the stunts as descript or non-descript.

NOTE: Please make every effort to insure that your numbers correspond across categories and among
Part I and Part II.

LOW–BUDGET
AFFIRMATIVE ACTION

SCREEN ACTORS GUILD
Casting Data Report

See Reverse
For Instructions

THIS FORM MUST BE COMPLETED FOR EACH MOTION PICTURE AND EACH EPISODE OF EACH SERIES PRODUCED FOR THE QUARTER IN WHICH PRINCIPAL PHOTOGRAPHY WAS COMPLETED.

1) PRODUCTION COMPANY

2) QUARTER and YEAR

3) PROJECT (Title, Prod. No., etc.)

4) DESCRIPTION (Feature, M.O.W., TV Series, etc.)

5) TOTAL NO. OF DAYS OF PRODUCTION (Principal Photography Only)

6) DATA SUBMITTED BY _____ NAME

TELEPHONE NUMBER

7) CHECK IF APPROPRIATE ☐ NO STUNTS

PART I

8)

CATEGORY		FORM OF HIRING			9) CAST TOTALS	10) NO. OF DAYS WORKED	11) AGE:		
		DAILY	WEEKLY	SERIES			UNDER 40	40 to 60	60 & Over
MALE	LEAD								
	SUPPORT								
FEMALE	LEAD								
	SUPPORT								

PART II

12)

CATEGORY		FORM OF HIRING							13) NO. OF DAYS WORKED		14) AGE					
		DAILY		WEEKLY		SERIES					UNDER 40		40 to 60		60 & Over	
		M	F	M	F	M	F	M	F	M	F	M	F	M	F	
ASIAN / PACIFIC	LEAD															
	SUPPORT															
BLACK	LEAD															
	SUPPORT															
CAUCASIAN	LEAD															
	SUPPORT															
LATINO / HISPANIC	LEAD															
	SUPPORT															
N. AMERICAN INDIAN	LEAD															
	SUPPORT															
UNKNOWN/OTHER	LEAD															
	SUPPORT															

INSTRUCTIONS

1. Indicate the Production Company (e.g. "THE ABC COMPANY").

2. Indicate the quarter/year (e.g. "1st quarter 1981").

   The quarters consist of:

January	— March	(1st)
April	— June	(2nd)
July	— September	(3rd)
October	— December	(4th)

3. Indicate the <u>name</u> of the film for which you are reporting.

4. Indicate the <u>type</u> of project (feature, television movie, television pilot, television series, animation).

5. Use a number to respond to this question.

6. Indicate the name of person completing this form and the telephone number for same.

7. Two separate reports are required, one for <u>Performers</u> only and one for <u>Stunt Performers</u> only. If there were no Stunt Performers employed on the film, check the "No Stunt" box. If Stunt Performers were employed, complete the casting data report form for Stunt Performers.

8. <u>Part I.</u> Indicate the total number of lead and supporting Performers in each of the applicable categories.

9. Use numbers only to indicate the total number of Performers in the category.

10. Use numbers only to indicate the total number of days worked by <u>ALL</u> Performers in the category.

11. Use numbers only to indicate how many Performers were in each age group.

12. <u>Part II.</u> Indicate the total number of males and females in each category.

13. Use number only to indicate the total number of days worked by <u>ALL</u> the Performers in male and female category.

14. Use numbers only to indicate how many performers were in each age group.

NOTE: PLEASE MAKE EVERY EFFORT TO INSURE THAT YOUR NUMBERS CORRESPOND ACROSS AND AMONG <u>PART I AND PART II.</u>

SCREEN ACTORS GUILD
7065 Hollywood Blvd.
Hollywood, CA 90028-7594

 # 10

FINAL CAST LIST INFORMATION SHEET

DATE
FILED: _____

PICTURE TITLE _____

SHOOTING LOCATION _____

PRODUCTION COMPANY _____

START DATE _____   COMPLETION DATE _____

ADDRESS _____

FEDERAL I.D.# _____   STATE I.D.# _____

PHONE ( ) _____   CONTACT _____

PICTURE # _____

Check
One: MP _____   MOW _____   OTHER TV _____   INDUSTRIAL _____   OTHER _____

DISTRIBUTOR _____

To establish Residual payments, see Section 5.2 of the 1980 Basic Agreement.

PLAYER NAME & SOCIAL SECURITY NUMBER	PLAYER ADDRESS INCLUDING ZIP	(1) PERIOD WORKED #DYS / #WKS	(1) Start Date	(1) Finish Date	(2) Contract Type	(3) Player Type	(4) TOTAL GROSS SALARY .	(5) BASE SALARY	Time Units	Salary Units	Total Units	FOR SAG USE ONLY

(1) Include days not worked, but considered worked under continuous employment provisions. Report contractually guaranteed work period or actual time worked, whichever is longer.

(2) Insert D for Daily or W for Weekly type of contract.

(3) Insert: A = Actor; ST = Stunt; P = Pilot; SG = Singer; ADR = Automated Dialogue Replacement.

(4) Include all salary, Overtime, Premium, and Stunt Adjustments. Do not include any Penalties paid (i.e. Meal Penalties, forced Calls, etc.).

(5) List base contractual salary (i.e. $1,500.00/week or $500.00/day).

To establish Residual payments, see Section 5.2 of the 1980 Basic Agreement.

PLAYER NAME & SOCIAL SECURITY NUMBER	PLAYER ADDRESS INCLUDING ZIP	(1) PERIOD WORKED # WKS	(1) PERIOD WORKED # DYS	(1) Start Date	(1) Finish Date	(2) Contract Type	(3) Player Type	(4) TOTAL GROSS SALARY	(5) BASE SALARY	Time Units	Salary Units	Total Units	FOR SAG USE ONLY

(1) Include days not worked, but considered worked under continuous employment provisions. Report contractually guaranteed work period or actual time worked, whichever is longer.
(2) Insert D for Daily or W for Weekly type of contract.
(3) Insert: A = Actor; ST = Stunt; P = Pilot; SG = Singer; ADR = Automated Dialogue Replacement.
(4) Include all salary, Overtime, Premium, and Stunt Adjustments. Do not include any Penalties paid (i.e. Meal Penalties, forced Calls, etc.).
(5) List base contractual salary (i.e. $1,500.00/week or $500.00/day).

It is the responsibility of the reporting member to file a copy of this report with the Screen Actors Guild within forty-eight (48) hours of each session and to deliver a copy to the employer or the employer's representative at the conclusion of each session. If there is a contractor, he shall assume these responsibilities with respect to each session.

Work Date _____ Title _____

Episode Title _____ Prod. No. _____

Production Co./   Studio   Sound Supervisor
Employer _____   Facility _____   Editor _____

Address _____   Address _____   Sound Engineer/
        _____   _____   Mixer _____

        _____   _____   ADR Supervisor _____

Phone # (   )   Phone # (   )   Employer Rep. _____

Type of Film: Theatrical _____ TV Series _____ TV MOW _____ TV Pilot _____ Other _____

Performer's Name	Performer's Social Security #	Character of 6+ Lines (sync)	Additional sets of up to 3 characters under 5 sync lines each	Hours Employed Studio Time Report/Dismiss	Meal Period From/To	Performer's Initials
_____	_____	_____	_____	_____	_____	_____
_____	_____	_____	_____	_____	_____	_____
_____	_____	_____	_____	_____	_____	_____
_____	_____	_____	_____	_____	_____	_____
_____	_____	_____	_____	_____	_____	_____
_____	_____	_____	_____	_____	_____	_____
_____	_____	_____	_____	_____	_____	_____
_____	_____	_____	_____	_____	_____	_____

Reel #s Recorded: _____

NOTES: _____

_____

This engagement shall be governed by and be subject to the applicable terms of the Screen Actors Guild Codified Basic or Television Agreement.

Production Co./EMPLOYER _____

Signature of Employer or
Employer Representative _____

SAG Reporter _____ (Print name) _____

SAG Reporter's Phone # (   )   Date _____   EXHIBIT I

DIRECTORS GUILD OF AMERICA
WEEKLY   WORK   LIST

From:_____

(signatory company)

_____

(address)

_____

Return to:
Directors Guild of America, Inc.

Week Ending:_____

Name	Soc. Sec.#	Cat.	Project

Prepared by _____

Phone #

RC314/031489

DGA EMPLOYMENT DATA REPORT

DATE: _____   PREPARED BY: _____   PHONE NO: _____

SIGNATORY COMPANY: _____

QUARTER COVERED: _____

PROJECT: _____

DIRECTOR

	C	B	H	A	AI	UNKNOWN
MALE						
FEMALE						

UNIT PRODUCTION MANAGER

	C	B	H	A	AI	UNKNOWN
MALE						
FEMALE						

FIRST ASSISTANT DIRECTOR

	C	B	H	A	AI	UNKNOWN
MALE						
FEMALE						

SECOND ASSISTANT DIRECTOR

	C	B	H	A	AI	UNKNOWN
MALE						
FEMALE						

FIRST TIME DIRECTOR

	C	B	H	A	AI	UNKNOWN
MALE						
FEMALE						

The minority codes utilized in this report represent the following:

C	—	CAUCASIAN
B	—	BLACK
H	—	HISPANIC
A	—	ASIAN
AI	—	AMERICAN INDIAN

When completing this report, the employment statistics must be reported in order that two (2) types of statistics can be obtained. The first statistic will indicate the number of persons employed in the respective category (referenced above) during that quarter. The second statistic will indicate the number of days worked or guaranteed in the respective categories for that quarter. Therefore in each category, there will be two separate sets of statistics: one of top of the other separated by a horizontal slash (example below). The top statistic will represent the number of employees working, the bottom statistic will be the number of days worked or guaranteed during the same quarter.

Example:

DIRECTOR

	C	B	H	A	AI	UNKNOWN
MALE	1/56					
FEMALE		1/25				

In the above example, there was one (1) male Caucasian Director working during the quarter for a total of fifty-six (56) days worked or guaranteed. There was one (1) female Black Director working for a total of twenty-five (25) days worked or guaranteed.

This report is to be submitted on a per-production basis not on a per episode basis. In instances where the same DGA employee is employed for multiple episodes in a continuing series, such employee shall only be counted once in the number of employees statistics, but such employee's cumulative days worked shall be included in that statistic.

DATE_____

TO: Writers Guild of America
          AND
     All Participating Writers (or to the current agent if that participant so elects)

NAMES OF PARTICIPATING WRITERS   ADDRESS

_____   _____
_____   _____
_____   _____
_____   _____

Title of Photoplay_____
Executive Producer_____
Producer_____
Director_____
Other Production Executives, including their titles, if
     Participating Writers_____

According to the provisions of Schedule A of the Writers Guild of America Theatrical and Television Basic Agreement of 1985 credits are now being determined on the above entitle production.

ON SCREEN, the tentative writing credits are as follows:

SOURCE MATERIAL upon which the photoplay is based, if any:

ON SCREEN, FORM of Source Material credit, if any:

PRESENTATION or PRODUCTION credits, if any, which are intended for use in advertising and/or on-screen:

The above tentative writing credits will become final unless a protest is communicated to the undersigned not later than 6:00 P.M. on _____

_____
          (Signatory Company)
BY_____
NAME_____
ADDRESS_____
PHONE_____

Revised
Feb. 1985

NOTICE OF TENTATIVE WRITING CREDITS - TELEVISION

DATE_____

TO: Writers Guild of America
         AND
       Participating Writers

NAMES OF PARTICIPATING WRITERS   ADDRESS

_____   _____

_____   _____

_____   _____

_____   _____

Title of Episode_____ Prod. No._____
          (If Pilot or MOW or other special or unit program,
           indicate Network and length.)

Series Title_____

Producing Company_____

Executive Producer_____

Producer_____   Assoc. Producer_____

Director_____   Story Editor_____
                     (or Consultant)

Other Production Executives, if
    Participating Writers_____

Writing credits on this episode are tentatively determined as follows:

ON SCREEN:

Source Material credit ON THIS EPISODE (on separate card, unless otherwise indicated) if any:

Continuing source material or Created By credit APPEARING ON ALL EPISODES OF SERIES (on separate card):

Revised final script was sent to participating writers on_____

The above tentative writing credits will become final unless a protest is communicated to the undersigned not later than 6:00 P.M. on _____

_____
        (Company)
BY_____

BREAKDOWN SHEET

BREAKDOWN PAGE# _____

SHOW _____

PRODUCTION# _____

EPISODE _____

DATE _____

LOCATION _____

SCENE #'S	DESCRIPTION		NO. OF PAGES
	(INT)(EXT)	(DAY)(NIGHT)	
		TOTAL	

NO.	CAST	BITS/DOUBLES	ATMOSPHERE
		WARDROBE	PROPS/SET DRESSING
		SPEC. EFFECTS	TRANS/PIC VEHICLES

STUNTS	MUSIC/SOUND/CAMERA	WRANGLERS/LIVESTOCK

HAIR/MAKE-UP	SPECIAL REQUIREMENTS

DAY-OUT-OF-DAYS

PRODUCTION COMPANY _____

PRODUCTION TITLE _____

EPISODE TITLE _____

PRODUCTION # _____

SCRIPT DATED _____

DATE _____

PRODUCER _____

DIRECTOR _____

UNIT PRODUCTION MGR. _____

FIRST ASST. DIRECTOR _____

MONTH ---->
DAY OF WEEK ---->
SHOOTING DAYS --->

NAME	CHARACTER														TRAVEL	START	FINISH	WORK	IDLE	TOTAL
1																				
2																				
3																				
4																				
5																				
6																				
7																				
8																				
9																				
10																				
11																				
12																				
13																				
14																				
15																				
16																				
17																				
18																				
19																				
20																				
21																				
22																				
23																				
24																				
25																				
26																				
27																				
28																				
29																				
30																				
31																				

© ELH Form #6

CALL SHEET

PRODUCTION COMPANY _____

SHOW _____

SERIES EPISODE _____

PROD# _____ DAY# _____ OUT OF _____

IS TODAY A DESIGNATED DAY OFF?   [ ] YES   [ ] NO

CREW CALL _____

LEAVING CALL _____

SHOOTING CALL _____

DATE _____

DIRECTOR _____

PRODUCER _____

LOCATION _____

SUNRISE _____ SUNSET _____

ANTICIPATED WEATHER _____

[ ] Weather Permitting   [ ] See Attached Map

[ ] Report to Location   [ ] Bus to Location

Set Description	Scene Nos.	Cast	D/N	Pages	Location

Cast	Part Of	Leave	Makeup	Set Call	Remarks

Atmosphere & Stand-ins

NOTE: No forced calls without previous approval of unit production manager or assistant director.   All calls subject to change.

Advance Schedule Or Changes

Assistant Director _____

Production Manager _____

PRODUCTION REQUIREMENT

SHOW: PROD#:   DATE:

NO	STAFF & CREW	TIME	NO	STAFF & CREW	TIME	NO	EQUIPMENT
	Production Mgr.			Gaffer			Cameras
	1st Asst. Dir.			Best Boy			
	2nd Asst. Dir.			Lamp Oper.			Dolly
	2nd 2nd Asst. Dir.			Lamp Oper.			Crane
	DGA Trainee			Lamp Oper.			Condor
	Script Supervisor			Local 40 Man			
	Dialogue Coach						Sound Channel
	Prod. Coordinator			Prod. Designer			
	Prod. Sect'y			Art Director			Video
	Prod. Accountant			Asst. Art Dir.			
	Asst. Accountant			Set Designer			Radio Mikes
	Location Manager			Sketch Artist			Walkie/talkies
	Asst. Location Mgr.						
	Teacher/Welfare Worker			Const. Coord.			Dressing Rooms
	Production Assts.			Const. Foreman			Schoolrooms
				Paint Foreman			Rm. for Parents
	Dir. of Photography			Labor Foremen			
	Camera Operator			Const. First Aid			Projector
	Camera Operator						Moviola
	SteadyCam Operator			Set Decorator			
	Asst. Cameraman			Lead Person			Air Conditioners
	Asst. Cameraman			Swing Crew			Heaters
	Asst. Cameraman			Swing Crew			Wind Machines
	Still Photographer			Swing Crew			
	Cameraman-Process			Drapery			
	Projectionist						
				Technical Advisor			**SUPPORT PERSONNEL** / TIME
	Mixer			Publicist			Policemen
	Boomman			**MEALS**			Motorcycles
	Cableman			Caterer			Fireman
	Playback			Breakfasts			Guard
	Video Oper.			Wlkg. Breakfasts rdy @			Night Watchman
				Gals. Coffee			
	Key Grip			Lunches rdy @ Crew @			
	2nd Grip			Box Lunches			
	Dolly Grip			Second Meal			
	Grip						
	Grip						**VEHICLES**
	Grip			**DRIVERS**			Prod. Van
				Trans. Coord.			Camera
	Greensman			Trans. Capt.			Grip
				Driver			Electric
	S/By Painter			Driver			Effects
	Craftservice			Driver			Props
	First Aid			Driver			Wardrobe
				Driver			Makeup
	Spec. Efx			Driver			Set Dressing
	Spec. Efx			Driver			Crew Bus
				Driver			Honeywagon
	Propmaster			Driver			Motorhomes
	Asst. Props			Driver			Station Wagons
	Asst. Props			Driver			Mini-buses
				Driver			Standby Cars
	Costume Designer			Driver			Crew Cabs
	Costume Supervisor			Driver			Insert Cars
	Costumer			Driver			Generators
	Costumer			Driver			Water Wagon
				Driver			Picture Cars
	Makeup Artist			Driver			
	Makeup Artist			Driver			
	Body Makeup						
	Hairstylist			Stunt Coord.			
	Hairstylist			Wranglers			
				Animal Handlers			Livestock
	Editor						Animals
	Asst. Editor						
	Apprentice Editor						

DEPARTMENT   **SPECIAL INSTRUCTIONS**

         © ELH Form #7A

DAILY PRODUCTION REPORT

	1st Unit	2nd Unit	Reh.	Test	Travel	Holidays	Change Over	Retakes & Add. Scs.	Total	Schedule	
No. Days Sched.										Ahead	
No. Days Actual										Behind	

Title_____ Prod#_____ Date_____

Producer_____ Director_____

Date Started_____ Scheduled Finish Date_____ Est. Finish Date_____

Sets_____

Location_____

Crew Call_____ Shooting Call_____ First Shot_____ Lunch_____ Til_____

1st Shot After Lunch_____ 2nd Meal_____ Til_____ Camera Wrap_____ Last Man Out_____

Company dismissed at [ ] Studio [ ] Location [ ] Headquarters   Round Trip Mileage_____   Is Today A Designated Day Off? [ ] YES [ ] NO

SCRIPT SCENES AND PAGES			MINUTES		SETUPS		ADDED SCENES		RETAKES		
	SCENES	PAGES	Prev.		Prev.		Prev.		PAGES	SCENES	
			Today		Today		Today		Prev.		
Script			Total		Total		Total		Today		
Taken Prev.			Scene No.						Total		
Taken Today											
Total to Date			Added Scenes								
To be Taken			Retakes				Sound Tracks				

FILM STOCK	FILM USE	GROSS	PRINT	NO GOOD	WASTE	1/4" ROLLS	FILM INVENTORY	
	Prev.						Starting Inv.	
	Today						Additional Rec'd.	
	To Date						Today	
							Total	
FILM STOCK	FILM USE	GROSS	PRINT	NO GOOD	WASTE		FILM INVENTORY	
	Prev.						Starting Inv.	
	Today						Additional Rec'd.	
	To Date						Today	
							Total	
FILM STOCK	FILM USE	GROSS	PRINT	NO GOOD	WASTE		FILM INVENTORY	
	Prev.						Starting Inv.	
	Today						Additional Rec'd.	
	To Date						Today	
							Total	

CAST - WEEKLY & DAY PLAYERS Worked - W Rehearsal - R Finished - F Started - S Hold - H Test - T Travel - TR		W S R H F T	MAKEUP WDBE.	WORKTIME		MEALS		TRAVEL TIME				STUNT ADJ.
CAST	CHARACTER	TR		REPORT ON SET	DISMISS ON SET	OUT	IN	LEAVE FOR LOC.	ARRIVE ON LOC.	LEAVE LOCATION	ARRIVE AT HDQ.	

XX = N.D. BREAKFAST   * = DISMISS TIME INCLUDES 15 MIN. MAKEUP / WARD. REMOVAL

X = NOT PHOTOGRAPHED   S = SCHOOL ONLY

EXTRA TALENT

No.	Rate	1st Call	Set Dismiss	Final Dismiss	Adj.	MPV	No.	Rate	1st Call	Set Dismiss	Final Dismiss	Adj.	MPV

Assistant Director_____ Production Manager_____

NO.	STAFF & CREW	TIME	NO.	STAFF & CREW	TIME	NO.	EQUIPMENT	
	Production Mgr.			Gaffer			Cameras	
	1st Asst. Dir.			Best Boy				
	2nd Asst. Dir.			Lamp Oper.			Dolly	
	2nd 2nd Asst. Dir.			Lamp Oper.			Crane	
	DGA Trainee			Lamp Oper.			Condor	
	Script Supervisor			Local 40 Man				
	Dialogue Coach						Sound Channel	
	Prod. Coordinator			Prod. Designer				
	Prod. Sect'y			Art Director			Video	
	Prod. Accountant			Asst. Art Dir.				
	Asst. Accountant			Set Designer			Radio Mikes	
	Location Manager			Sketch Artist			Walkie/talkies	
	Asst. Location Mgr.							
	Teacher/Welfare Worker			Const. Coord.			Dressing Rooms	
	Production Assts.			Const. Foreman			Schoolrooms	
				Paint Foreman			Rm. for Parents	
	Dir. of Photography			Labor Foremen				
	Camera Operator			Const. First Aid			Projector	
	Camera Operator						Moviola	
	SteadiCam Operator			Set Decorator				
	Asst. Cameraman			Lead Person			Air Conditioners	
	Asst. Cameraman			Swing Crew			Heaters	
	Asst. Cameraman			Swing Crew			Wind Machines	
	Still Photographer			Swing Crew				
	Cameraman-Process			Drapery				
	Projectionist							
				Technical Advisor			SUPPORT PERSONNEL	TIME
	Mixer			Publicist			Policemen	
	Boomman			MEALS			Motorcycles	
	Cableman			Caterer			Fireman	
	Playback			Breakfasts			Guard	
	Video Oper.			Wlkg. Breakfasts rdy @			Night Watchman	
				Gals. Coffee				
	Key Grip			Lunches rdy @ Crew @				
	2nd Grip			Box Lunches				
	Dolly Grip			Second Meal				
	Grip							
	Grip						VEHICLES	
	Grip			DRIVERS			Prod. Van	
				Trans. Coord.			Camera	
	Greensman			Trans. Capt.			Grip	
				Driver			Electric	
	S/By Painter			Driver			Effects	
	Craftservice			Driver			Props	
	First Aid			Driver			Wardrobe	
				Driver			Makeup	
	Spec. Efx			Driver			Set Dressing	
	Spec. Efx			Driver			Crew Bus	
				Driver			Honeywagon	
	Propmaster			Driver			Motorhomes	
	Asst. Props			Driver			Station Wagons	
	Asst. Props			Driver			Mini-buses	
				Driver			Standby Cars	
	Costume Designer			Driver			Crew Cabs	
	Costume Supervisor			Driver			Insert Cars	
	Costumer			Driver			Generators	
	Costumer			Driver			Water Wagon	
				Driver			Picture Cars	
	Makeup Artist			Driver				
	Makeup Artist			Driver				
	Body Makeup							
	Hairstylist			Stunt Coord.				
	Hairstylist			Wranglers				
				Animal Handlers			Livestock	
	Editor						Animals	
	Asst. Editor							
	Apprentice Editor							

COMMENTS - DELAYS (EXPLANATION) - CAST, STAFF & CREW ABSENCE

☐ NO ACCIDENTS REPORTED TODAY

CHECK REQUEST

SHOW_____   PROD#_____

COMPANY_____

ADDRESS_____   PHONE#_____

_____   FAX#_____

DATE_____   AMOUNT $_____

CHECK PAYEE_____

ADDRESS_____

_____

PHONE#_____   FAX #_____

ATTN:_____

PAYEE SS# OR FED. ID#_____

DESCRIPTION	CODING	AMOUNT

[ ] PURCHASE
[ ] RENTAL   CHECK NEEDED: [ ] IMMEDIATELY   TOTAL:
[ ] DEPOSIT   [ ] WITHIN NEXT DAY OR TWO
[ ] ADVANCE   [ ] WITHIN NORMAL PROCESSING TIME
[ ] 1099
[ ] INVENTORY

WHEN READY: [ ] PLEASE MAIL CHECK
                [ ] PLEASE GIVE CHECK TO_____

CHECK REQUESTED BY_____ DEPT._____

APPROVED BY_____ DATE_____

(INVOICE SUBSTANTIATION MUST FOLLOW THIS REQUEST)

PAID BY CHECK # _____   DATE _____

PURCHASE ORDER

DATE_____   P.O.#_____

SHOW_____   PROD#_____

COMPANY_____

ADDRESS_____   PHONE#_____

_____   FAX#_____

VENDOR_____

ADDRESS_____   PHONE#_____

_____   FAX#_____

CONTACT_____

[ ] PURCHASE   [ ] RENTAL   [ ] SERVICE

DESCRIPTION	CODING	AMOUNT

SET #(s)_____   TOTAL COST: $_____ Per Show [ ]
                                                                         Day   [ ]
IF TOTAL COST CANNOT BE DETERMINED   Week   [ ]
AT THIS DATE, ESTIMATE OF COSTS WILL   Month   [ ]
NOT EXCEED $_____

IF P.O. IS FOR A <u>RENTAL</u>, PLEASE ESTIMATE DATE OF RETURN_____

ORDER PLACED BY_____   DEPT._____

APPROVED BY_____   DATE_____

cc: Vendor (Orig)
       Production Manager
       Accounting Dept.
       Department Head

© ELH Form #10

PETTY CASH ACCOUNTING

NAME _____

DEPARTMENT _____

SHOW _____   AMOUNT RECEIVED $ _____

FROM _____ 19____   TO _____ 19____

ENVELOPE # _____

* DATE _____

CHECK # _____

FOR ACCOUNTING USE ONLY

ACCOUNT	AMOUNT

DATE	NO.	PAID TO	FOR	ACCOUNT	AMOUNT
				TOTAL: **	

NOTE: EACH RECEIPT SHOULD BE CLEARLY LABELED WITH A DATE AND DESCRIPTION AS TO WHAT THEY ARE FOR AND ATTACHED IN THE SAME ORDER IN WHICH THEY APPEAR ON THE ENVELOPE.

APPROVED _____

AUDITED _____   ENTERED _____

AMOUNT ADVANCED *

TOTAL ACCOUNTED FOR **

CASH ON HAND

-OR-

AMT. TO BE REIMBURSED

PETTY CASH ADVANCE/REIMBURSEMENT	SIGNATURE
RECEIVED IN CASH $ ON , 19	

AMOUNT $ _____   NO. _____

RECEIVED OF PETTY CASH

DATE _____

NAME _____

DEPARTMENT _____

DESCRIPTION _____
_____
_____
_____

☐ *PETTY CASH TO BE ACCOUNTED FOR*

APPROVED BY   RECEIVED BY

_____   _____

© ELH Form #12

CAST DEAL MEMO

PRODUCTION COMPANY_____   DATE_____

ADDRESS_____   PHONE#_____

_____   FAX#_____

SHOW_____   EPISODE_____

CASTING DIRECTOR_____   PROD#_____

ARTIST_____   SOC.SEC.#_____

ADDRESS_____   PHONE#_____

_____   MESSAGES_____

ROLE_____   START DATE_____

[ ] ACTOR	[ ] THEATRICAL	[ ] DAY PLAYER
[ ] SINGER	[ ] TELEVISION	[ ] 3-DAY PLAYER
[ ] STUNT	[ ] OTHER_____	[ ] WEEKLY
[ ] OTHER_____		

COMPENSATION $_____ PER   [ ] DAY   [ ] WEEK   [ ] SHOW

	#DAY/WEEKS	DATES
TRAVEL	_____	_____
REHEARSAL/FITTINGS	_____	_____
PRINCIPLE PHOTOGRAPHY	_____	_____
ADDITIONAL SHOOT DAYS	_____	_____
POST PRODUCTION DAYS	_____	_____

PER DIEM/EXPENSES_____

_____

TRANSPORTATION/TRAVEL_____

_____

ACCOMMODATIONS_____

_____

OTHER_____

_____

BILLING_____

_____

[ ] PAID ADVERTISING

AGENT_____   HOME#_____

AGENCY_____   OFFICE#_____

ADDRESS_____   FAX#_____

_____

[ ] LOAN OUT

CORPORATION NAME_____

Address_____

_____

Federal I.D.#_____

CONTRACT PREPARED BY_____   DATE SENT OUT_____

SENT: [ ] To Agent   [ ] To Artist   [ ] To Set

[ ] SENT SCRIPT   [ ] NOTIFIED WARDROBE   [ ] STATION 12   [ ] INSURANCE PHYSICAL

APPROVED BY_____   TITLE_____

CREW DEAL MEMO

PRODUCTION CO._____   DATE_____

SHOW_____   PROD#_____

NAME_____   SOC.SEC.#_____

ADDRESS_____   PHONE (Home)_____

_____   (Beeper)_____

START DATE_____   (Fax)_____

JOB TITLE_____   ACCOUNT#_____

UNION/GUILD_____   GUARANTEE_____wks.

RATE (In Town) _____   Per [Hour] [Day] [Week] for a [5] [6]_____ -day week

(Distant Loc.)_____   Per [Hour] [Day] [Week] for a [5] [6]_____ -day week

ADDITIONAL DAY(S) PRO-RATED @_____(th)   Of a week

OVERTIME_____   After_____hours   _____   After_____hours

BOX RENTAL_____   Per Day/Week

EQUIPMENT/VEHICLE RENTAL_____   Per Day/Week

MILEAGE ALLOWANCE_____   Per Day/Week

> NOTE: Box & Equipment rental & mileage allowance are subject to 1099 reporting. -- Any equipment rented by the Production Co. from the employee must be listed or inventoried before rental can be paid.

TRAVEL/ACCOMODATIONS_____

_____

_____

EXPENSES/PER DIEM_____

_____

_____

OTHER_____

_____

_____

[ ] LOAN OUT

CORP. NAME_____   FED. ID#_____

ADDRESS (If Different From Above)_____

AGENT_____   AGENCY_____

ADDRESS_____   PHONE#_____

_____   Fax#_____

EMPLOYER OF RECORD_____

ADDRESS_____   PHONE#_____

_____   FAX#_____

IF AWARDED SCREEN CREDIT, HOW WOULD YOU LIKE YOUR NAME TO READ_____

APPROVED BY_____   TITLE_____

ACCEPTED_____   DATE_____

© ELH Form #14

WRITER'S DEAL MEMO

PRODUCTION COMPANY_____ DATE_____

ADDRESS_____ PHONE#_____

_____ FAX#_____

SHOW_____ PROD#_____

EPISODE_____

WRITER_____ PHONE#_____

SOC. SEC.#_____ MESSAGES_____

ADDRESS_____ FAX#_____

_____

DATES OF EMPLOYMENT_____

_____

_____

COMPENSATION_____

_____

_____

ADDITIONAL TERMS OF EMPLOYMENT_____

_____

_____

_____

BILLING_____

_____

_____

[ ] PAID ADVERTISING

WRITER'S AGENT_____ DIRECT#_____

AGENCY_____ PHONE#_____

ADDRESS_____ FAX#_____

_____

[ ] LOAN OUT

CORPORATION NAME_____

ADDRESS_____

_____

FEDERAL I.D.#_____

CONTRACT PREPARED BY_____

DATE SENT OUT_____

APPROVED BY_____

TITLE_____ DATE_____

WRITING TEAM DEAL MEMO

PRODUCTION COMPANY_____ DATE_____

ADDRESS_____ PHONE#_____

_____ FAX#_____

SHOW_____ PROD#_____

EPISODE_____

WRITERS_____ _____

SOC.SEC#_____ _____

ADDRESS_____ _____

_____ _____

PHONE#_____ _____

FAX#_____ _____

DATES OF EMPLOYMENT_____

_____

COMPENSATION_____

_____

_____

ADDITIONAL TERMS OF EMPLOYMENT_____

_____

_____

BILLING_____

_____

[ ] PAID ADVERTISING

WRITER'S AGENTS_____ _____

AGENCY   _____ _____

ADDRESS   _____ _____

               _____ _____

PHONE#   _____ _____

[ ] LOAN OUT   [ ] LOAN OUT

CORP. NAME_____ _____

ADDRESS_____ _____

_____ _____

FED. I.D.#_____ _____

CONTRACT PREPARED BY_____

DATE SENT OUT_____

APPROVED BY_____

TITLE_____ DATE_____

© ELH Form #16

DGA—Director Deal Memorandum

Director Deal Memorandum

This confirms our agreement to employ you to direct the project described as follows:

Name:_____ SS#:_____
Loanout (if applicable):_____ Tel. #: _____
Address: _____
Salary: $ _____ ❏ per week ❏ per day ❏ per show
Additional Time: $_____ ❏ per week ❏ per day
Start Date: _____ Guaranteed Period: _____ ❏ pro rata

Project Information:
   Picture or Series Title: _____
   Episode/Segment Title: _____ Epsd.#_____
   Length of Program: _____ Is this a Pilot? ❏Yes   ❏No

Produced Primarily/Mainly for:
   ❏ Theatrical   ❏ Network   ❏ Syndication
   ❏ Basic Cable   ❏ Disc/Cassette   ❏ Pay/TV: _____
                                                        (service)

Theatrical Film Budget (check one)   Free Television/Pay Television
   ❏ A. Under $500,000   ❏ Network Prime Time (type)
   ❏ B. Between $500,000 and $1,500,000   ❏ Other than Network Prime Time (type)
   ❏ C. Over $1,500,000

Check one (if applicable): ❏ Segment   ❏ Second Unit

The **INDIVIDUAL** having final cutting authority over the film is : _____

Other conditions (including credit above minimum): _____

_____

This employment is subject to the provisions of the Directors Guild of America Basic Agreement of 1993.

Accepted and Agreed: Signatory Co: _____
Employee: _____   By: _____
Date: _____   Date: _____

RC300/070193

Addendum to the Director's Deal Memorandum Post Production Schedule
(for a Theatrical Motion Picture or a Television Motion Picture 90 minutes or longer)

Director's Name: _____

Project Title: _____

Company Name: _____

Directors Cut: Start Date: _____

              Finish Date: _____

Please Indicate Dates Below:
Special Photography
        & Processes (if any): _____

Delivery of Answer Print: _____

Release (Theatrical Film): _____

Network Broadcast (if applicable): _____

DGA—Unit Production Manager &
Assistant Director Film Deal Memorandum

Unit Production Manager &
Assistant Director Film Deal Memorandum

This confirms our agreement to employ you on the project described below as follows:

Name:_____   SS#:_____

Loanout (if applicable):_____   Tel. #: _____

Address: _____

_____   ❏ Unit Production Manager
                                          ❏ First Assistant Director
                                          ❏ Key Second Assistant Director
❏ Principal Photography   ❏ 2nd Second Assistant Director
❏ Second Unit   ❏ Additional Second Assistant Director
❏ Both   ❏ Technical Coordinator

Salary: $ _____ $ _____   ❏ per week   ❏ per day
                   (STUDIO)   (LOCATION)

Production Fee: $ _____ $ _____
                   (STUDIO)   (LOCATION)

Start Date: _____   Guaranteed Period: _____

Film or Series Title: _____
Episode/Segment Title: _____
Length of Program: _____   Is this a Pilot?   ❏ Yes   ❏ No

Intended Primary Market:
   ❏ Theatres   ❏ Network   ❏ Syndication
   ❏ Basic Cable   ❏ Disc/Cassette   ❏ Pay/TV: _____
                                                            (service)

Other Terms (e.g., credit, suspension, per diem, etc.): _____

_____

_____

   ❏ Studio   ❏ Distant Location   ❏ Both

   ❏ Check if New York Area Amendment Applies

This employment is subject to the provisions of the Directors Guild of America Basic Agreement of 1993.

Accepted and Agreed: _____   Signatory Co: _____

Employee: _____   By: _____

Date: _____   Date: _____

RC301/070193

EXTRA TALENT VOUCHER

DATE WORKED_____

PRODUCTION_____ PROD#_____

EXTRA CASTING AGENCY_____

CONTACT_____ PHONE#_____

EMPLOYER OF RECORD_____

       ADDRESS_____

       PHONE#_____

_____

NAME (Please Print)_____

     ADDRESS_____

        _____

     PHONE#_____

  SOC. SEC.#_____

    [ ] Married   [ ] Single   _____ Exemptions   [ ] Completed I-9

REPORTING TIME _____ MEAL _____ 2ND MEAL _____ DISMISSAL TIME _____ TOTAL HRS. WORKED:	**BASE RATE** _____ HRS. of S.T. @_____per. hr. _____ _____ HRS. of 1 1/2X @_____per. hr. _____ _____ HRS. of 2X @_____per. hr. _____ ADJUSTMENT(S) _____ _____ _____ _____ GROSS TOTAL:

      MILEAGE REIMBURSEMENT   _____
      WARDROBE REIMBURSEMENT   _____
      OTHER REIMBURSEMENT   _____

I acknowledge receipt of the compensation stated herein as payment in full for all services rendered by me on the days indicated. I hereby grant to my employer permission to photograph me and to record my voice, performances, poses, acts, plays and appearances, and use my picture, photograph, silhouette and other reproductions of my physical likeness and sound in the above-named production and in the unlimited distribution, advertising, promotion, exhibition and exploitation of the production by any method or device now known or hereafter devised in which the same may be used. I agree that I will not assert or maintain against you, your successors, assigns and licensees, any claim, action, suit or demand of any kind or nature whatsoever in connection with your authorized use of my physical likeness and sound in the production as herein provided.

SIGNATURE_____
        (If minor, parent or guardian must sign)

APPROVED BY_____

   TITLE_____

LOCATION AGREEMENT

Date

(Your company name)
(Company Address)

Gentlemen:

You have advised the undersigned that you are producing a motion picture/television (movie) (series) tentatively entitled_____, (the "Picture"). In consideration of your payment to the undersigned for the sum of $_____, you and the undersigned hereby agree as follows:

1.   The undersigned hereby irrevocably grants you and your agents, employees, licensees, successors and assigns:

(a)   The right to enter and remain upon the property, which shall include not only real property but any fixtures, equipment or other personal property thereat or thereon, located at: (the "Property"), with personnel and equipment (including without limitations, props, temporary sets, lighting, camera and special effects equipment) for the purpose of photographing scenes and making recordings of said Property in connection with the production of the Picture on the following date(s): _____. If the weather or other conditions are not favorable for such purpose on such date(s), the date(s) shall be postponed to _____.

(b)   The right to take motion pictures, videotapes, still photographs and/or sound recordings on and of any and all portions of the Property and all names associated there- with or which appear in, on or about the Property.

(c)   All rights of every nature whatsoever in and to all films and photographs taken and recordings made hereunder, including without limitation of all copyrights therein and renewals and extensions thereof, and the exclusive right to reproduce, exhibit, distribute, and otherwise exploit in perpetuity throughout the universe (in whole or in part) such films, photographs and recordings in any and all media, whether now known or hereafter devised, including without limitation in and in connection with the Picture and the advertising and other exploitation thereof.

2. You agree to indemnify and to hold the undersigned harmless from and against all liability or loss which the undersigned may suffer or incur by reason of any injury to or death of any person, or damage to any property (ordinary wear and tear excepted), directly caused by any of your agents or employees when present on the Property or by reason of the use by any of your agents or employees or any equipment brought by them on to the property.

3. The undersigned warrants and represents (as a condition to the payment of the compensation referred to above), that the undersigned has the full right and authority to enter into this agreement and grant the rights herein granted, and that the consent or permission of no other person, firm, or entity is necessary in order to enable you to exercise or enjoy the rights herein granted.

4. The undersigned hereby releases you from, and covenants not to sue you for, any claim or cause of action, whether known or unknown, for defamation, invasion of his

(continued on the following page)

privacy, right of publicity or any similar matter, or any other claim or cause of action, based upon or relating to the exercise of any of the rights referred to in Paragraph 1 hereof; provided, however, that the foregoing shall not affect your obligations to indemnify the undersigned pursuant to Paragraph 2 hereof.

5. The undersigned further warrants neither he/she or anyone acting for him/her, gave or agreed to give anything of value, except for use of the Property, to anyone at (THE NAME OF YOUR PRODUCTION COMPANY) or anyone associated with the production for using the Property as a shooting location.

6. This agreement shall inure to benefit of and shall be binding upon your and our respective successors, licensees, assigns, heirs and personal representatives. You shall not be obligated actually to exercise any of the rights granted to you hereunder; it being understood that your obligations shall be fully satisfied hereunder by payment of the compensation referred to above. The agreement constitutes the entire agreement between the parties with respect to the subject matter hereof and cannot be amended except by a written instrument signed by the parties.

Yours very truly,

ACCEPTED & AGREED TO:

_____

(Signature)

BY_____   _____

(Please Print Name)

_____

(Title)

_____

(Address)

_____

(Phone Number)

_____

(Business Phone)

PERSONAL RELEASE

Date

(Your company name)
(Company address)

Gentlemen:

I, the undersigned, hereby grant permission to _____
_____ to photograph me and to record my voice, performances, poses, acts, plays and appearances, and use my picture, photograph, silhouette and other reproductions of my physical likeness and sound as part of the motion picture/ television (movie) (series) tentatively entitled _____ (the "Picture") and the unlimited distribution, advertising, promotion, exhibition and exploitation of the Picture by any method or device now known or hereafter devised in which the same may be used, and/or incorporated and/or exhibited and/or exploited.

I agree that I will not assert or maintain against you, your successors, assigns and licensees, any claim, action, suit or demand of any kind or nature whatsoever, including but not limited to, those grounded upon invasion of privacy, rights of publicity or other civil rights, or for any other reason in connection with your authorized use of my physical likeness and sound in the Picture as herein provided. I hereby release you, your successors, assigns and licensees, and each of them, from and against any and all claims, liabilities, demands, actions, causes of action(s), costs and expenses whatsoever, at law or in equity, known or unknown, anticipated or unanticipated, which I ever had, now have, or may, shall or hereafter have by reason, matter, cause or thing arising out of your use as herein provided.

I affirm that neither I, nor anyone acting for me, gave or agreed to give anything of value to any of your employees or any representative of any television station, network or production entity for arranging my appearance on the Picture.

I have read the foregoing and fully understand the meaning and effect thereof and, intending to be legally bound, I have signed this release

Very truly yours,

_____
(Signature)

_____
(Please print name)

_____

_____
(Address)

_____
(Phone number)

PERSONAL RELEASE—PAYMENT

Date

(Your company name)
(Company address)

Gentlemen:

In consideration of payment to me of the sum of $_____, receipt of which is hereby acknowledged, I, the undersigned, hereby grant permission to _____ to photograph me and to record my voice, performances, poses, acts, plays and appearances, and use my picture, photograph, silhouette and other reproductions of my physical likeness and sound as part of the motion picture/television (movie) (series) tentatively entitled _____ (the "Picture") and the unlimited distribution, advertising, promotion, exhibition and exploitation of the Picture by any method or device now known or hereafter devised in which the same may be used, and/or incorporated and/or exhibited and/or exploited.

I agree that I will not assert or maintain against you, your successors, assigns and licensees, any claim, action, suit or demand of any kind or nature whatsoever, including but not limited to, those grounded upon invasion of privacy, rights of publicity or other civil rights, or for any other reason in connection with your authorized use of my physical likeness and sound in the Picture as herein provided. I hereby release you, your successors, assigns and licensees, and each of them, from and against any and all claims, liabilities, demands, actions, causes of action(s), costs and expenses whatsoever, at law or in equity, known or unknown, anticipated or unanticipated, which I ever had, now have, or may, shall or hereafter have by reason, matter, cause or thing arising out of your use as herein provided.

I affirm that neither I, nor anyone acting for me, gave or agreed to give anything of value to any of your employees or any representative of any television station, network or production entity for arranging my appearance on the Picture.

I have read the foregoing and fully understand the meaning and effect thereof and, intending to be legally bound, I have signed this release

Very truly yours,

_____
(Signature)

_____
(Please print name)

_____

_____
(Address)

_____
(Phone number)

GROUP RELEASE

(Your company name)
(Company address)

Gentlemen:

I, the undersigned, hereby grant permission to _____ to photograph me and to record my voice, performances, poses, acts, plays and appearances, and use my picture, photograph, silhouette and other reproductions of my physical likeness and sound as part of the motion picture/television (movie) (series) tentatively entitled _____ (the "Picture") and the unlimited distribution, advertising, promotion, exhibition and exploitation of the Picture by any method or device now known or hereafter devised in which the same may be used, and/or incorporated and/or exhibited and/or exploited.

I agree that I will not assert or maintain against you, your successors, assigns and licensees, any claim, action, suit or demand of any kind or nature whatsoever, including but not limited to, those grounded upon invasion of privacy, rights of publicity or other civil rights, or for any other reason in connection with your authorized use of my physical likeness and sound in the Picture as herein provided. I hereby release you, your successors, assigns and licensees, and each of them, from and against any and all claims, liabilities, demands, actions, causes of action(s), costs and expenses whatsoever, at law or in equity, known or unknown, anticipated or unanticipated, which I ever had, now have, or may, shall or hereafter have by reason, matter, cause or thing arising out of your use as herein provided.

I affirm that neither I, nor anyone acting for me, gave or agreed to give anything of value to any of your employees or any representative of any television station, network or production entity for arranging my appearance on the Picture.

I have read the foregoing and fully understand the meaning and effect thereof and, intending to be legally bound, I have signed this release

NAME   ADDRESS   SOC. SEC.#

_____   _____   _____

_____   _____   _____

_____   _____   _____

_____   _____   _____

_____   _____   _____

_____   _____   _____

_____   _____   _____

_____   _____   _____

USE OF NAME

Date

(Your company name)
Ccompany address)

Gentlemen:

For good and valuable consideration, receipt of which I hereby acknowledge, I hereby grant to you and to your successors, assigns, distributees and licensees forever, throughout the universe, the sole, exclusive and unconditional right and license to use, simulate and portray my name to such extent and in such manner as you in your sole discretion may elect, in or in connection with your motion picture/television (movie) (series) tentatively entitled _____ (including reissues, remakes of and sequels to any such production) prepared by you or any successor to your interest therein, together with the right to publish synopses thereof, and to advertise, exploit, present, release, distribute, exhibit and/or otherwise utilize said productions and publications throughout the world.

I agree that I will not bring, institute or assert or consent that others bring, institute or assert any claim or action against you or your successors, licensees, distributees, or assigns, on the ground that anything performed in any such production or contained in the advertising or publicity issued in connection therewith is libelous, reflects adversely upon me, violates my right of privacy, or violates any other rights, and I hereby release, discharge, and acquit you and them of and from any and all such claims, actions, causes of action, suits and demands whatsoever that I may now or hereafter have against you or them.

In granting of the foregoing rights and licenses, I acknowledge that I have not been induced so to do by any representation or assurance by you or on your behalf relative to the manner in which any of the rights or licenses granted hereunder may be exercised; and I agree that you are under no obligation to exercise any of the rights or licenses granted hereunder.

Very truly yours,

_____
(Signature)

ACCEPTED & AGREED TO:

_____
(Please Print Name)

_____
(Address)

By _____

_____
(Phone Number)

Use of Trademark or Logo

Date

(Your company name)
(Company address)

Gentlemen:

For good and valuable consideration, receipt of which is hereby acknowledged, the undersigned hereby grants to you, your successors, licensees and assigns, the non-exclusive right, but not the obligation to use and include all or part of our trademark(s), logo(s), and/or animated or identifiable characters (the Mark(s)) listed below in the motion picture/television (movie) (series) tentatively entitled _____ (the "Picture"), and to utilize and reproduce the Mark(s) in connection with the Picture, without limitation as to time or number of runs, for reproduction, exhibition and exploitation, throughout the world, in any and all manner, methods and media, whether now known or hereafter known or devised, and in the advertising, publicizing, promotion, trailers and exploitation thereof.

The undersigned acknowledges, as does the company which he represents, that, under the Federal Communications Act, it is a federal offense to give or agree to give anything of value to promote any product, service or venture in connection with the Picture on the air, and warrants and represents that neither he nor they have done or will do so.

The undersigned and the company he represents, hereby warrant, represent and affirm that he and the company have the right to grant the rights granted herein, free of claims by any person or entity.

Mark(s): _____

_____

Very truly yours,

ACCEPTED & AGREED TO:

_____
(Signature)

_____
(Please print name)

_____
(Title)

By_____

_____
(Address)

_____
(Phone #)

Use of Literary Material

Date

(Your company name)
(Company address)

Gentlemen:

I am informed that you are producing a motion picture/television (movie)(series) presently entitled_____ (the "Picture") and that you have requested that I grant you the right to use the title and/or portions of the following literary material owned and published by the undersigned for inclusion in the Picture:

_____

For good and valuable consideration, receipt of which is hereby acknowledged, I (the undersigned) do hereby confirm the consent hereby given you with respect to your use of the above title and/or literary material (the "Materials") in connection with the Picture, and I do hereby grant to you, your successors, assigns and licensees, the perpetual right to use the Materials in connection with the Picture. I agree that you may record the Materials on tape, film or otherwise and use the Materials and recordings in and in connection with the exhibition, advertising, promotion, exploitation, and any other use of the Picture as you may desire.

I hereby release you, your agents, successors, licensees and assigns, and each of them, from and against any and all claims, liabilities, demands, actions, causes of action, costs and expenses, whatsoever, at law or in equity, known or unknown, anticipated or unanticipated, suspected or unsuspected, with I ever had, now have, or may, shall or hereafter have by any reason, matter, cause or thing whatsoever, arising out of your use of the Materials as provided herein in connection with the Picture. I realize that in using the Materials, you are relying upon the rights granted to you hereunder.

Very truly yours,

ACCEPTED & AGREED TO:

By_____

_____
(Signature)

_____
(Please Print Name)

_____
(Address)

_____
(Phone Number)

USE OF STILL PHOTOGRAPH(S)

PERSON IN PHOTO/FREE

Date

(Your company name)
(Company address)

Gentlemen:

For good and valuable consideration, receipt of which is hereby acknowledged, I, the undersigned, hereby grant to you, your successors, licensees and assigns, the non-exclusive right, but not the obligation to use and include my physical likeness in the form of still photograph(s) (the Still(s)) as described below in the motion picture/television (movie) (series) tentatively entitled:
_____ (the "Picture"), and to utilize and reproduce the Still(s) in connection with the Picture, without limitation as to time or number of runs, for reproduction, exhibition and exploitation, throughout the world, in any and all manner, methods and media, whether now known or hereafter known or devised, and in the advertising, publicizing, promotion, trailers and exploitation thereof.

I agree that I will not assert or maintain against you, your successors, assigns and licensees, a claim, action, suit or demand of any kind or nature whatsoever, including but not limited to, those grounded upon invasion of privacy, rights of publicity or other civil rights, or for any other reason in connection with your authorized use of the Still(s) in the Picture as herein provided. I hereby release you, your successors, assigns and licensees from any and all such claims, actions, causes of action, suits and demands whatsoever that I may now or hereafter have against you or them.

In the granting of the foregoing rights and licenses, I acknowledge that I have not been induced to do so by any representative or assurance by you or on your behalf relative to the manner in which any of the rights or licenses granted hereunder may be exercised; and I agree that you are under no obligation to exercise any of the rights or licenses granted hereunder.

Description of the Still(s):

_____

Very truly yours,

_____
(Signature)

ACCEPTED & AGREED TO:

_____
(Please print name)

_____

By_____

_____
(Address)

_____
(Phone Number)

USE OF STILL PHOTOGRAPH(S)

(PERSON IN PHOTO/PAYMENT)

Date

(Your company name)
(Company address)

Gentlemen:

In consideration of the payment of the sum of $_____ and other good and valuable consideration, receipt of which is hereby acknowledged, I, the undersigned hereby grant to you, your successors, licensees and assigns, the non-exclusive right, but not the obligation to use and include my physical likeness in the form of the still photograph(s) (the Still(s)) as described below in the motion picture/television (movie) (series) tentatively entitled _____ (the "Picture"), and to utilize and reproduce the Still(s) in connection with the Picture, without limitation as to the number of runs, for reproduction, exhibition and exploitation, throughout the world, in any and all manner, methods and media, whether now known or hereafter known or devised, and in the advertising, publicizing, promotion, trailers and exploitation thereof.

I agree that I will not assert or maintain against you, your successors, assigns and licensees, a claim, action, suit or demand of any kind or nature whatsoever, including but not limited to, those grounded upon invasion of privacy, rights of publicity or other civil rights, or for any other reason in connection with your authorized use of the Still(s) in the Picture as herein provided. I hereby release you, your successors, assigns and licensees from any and all such claims, actions, causes of action, suits and demands whatsoever that I may now or hereafter have against you or them.

In the granting of the foregoing rights and licenses, I acknowledge that I have not been induced to do so by any representative or assurance by you or on your behalf relative to the manner in which any of the rights or licenses granted hereunder may be exercised; and I agree that you are under no obligation to exercise any of the rights or licenses granted hereunder.

Description of the Still(s):

_____

Very truly yours,

ACCEPTED & AGREED TO:

_____
(Signature)

By_____
_____
(Please Print Name)

_____
_____
(Address)

_____
(Phone Number)

USE OF STILL PHOTOGRAPH(S)

(COPYRIGHTED OWNER—NOT PERSON IN PHOTO/FREE)

Date

(Your company name)
(Company address)

Gentlemen:

For good and valuable consideration, receipt of which is hereby acknowledged, the undersigned hereby grants to you, your successors, licensees and assigns, the non-exclusive right, but not the obligation to use and include the still photograph(s) (the Still(s)) as described below in the motion picture/television (movie) (series) tentatively entitled _____ (the "Picture"), and to utilize and reproduce the Still(s) in connection with the Picture, without limitation as to time or number of runs, for reproduction, exhibition and exploitation, throughout the world, in any and all manner, methods and media, whether now known or hereafter known or devised, and in the advertising, publicizing, promotion, trailers and exploitation thereof.

The undersigned acknowledges, as does the company which he represents, that, under the Federal Communications Act, it is a federal offense to give or agree to give anything of value to promote any product, service or venture in connection with the Picture on the air, and warrants and represents that neither he nor they have done or will do so.

The undersigned and the company he represents, hereby warrant, represent and affirm that he and the company have the right to grant the rights granted herein, free of claims by any person or entity.

Description of the Still(s):

_____

Very truly yours,

ACCEPTED & AGREED TO:

_____
(Signature)

_____
(Please print name)

By_____

_____

_____
(Address)

_____
(Phone Number)

USE OF STILL PHOTOGRAPH(S)

(COPYRIGHTED OWNER—NOT PERSON IN PHOTO/PAYMENT)

Date

(Your company name)
(Company address)

Gentlemen:

In consideration of the payment of the sum of $_____ and other good and valuable consideration, receipt of which is hereby acknowledged, the undersigned hereby grants to you, your successors, licensees and assigns, the non-exclusive right, but not the obligation to use and include the still photograph(s) (the Still(s)) as described below in the motion picture/television (movie) (series) tentatively entitled _____(the "Picture"), and to utilize and reproduce the Still(s) in connection with the Picture, without limitation as to time or number of runs, for reproduction, exhibition and exploitation, throughout the world, in any and all manner, methods and media, whether now known or hereafter known or devised, and in the advertising, publicizing, promotion, trailers and exploitation thereof.

The undersigned acknowledges, as does the company which he represents, that, under the Federal Communications Act, it is a federal offense to give or agree to give anything of value to promote any product, service or venture in connection with the Picture on the air, and warrants and represents that neither he nor they have done or will do so.

The undersigned and the company he represents, hereby warrant, represent and affirm that he and the company have the right to grant the rights granted herein, free of claims by any person or entity.

Description of the Still(s):

_____

Very truly yours,

_____
(Signature)

ACCEPTED & AGREED TO:

_____
(Please print name)

_____
(Title)

By_____

_____
(Address)

_____
(Phone Number)

WORDING FOR MULTIPLE SIGNS

PLACE IN A STUDIO WHEN TAPING OR FILMING BEFORE A LIVE AUDIENCE:

Please be advised that your presence as a member of the studio audience during the taping/ filming of the program entitled _____ constitutes your permission to ** _____ to use your likeness on the air in any form and as often as they deem appropriate and desirable for promotional or broadcast purposes.

If for any reason you object to your likeness being so used, you should leave the studio at this time. If you remain, your presence at this taping/filming will constitute your approval of the foregoing.

PLACE IN AN "AREA" DURING THE TAPING OR FILMING OF A SHOW:

Please be advised that (filming) (taping) is taking place in connection with the production of a (motion picture) (television movie) (television series) tentatively entitled _____. People entering this area may appear in the picture. By entering this area, you grant to ** _____ the right to film and photograph you and record your voice and to use your voice and likeness in connection with the picture and the distribution and exploitation thereof, and you release ** _____ and its licensees from all liability in connection therein. You agree and understand that ** _____ will proceed in reliance upon such grant and release. ** _____ does not assume responsibility for any injury to your person or damage or loss to your property.

The use of cameras and recording equipment is prohibited due to union and copyright regulations.

Smoking is prohibited in this area... Thank you!

** Fill in the name of your production company

SUPPLYING A FILM/TAPE CLIP FOR PROMOTIONAL PURPOSES

Date

(Address to the person and/or
company requesting the clip)

Gentlemen:

The undersigned hereby authorizes you to use a FILM/TAPE CLIP from the motion picture/
television (movie) (series) tentatively entitled _____
for promotional purposes only in the program entitled _____
currently scheduled for broadcast on _____.

The undersigned hereby affirms that neither he nor anyone acting on his behalf or
any company which he may represent, gave or agreed to give anything of value (except
for the FILM/TAPE CLIP) which was furnished for promotional purposes solely on or
in connection with (THE NAME OF THE SHOW YOUR CLIP WILL APPEAR ON) to any member of
the production staff, anyone associated in any manner with the program or any
representative of (THE PRODUCTION COMPANY RECEIVING THE CLIP) for mentioning or
displaying the name of any company which he may represent or any of its products,
trademarks, trade-names or the like.

The undersigned understands that any broadcast identification of the FILM/TAPE CLIP
(or the name of any company, product, etc. which he may represent) which (THE NAME
OF YOUR PRODUCTION COMPANY) may furnish, shall, in no event, be beyond that which
is reasonable related to the program content.

The undersigned is aware, as is the company which he may represent, that it is a federal
offense unless disclosed to (THE PRODUCTION COMPANY RECEIVING THE CLIP) prior to
broadcast if the undersigned gives or agrees to give anything of value to promote
any product, service or venture on the air.

The undersigned represents that he is fully empowered to execute this letter on behalf
of any company which he may represent.

The undersigned warrants that he or the company which he may represent has the right
to grant the license herein granted, and agrees to indemnify you for all loss, damage
and liability, excluding the payment of any guild related talent fees or performing
rights fees in the music included in said clip, if any (which you agree to pay or
cause to be paid), arising out of the use of the above material.

Very truly yours,

ACCEPTED & AGREED:

By_____   _____
                                            (Please Print Name)

                                            _____
                                            (Title)

PRODUCT PLACEMENT RELEASE

Date

(Your production company)
(company address)

Gentlemen:

The undersigned ("Company") agrees to provide the following product(s) and/or service(s) to (THE NAME OF YOUR PRODUCTION COMPANY) for use in the motion picture/ movie for television/television series now entitled _____ (the "Picture"):

_____
_____
_____

The Company grants to you, your successors, licensees and assigns, the non-exclusive right, but not the obligation to use and include all or part of the trademark(s), logo(s) and/or identifiable characters (the "Mark(s)") associated with the above listed product(s) and/or service(s) in the Picture, without limitation as to time or number of runs, for reproduction, exhibition and exploitation, throughout the world, in any and all manner, methods and media, whether now known or hereafter known or devised, and in the advertising, publicizing, promotion, trailers and exploitation thereof.

The Company warrants and represents that it is the owner of the product(s) or direct provider of the service(s) as listed above or a representative of such and has the right to enter this agreement and grant the rights granted to (YOUR PRODUCTION COMPANY) hereunder.

In full consideration of the Company providing the product(s) and/or service(s) to (YOUR PRODUCTION COMPANY), (YOUR PRODUCTION COMPANY) agrees to accord the Company screen credit in the end titles of the positive prints of the Picture in the following form: "_____ furnished by _____".

The Company understands that any broadcast identification of its products, trademarks, trade names or the like which (YOUR PRODUCTION COMPANY) may furnish, shall in no event, be beyond that which is reasonably related to the program content.

As it applies to any and all television broadcasts of the Picture, the Company is aware that it is a federal offense to give or agree to give anything of value to promote any product, service or venture on the air. The Company affirms that it did not give or agree to give anything of value, except for the product(s) and/or service(s) to any member of the production staff, anyone associated in any manner with the Picture or any representative of (YOUR PRODUCTION COMPANY) for mentioning or displaying the name of the Company or any of its products, trademarks, trade names, or the like.

I represent that I am an officer of the Company and am empowered to execute this form on behalf of the Company.

I further represent that neither I nor the Company which I represent will directly or indirectly publicize or otherwise exploit the use, exhibition or demonstration

(continued on the following page)

of the above product(s) and/or service(s) in the Picture for advertising, merchandising or promotional purposes without the express written consent of (YOUR PRODUCTION COMPANY).

Sincerely yours,

AGREED & ACCEPTED BY

By_____

_____
(Authorized Signatory)

_____
(Please Print Name)

_____
(Title)

_____
(Name of Company)

_____

_____
(Address)

_____
(Phone Number)

FILM/TAPE FOOTAGE RELEASE

Date

LICENSOR: _____

LICENSEE: _____

DESCRIPTION OF THE FILM/TAPE FOOTAGE: _____

_____

LENGTH OF FOOTAGE: _____

PRODUCTION: _____

(The "Picture")

LICENSE FEE, if any: _____

Licensor hereby grants to Licensee, Licensor's permission to edit and include all or portion of the above-mentioned Footage in the Picture as follows:

1. Licensor grants to Licensee a non-exclusive license to edit and incorporate the Footage in the Picture. Licensee may broadcast and otherwise exploit the Footage in the Picture, and in customary advertising and publicity thereof, through-out the world in perpetuity in any media now known or hereafter devised.

2. Licensee shall not make any reproductions whatsoever of or from the Footage except as described hereunder.

3. Licensee agrees to obtain, at Licensee's expense, all required consents of any person whose appearances are contained in the Footage pursuant to this agreement, and to make any payments to such persons, guilds or unions to the extent required under applicable collective bargaining agreements for such use.

4. Licensor represents and warrants that: (1) Licensor has the right and power to grant the rights herein granted, and (2) neither Licensee's use of the Footage pursuant to this license nor anything contained therein infringes upon the rights of any third parties.

5. Licensor and Licensee each agree to indemnify and hold the other harmless from and against any and all claims, losses liabilities, damages and expenses, including reasonable attorneys' fees, which may result from any breach of their respective representations and warranties hereunder.

6. As between Licensor and Licensee, the Picture shall be Licensee's sole and exclusive property. Licensee shall not be obligated to use the Footage or the rights herein granted or to produce or broadcast the Picture.

7. Licensor acknowledges that, under the Federal Communications Act, it is a Federal offense to give or agree to give anything of value to promote any product, service or venture in the Picture, and Licensor warrants and represents that Licensor has not and will not do so.

(continued on the following page)

8. This agreement constitutes the entire understanding between the parties, supersedes any prior understanding relating thereto and shall not be modified except by a writing signed by the parties. This agreement shall be irrevocable and shall be binding upon and inure to the benefit of Licensor's and Licensee's respective successors, assigns and licensees.

Kindly sign below to indicate your acceptance of the foregoing.

Licensor:

CONFIRMED

By_____

_____
(Signature)

_____
(Please Print Name)

_____
(Title)

_____
(Company)

_____

_____
(Address)

_____
(Phone Number)

REQUEST FOR VIDEOCASSETTE

Date

(Address to the person requesting the videocassette)

Dear _____:

You accept delivery of the (1/2") (3/4") videocassette ("Recording") of _____ (the "Picture"), and in consideration of our delivery of it, agree as follows:

1. You warrant, represent and agree that the Recording shall be used solely for your private, personal library purpose or for screenings in connection with an in-house demo reel; and the Recording will never be publicly exhibited in any manner or medium whatsoever. You will not charge or authorize the charge of a fee for exhibiting the Recording. You will not duplicate or permit the duplication of the Recording. You will retain possession of the Recording at all times.

2. All other rights in and to the Picture, under copyright or otherwise, including but not limited to title to, are retained by (THE NAME OF YOUR PRODUCTION COMPANY).

3. The permission which we have granted to you for the use of the Recording itself will be non-assignable and non-transferable.

4. You agree to indemnify us against and hold us harmless from claims, liabilities and actions arising out of your breach of this agreement.

5. You agree to reimburse us for the cost of making the Recording available to you.

This will become a contract between you and us upon your acceptance of delivery of the Recording.

Sincerely yours,

ACCEPTED & AGREED:

By_____

_____
(Signature)

_____
(Please Print Name)

_____

_____

_____
(Phone Number)

ABBREVIATED PRODUCTION REPORT

SHOW_____ PROD#_____

DAY_____ DATE_____ DAY#_____ OUT OF_____

LOCATION_____

CREW CALL _____

FIRST SHOT _____ MEAL PENALTY_____

LUNCH _____ TO _____ OVERTIME_____

SECOND MEAL _____ TO _____

WRAP _____

SCENES_____

_____

SCENES SCHEDULED BUT NOT SHOT_____

_____

	SCENES	PAGES	MINUTES	SETUPS
PREVIOUS				
TODAY				
TOTAL				

FILM FOOTAGE

GROSS_____ GROSS TO DATE_____

PRINT_____ PRINT TO DATE_____

N.G._____

WASTE_____

NOTES_____

_____

_____

_____

_____

   © ELH Form #18

DAILY COST OVERVIEW

SHOW_____   PROD#_____

DATE_____   DAY#_____

START DATE_____

SCHEDULED FINISH DATE_____

REVISED FINISH DATE_____

	PER CALL SHEET	SHOT	AHEAD/BEHIND
# OF SCENES			
# OF PAGES			

	AS BUDGETED AND/OR SCHEDULED	ACTUAL	COST OVER/UNDER
CAST OVERTIME	_____	_____	_____
COMPANY SHOOTING HOURS	_____	_____	_____
MEAL PENALTY	_____	_____	_____
EXTRAS & STAND-INS	_____	_____	_____
CATERING	_____	_____	_____
RAW STOCK	_____	_____	_____
UNANTICIPATED EXPENSES:			
_____	_____	_____	_____
_____	_____	_____	_____
_____	_____	_____	_____
_____	_____	_____	_____
_____	_____	_____	_____

TOTAL FOR TODAY _____

PREVIOUS TOTAL _____

GRAND TOTAL _____

PREPARED BY_____   APPROVED BY_____

CAST INFORMATION

(Please fill squares in with dates)

SHOW				START DATE	# OF DAYS WORKING	DEAL MEMO	STATION 12	TRAVEL/HOTEL ACCOMMODATIONS	MEDICAL EXAM	SENT SCRIPT	NOTIFIED WARDROBE	SCRIPT REVISIONS (BLUE)	SCRIPT REVISIONS (PINK)	SCRIPT REVISIONS (GREEN)	CONTRACT RECEIVED	CONTRACT TO AGENT/ACTOR	CONTRACT RETURNED	CONT. SIGNED BY PRODUCER	COPIES DISTRIBUTED	NOTES
EPISODE	PROD#																			
ACTOR		ROLE																		

BOX/EQUIPMENT RENTAL INVENTORY

PRODUCTION COMPANY_____

SHOW_____   PROD#_____

EMPLOYEE_____   POSITION_____

    Address_____   SOC.SEC.#_____

    _____   PHONE#_____

LOAN OUT COMPANY_____   FED.I.D.#_____

RENTAL RATE $_____   PER   [ ] DAY   [ ] WEEK
                                             [ ] SUBMIT WEEKLY INVOICE
                                           [ ] RECORD ON WEEKLY TIME CARD

RENTAL COMMENCES ON_____

INVENTORIED ITEMS:_____
_____
_____
_____
_____
_____
_____
_____
_____
_____
_____
_____
_____
_____
_____
_____
_____
_____
_____
_____
_____

Please note: 1. *Box and equipment rentals are subject to 1099 reporting.*

               2. *The Production Company is not responsible for any claims of loss or damage to box/equipment rental items that are not listed on the above inventory.*

_____   _____
EMPLOYEE SIGNATURE   DATE

_____   _____
APPROVED BY   DATE

INVENTORY LOG

SHOW _____ PROD# _____ DEPARTMENT _____

ITEM(S)	PURCHASED FROM (Name/Address)	PURCHASE DATE	PURCHASE PRICE	P.O.#	AT COMPLETION OF PRINCIPAL PHOTOGRAPHY			LOCATION OF ITEM
					IF PORTION USED, HOW MUCH REMAINS	IF SOLD, FOR HOW MUCH	IF RET'D. TO COMPANY, IN WHAT CONDITION	

© ELH Form #22

PURCHASE ORDER LOG

SHOW _____

PROD# _____

| P.O.# | DATE | TO | FOR | PRICE | CHECK ONE | | | RENTAL RET'D | TO INVENTORY | P.O. ASSIGNED TO |
					PURCHASE	RENTAL	SERVICE			

CREW START-UP AND DATA SHEET

NAME	POSITION	SOC. SEC. #	NAME OF CORP. FED. I.D. #	DEAL MEMO	START SLIP	W-4 I-9	START DATE	WRAP DATE	PAYCHECK TO	
									EMPLOYEE	MAIL

© ELH Form #24

TIME CARDS/INVOICES
WEEKLY CHECK LIST

NAME	POSITION	SOC. SEC. # FED. I.D. #	TIME CARDS AND/OR INVOICES TURNED IN EACH WEEK								
			W/E	W/E	W/E	W/E	W/E	W/E	W/E	W/E	W/E

INDIVIDUAL PETTY CASH ACCOUNT

NAME _____   DEPARTMENT _____

SHOW _____   PROD# _____

FLOAT $ _____

DATE	CHECK#/CASH RECV'D FROM	AMOUNT RECV'D	ACCOUNTED FOR	BALANCE

© ELH Form #26

INVOICE

TO: _____
_____
_____
_____

FROM: _____   DATE _____
(Address) _____
_____
(Phone #) _____

PAYEE SS# OR FED. ID# _____   1099 _____

FOR SERVICES RENDERED ON _____ OR WEEK/ENDING _____

DESCRIPTION OF SERVICE/RENTAL/CAR ALLOWANCE

TOTAL AMOUNT DUE $ _____

EMPLOYEE SIGNATURE _____

APPROVED BY _____

PD. BY CHECK # _____   DATE _____

CASH OR SALES RECEIPT DATE _____ No. _____

RECIPIENT/
SOLD TO: _____

ADDRESS: _____

_____

PHONE# _____

FOR PURCHASE OF: _____

_____

WRITTEN
AMOUNT _____ $ _____

☐ CASH   ☐ 1099   Soc.Sec.# _____

☐ CHECK   Fed.I.D.# _____

ACCOUNT CODING _____

APPROVED BY _____ RECV'D BY _____

THE CHECK'S IN THE MAIL

CHECK MADE OUT TO	CHECK NUMBER	CHECK DATED	ADDRESS SENT TO	DATE MAILED	PAY-ROLL	INV.

MILEAGE LOG

NAME: _____   WEEK ENDING _____

SHOW: _____   PROD# _____

| DATE | LOCATION | | PURPOSE | MILEAGE |
	FROM	TO		

TOTAL MILES: _____

_____MILES @ _____ ¢ Per Mile = $ _____

Approved By: _____   Date: _____

Pd. By Check # _____   Date _____

© ELH Form #30

RAW STOCK INVENTORY

SHOW_____ PROD#_____

WEEK ENDING_____

	52_____	52_____	52_____	52_____

EPISODE/WEEKLY TOTALS

Print	_____	_____	_____	_____
No Good	_____	_____	_____	_____
Waste	_____	_____	_____	_____
Total **	_____	_____	_____	_____

PURCHASED

Previously Purchased	_____	_____	_____	_____
Purchased This Episode/Week	+ _____	_____	_____	_____
Total Stock Purchased	_____	_____	_____	_____

USED

Stock Used To Date	_____	_____	_____	_____
Used This Episode/Week **	+ _____	_____	_____	_____
Total Stock Used	_____	_____	_____	_____

Total Purchased	_____	_____	_____	_____
Total Used	− _____	_____	_____	_____
Estimated Remaining Stock	_____	_____	_____	_____
(Remaining Stock As Per Assistant Cameraman)	_____	_____	_____	_____

RAW STOCK PURCHASES MADE DURING
THIS EPISODE/WEEK:

P.O.#_____	_____	_____	_____	_____
P.O.#_____	_____	_____	_____	_____
P.O.#_____	_____	_____	_____	_____
P.O.#_____	_____	_____	_____	_____
TOTAL	_____	_____	_____	_____

NOTES:

DAILY RAW STOCK LOG

SHOW _____   PROD# _____

DATE _____   DAY # _____

CAMERA	ROLL #	GOOD	N.G.	WASTE	TOTAL

	DRAWN	GOOD	N.G.	WASTE	TOTAL
PREVIOUS					
TODAY					
TOTAL					

UNEXPOSED ON HAND	TOTAL EXPOSED

© ELH Form #32

REQUEST FOR PICK UP

DATE_____

SHOW_____   PROD#_____

PICK UP REQUESTED BY_____

ITEM(S) TO BE PICKED UP_____

_____

_____

_____

_____

PICK UP FROM_____

(COMPANY)_____   PHONE#_____

ADDRESS _____

_____

DIRECTIONS (if needed)_____

_____

_____

_____

☐ MUST BE PICKED UP AT _____ (A.M.) (P.M.)

☐ PICK UP AS SOON AS POSSIBLE

☐ PICK UP TODAY. NO SPECIFIC TIME

☐ NO RUSH -- WHENEVER YOU CAN

COMMENTS/SPECIAL INSTRUCTIONS_____

_____

_____

_____

DATE & TIME OF PICK UP_____

ITEM(S) DELIVERED TO_____

(ALL PICK UP SLIPS ARE TO BE KEPT ON FILE IN THE PRODUCTION OFFICE)

REQUEST FOR DELIVERY

DATE_____

SHOW_____ PROD#_____

DELIVERY REQUESTED BY_____

ITEM(S) TO BE DELIVERED_____

_____

_____

_____

_____

DELIVER TO_____

(COMPANY)_____ PHONE#_____

ADDRESS _____

_____

DIRECTIONS (if needed)_____

_____

_____

_____

☐   MUST BE DELIVERED BY _____ (A.M.) (P.M.)

☐   DELIVER AS SOON AS POSSIBLE

☐   DELIVER TODAY, NO SPECIFIC TIME

☐   NO RUSH -- WHENEVER YOU CAN

COMMENTS/SPECIAL INSTRUCTIONS:_____

_____

_____

_____

DATE & TIME OF DELIVERY_____

RECEIVED BY_____

(ALL DELIVERY SLIPS ARE TO BE KEPT ON FILE IN THE PRODUCTION OFFICE)

© ELH Form #34

DRIVE-TO

SHOW _____ DATE _____

EPISODE _____ PROD# _____

LOCATION _____

MILEAGE: _____ MILES @ _____ ¢ PER MILE = $ _____

NAME	SOC. SEC.#	POSITION	SIGNATURE
1.			
2.			
3.			
4.			
5.			
6.			
7.			
8.			
9.			
10.			
11.			
12.			
13.			
14.			
15.			
16.			
17.			
18.			
19.			
20.			
21.			
22.			
23.			
24.			
25.			
26.			
27.			
28.			
29.			
30.			

TOTAL ALLOCATION: _____ People X $ _____ = $ _____

APPROVED _____ DATE _____

WALKIE-TALKIE SIGN-OUT SHEET

SHOW _____   PROD# _____

SERIAL #	PRINT NAME	DATE OUT	DATE IN	SIGNATURE

WALKIE-TALKIES RENTED FROM: _____

ADDRESS _____   PHONE# _____

_____   FAX# _____

CONTACT _____   HOURS _____

BEEPER SIGN-OUT SHEET

SHOW _____ PROD# _____

SERIAL #	PRINT NAME	DATE OUT	DATE IN	SIGNATURE

BEEPERS RENTED FROM: _____

ADDRESS _____ PHONE# _____

_____ FAX# _____

CONTACT _____ HOURS _____

VEHICLE RENTAL SHEET

PRODUCTION COMPANY_____ DATE_____

ADDRESS_____

_____

PHONE#_____

The vehicle as described below is to be rented for use on the film tentatively entitled:_____

YEAR, MAKE, MODEL_____

LICENSE NUMBER_____

SERIAL ID#_____

VALUE_____

SPECIAL EQUIPMENT/ATTACHMENTS_____

_____

RENTAL PRICE $_____ Per Day/Week/Month

OWNER'S NAME_____

    ADDRESS_____

_____

    PHONE#_____

DRIVER OF VEHICLE (if not owner)_____

START DATE_____ COMPLETION DATE_____

INSURANCE TO BE SUPPLIED BY_____

INSURANCE COMPANY_____

POLICY #_____

INSURANCE AGENCY REP._____

    PHONE#_____

REQUIRED MAINTENANCE_____

    FUEL_____

VEHICLE TO BE USED FOR_____ (DEPARTMENT)

CERTIFICATE OF INSURANCE   [ ] TO OWNER   [ ] IN VEHICLE   [ ] ON FILE

AGREED TO:

BY:_____   BY:_____
    OWNER   TRANSPORTATION COORDINATOR

     © ELH Form #38

LOCATION INFORMATION SHEET

SHOW_____

LOCATION MANAGER_____

PERMIT SERVICE_____

      CONTACT_____

      PHONE #_____

PRODUCTION #_____

(SCRIPTED)LOCATION_____

_____

DATE(S)_____

[ ] INT.   [ ] EXT.   [ ] DAY   [ ] NIGHT

ACTUAL LOCATION
(Address & Phone #)

_____

DATE & DAYS

	# of days	dates
Prep:	_____	_____
Shoot:	_____	_____
Strike:	_____	_____

LOCATION OF NEAREST EMERGENCY MEDICAL FACILITY

CONTACTS

Owner(s)   Name(s)_____

            Address_____

                     _____

Phone/FAX#   _____

Beeper #   _____

Representative(s)

Company: _____

Contact: _____

Address: _____

             _____

Phone/FAX#   _____

Beeper #   _____

LOCATION SITE RENTAL FEE

Full Amount $_____

Amount for PREP days $_____

Amount for SHOOT days $_____

Amount for STRIKE days $_____

Deposit $_____   Due on_____

[ ] Refundable   [ ] Apply to total fee

Balance $_____   Due on_____

O.T. after_____hrs. per day @ $_____per hr.

_____Additional days @ $_____per day

Additional charges: Phone $_____

                       Utilities $_____

                       Parking $_____

(Other)_____ $_____

CHECK OFF LIST

[ ]   Location Agreement
[ ]   Certificate of Insurance
[ ]   Permit
[ ]   Fire Safety Officer(s)
[ ]   Police
[ ]   Location Fee
[ ]   Security
[ ]   Intermittent Traffic Control
[ ]   Post for Parking

[ ] Signed Release from Neighbors
[ ] Prepared map to Location
[ ] Heaters/Fans/Air Conditioners
[ ] Lay-out Board/Drop Clothes
[ ] Utilities/Power Supply

Allocated Areas For
[ ]   Extras
[ ]   Dressing Rms.
[ ]   Eating
[ ]   Hair/Makeup

Allocated Parking For
[ ]   Equipment
[ ]   Honeywagons
[ ]   Cast Vehicles
[ ]   Crew Vehicles
[ ]   Buses
[ ]   Picture Vehicles
[ ]   Extra Tables & Chairs/Tent
[ ]   Locate Parking Lot if
        Shuttle is Necessary

© ELH Form #39

LOCATION LIST

SHOW _____

PRODUCTION # _____

SET LOCATION	ACTUAL LOCATION (ADDRESS & PHONE)		DATE & DAYS (PREP/SHOOT/STRIKE)	CONTACTS (OWNER & REPRESENTATIVE)

REQUEST TO FILM DURING EXTENDED HOURS

Dear Resident:

    This is to inform you that _____ will be shooting a film entitled "_____" in your neighborhood at _____.

Filming activities in residential areas is normally allowed only between the hours of _____ and _____. In order to extend the hours before and/or after these times, the City requires that we obtain a signature of approval from the neighbors. The following information pertains to the dates and times of our scheduled shoot and any specific information you may need to know regarding our filming activities.

We have obtained or applied for all necessary City permits and maintain all legally required liability insurance. A copy of our film permit will be on file at the City Film Office and will also be available at our shooting location.

FILMING DAYS/HOURS REQUESTED: on_____ (date(s))
from _____ (a.m.) (p.m.) to _____ (a.m.) (p.m.)
and _____ (date(s))
from _____ (a.m.) (p.m.) to _____ (a.m.) (p.m.)

THE FOLLOWING ACTIVITIES ARE PLANNED FOR THE EXTENDED HOURS:
_____

We appreciate your hospitality and cooperation. We wish to make filming on your street a pleasant experience for both you and us. If you have any questions or concerns before or during the filming, please feel free to call our Production Office and ask for me or the Production Manager.

Sincerely yours,

_____
Location Manager

_____
Production Company

_____
Phone No.

    We would very much appreciate it if you would complete and sign where indicated below. A representative from our company will be by within the next day or two to pick-up this form.
_____

❑   I DO NOT OBJECT TO THE EXTENDED FILMING HOURS
❑   I DO OBJECT TO THE EXTENDED FILMING HOURS

COMMENTS:

NAME: _____
ADDRESS: _____
PHONE #: (Optional) _____

TRAVEL MOVEMENT

PROD# _____

SHOW _____
TRAVEL FROM _____ TO _____
DAY/DATE _____ AIRLINE _____
TYPE OF AIRCRAFT _____ MEAL(S) _____ MOVIE _____
FLIGHT# _____ DEPARTURE TIME _____ ARRIVAL _____ FLIGHT STOPS IN _____
CHANGE TO FLIGHT # _____ DEPARTURE _____ ARRIVAL _____

NAME	POSITION	GROUND TRANSPORTATION TO AIRPORT	TO BE PICKED UP @	GROUND TRANSPORTATION FROM AIRPORT

DIRECT # TO PRODUCTION OFFICE _____
FAX# _____
ADDITIONAL INFO. _____

HOTEL _____
Address _____
Phone # _____

© ELH Form #41

HOTEL ROOM LOG

SHOW _____
HOTEL _____
LOCATION _____

PROD# _____
CONTACT _____
PHONE# _____

NAME	POSITION	ROOM #	TYPE OF ROOM	RATE	DATE IN	DATE OUT	TOTAL DAYS

HOTEL ROOM LIST

SHOW _____ PROD# _____

HOTEL _____ LOCATION _____

ADDRESS _____

_____ LOCATION DATES _____

Through

PHONE# _____ FAX# _____ _____

NAME	POSITION	ROOM #	DIRECT #
Production Office	--------		
Accounting Office	--------		
Transportation Office	--------		
Editing Room	--------		

© ELH Form #43

MEAL ALLOWANCE

SHOW _____

LOCATION _____

PROD# _____

WEEK OF _____

MEAL RATES

BREAKFAST $ _____
LUNCH $ _____
DINNER $ _____

NAME	DAY	MON			TUE			WED			THUR			FRI			SAT			SUN			TOTAL	SIGNATURE
	DATE																							
		B	L	D	B	L	D	B	L	D	B	L	D	B	L	D	B	L	D	B	L	D		

TOTAL: _____

APPROVED _____

TRAVEL MEMO TO CAST AND CREW

TO: _____

FROM: _____

RE: TRAVEL & HOTEL ACCOMMODATIONS/LOCATION INFORMATION FOR
    CAST & CREW TRAVELING TO _____

As per your []contract []deal memo, you will be provided with _____(# of tickets), _____-class, round-trip airfare(s) to _____(destination).

At the present time, you are scheduled to travel on _____ (day & date) with plane reservations as follows:

    AIRLINE:_____ FLIGHT #_____
    DEPARTS FROM:_____ AT:_____(a.m.)(p.m.)
    ARRIVAL TIME:_____ (a.m.)(p.m.)

The following meals will be served during your flight:
    [ ] Breakfast [ ] Lunch [ ] Dinner [ ] Snack

There [ ] will [ ] will not be a movie shown during your flight.

The following ground transportation will be provided for you:
    TO AIRPORT:_____
    You will be picked-up at _____(a.m.)(p.m.)
    FROM AIRPORT:_____

You will be staying at:
    _____(hotel)
    _____(address)
    _____(phone #)

The following accommodations have been reserved for you:
    [ ] Condo/Apartment [ ] Hotel Suite [ ] Rm. w/a kitchenette
    [ ] Rm. w/a king-sz. bed [ ] Rm. w/a queen sz. bed
    [ ] Rm. w/two beds [ ] Rm. on the ground floor
    [ ] Other_____

On location, [ ] you will be provided with a vehicle
      [ ] we're not able to provide you with a vehicle
      [ ] you will be sharing the use of a vehicle

Your per diem will be $_____ per day.

Please be aware that upgrading your air fare, bringing guests, reserving a larger room, etc. is to be done at your expense. You can make additional plane reservations through_____ at _____(phone #), and you will be informed as to the additional costs. All hotel incidental charges (room service, long distance phone calls, etc.) will be charged directly to you by the hotel.

(continued on the following page)

All department heads are requested to supply _____ with a list of any equipment/wardrobe/props, etc., that will need to be shipped to location. We will need to know how many pieces each department will be shipping and if any of the pieces are oversized. Shipping tags and labels can be picked-up at the production office.

Also, please let _____ know as soon as possible as to any special requests you might have such as renting a car (if one is not provided for you) or a small refrigerator for your room. Every effort will be made to accommodate your requests.

Reports indicate that current weather conditions in _____(location) are _____ and will become [ ] warmer [ ] much warmer [ ] cooler [ ] much colder [ ] wetter as our schedule progresses. We will be shooting _____ nights and the weather at night for this time of year is anticipated to be _____. Please pack accordingly.

At the present, your return flight is scheduled for _____(day & date) on _____(airline), Flight #_____, leaving _____ at ____(a.m.)(p.m.) and arriving in _____ at _____(a.m.)(p.m.)

If there are changes in our shooting schedule or unforeseen delays that would extend our location shooting, you will be informed and your return reservations updated.

Your room will be reserved until the completion of [] your role [] production, and your return flight will be booked accordingly. If you wish to remain in _____, or to travel elsewhere at the completion of [] principal photography [] your role, please check with us first as your services may be needed for looping and/or pick-up shots. We may not know immediately if and/or when, but would let you know ASAP. If you choose to remain in _____, however, it will be your responsibility to make further arrangements with the hotel and to re-book your own airline tickets. Please just let us know of your plans and that you will not be returning with the rest of the company.

If you have any additional questions regarding your travel or location accommodations, please contact _____ at _____ (phone #).

ESSENTIAL PRODUCTION BOOKS FROM LONE EAGLE PUBLISHING CO.

THE HOLLYWOOD JOB-HUNTER'S SURVIVAL GUIDE
AN INSIDER'S WINNING STRATEGIES FOR GETTING THAT (ALL-IMPORTANT) FIRST JOB ...AND KEEPING IT
Hugh Taylor
$16.95
ISBN 0-943728-51-7, 314 pp, illustrations

There are currently over 250,000 students taking film courses in colleges and universities in the United States. Many of them will be making their way to Hollywood to try to get a job in "the business." For those of you who have no "uncle in production," "a cousin who's a director," "or a friend at the studio," Taylor offers insider's advice on getting that all-important first job in the entertainment industry.
Taylor's well-written guide discusses Getting The Job, Setting up the Office and Getting To Work, The Script and Story Development Process, Production, Information, Putting It all Together, Issues and Perspectives.

HUGH TAYLOR recently received his MBA in Business from Harvard's School of Business Administration. He has worked for the past two summers as an assistant to one of Hollywood's top producers moving up from the job of "gofer" to his current position as a development executive. In his tenure at his job, he has come up with his strategies for finding the right job and keeping it.

THE LANGUAGE OF VISUAL EFFECTS
Micheal J. McAlister
$18.95
ISBN 0-943728-47-9, 4.5 x 8.5, 176 pp
illustrations, hologram on cover

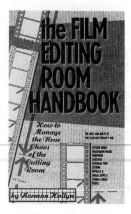

"...for people in the technical side of the business as well as for those in the academic arena."
—George Lucas

"Oscar-winning effects artist Micheal McAlister has provided the perfect reference to provide a comprehensive listing of hundreds of effects terms with concise explanations understandable to the layman. It will be a pleasure to refer my readers to this valuable volume.
—Don Shay, Editor/Publisher, Cinefex Magazine

"A visual effects 'Bible' that will soon be in every filmmaker's library as an excellent reference guide to visual effects work."
—Tom Joyner, Executive Production Manager/Feature Production,
Warner Bros., Inc.

MICHEAL J. MCALISTER is recognized as one of the industry's top Visual Effects Supervisors. He spent eleven years at Lucasfilm's Industrial Light and Magic where he garnered an Academy Award, an Emmy, a British Academy Award, a second Academy Award nomination and a second British Academy Award nomination. His work has been the subject of many television reports including *Entertainment Tonight, The Today Show, Nova* and various documentary specials both in the United States and abroad.

THE FILM EDITING ROOM HANDBOOK
HOW TO MANAGE THE NEAR CHAOS OF THE CUTTING ROOM
Norman Hollyn
$19.95
ISBN 0-943728-33-9, 6 x 9
445 pp, illustrations, bibliography, index

A well-written, semi-technical and profusely illustrated book which covers the editing process from pre-production image and sound, opticals, mixing and music editing through post-production answer print and previews. Perhaps most important, Hollyn tells how to get an editing job. An experienced editor who has worked on *Fame, Hair, Lenny, Network, Heathers* and, most recently, *Jersey Girl*, Hollyn knows his subject well. A book for movie fans as well as specialists.

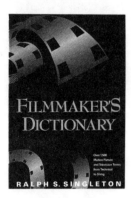

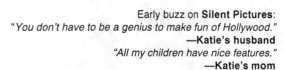

ESSENTIAL PRODUCTION BOOKS FROM LONE EAGLE PUBLISHING CO.

ANNUAL REFERENCE DIRECTORIES

1.   FILM DIRECTORS: A COMPLETE GUIDE $50
2.   FILM WRITERS GUIDE $45
3.   FILM PRODUCERS, STUDIOS, AGENTS & CASTING DIRECTORS GUIDE $45
4.   CINEMATOGRAPHERS, PRODUCTION DESIGNERS, COSTUME DESIGNERS &
         EDITORS GUIDE $45
5.   SPECIAL EFFECTS & STUNTS GUIDE $45
6.   FILM COMPOSERS GUIDE $45
7.   FILM ACTORS GUIDE $50
8.   TELEVISION WRITERS GUIDE $45
9.   TELEVISION DIRECTORS GUIDE $45

These credit and contact directories feature:
- working professionals of the film and television industry
- contact information
- credits
- releasing information (date/studio or date/network)
- Academy & Emmy Awards & nominations
- Index of Names
- Index of Film (Television) Titles, cross-referenced (except Actors)
- Index of Agents & Managers
- Interviews (selected volumes)
- and more

CALL 1-800 FILMBKS
FOR CURRENT EDITIONS AND PRICES.

HOW TO ORDER

1.   CALL 1-800-FILMBKS. HAVE YOUR CREDIT CARD READY (VISA, MC OR AMERICAN EXPRESS.) YOUR ORDER WILL BE TAKEN AND YOUR BOOKS SHIPPED TO YOU **ASAP**. WE USUALLY SHIP BY **UPS** GROUND, BUT OTHER ARRANGEMENTS CAN BE MADE.

2.   MAIL US YOUR REQUEST WITH A CHECK, MONEY ORDER OR CREDIT CARD INFORMATION. CALIFORNIA RESIDENTS ADD IN 8.25% SALES TAX. ALL ORDERS SHOULD ADD IN SHIPPING CHARGES: $4.00 FIR FIRST BOOK, $1.50 EACH ADDITIONAL BOOK. DO NOT FORGET TO PUT EXPIRATION DATE AND SIGN THE REQUEST. INCLUDE YOUR PHONE NUMBER. OUR MAILING ADDRESS IS:

> LONE EAGLE PUBLISHING CO.
> DEPT. EH
> 2337 ROSCOMARE ROAD #9
> LOS ANGELES, CA 90077-1851
> 310/471-8066

3.   **FAX** US YOUR REQUEST WITH ALL THE INFORMATION LISTED ABOVE. OUR FAX IS 310/471-4969.